Assembling Flowers and Cultivating Homes

Assembling Flowers and Cultivating Homes

Labor and Gender in Colombia

Greta Friedemann-Sánchez

LEXINGTON BOOKS

A division of

ROWMAN & LITTLEFIELD PUBLISHERS, INC.

Lanham • Boulder • New York • Toronto • Plymouth, UK

Some of the material in this book originally appeared as a journal article. This material is reprinted by permission from "Assets in Intrahousehold Bargaining among Women Workers in Colombia's Cut-Flower Industry," *Feminist Economics* 12, nos. 1–2 (January 2006): 247–69. See http://www.tandf.co.uk.

LEXINGTON BOOKS

A division of Rowman & Littlefield Publishers, Inc.
A wholly owned subsidiary of The Rowman & Littlefield Publishing Group, Inc.
4501 Forbes Boulevard, Suite 200
Lanham, MD 20706

Estover Road
Plymouth PL6 7 PY
United Kingdom

First paperback edition 2009

British Library Cataloguing in Publication Information Available

Library of Congress Cataloging-in-Publication Data

Friedemann-Sánchez, Greta, 1966-
Assembling flowers and cultivating homes : labor and gender in Colombia / Greta Friedemann-Sánchez.
p. cm.
Includes bibliographical references (p.) and index.
1. Cut flower industry—Colombia. 2. Women—Employment—Colombia. 3. Sex role—Colombia. I. Title.
SB443.4.C7F75 2006
338.1'7596609861—dc22 2005033716

ISBN-13: 978-0-7391-0979-3 (cloth : alk. paper)
ISBN-10: 0-7391-0979-0 (cloth : alk. paper)
ISBN-13: 978-0-7391-3296-8 (pbk : alk. paper)
ISBN-10: 0-7391-3296-2 (pbk : alk. paper)
eISBN-13: 978-0-7391-3297-5
eISBN-10: 0-7391-3297-0

Printed in the United States of America

∞™ The paper used in this publication meets the minimum requirements of American National Standard for Information Sciences—Permanence of Paper for Printed Library Materials, ANSI/NISO Z39.48–1992.

Dedicado a mis padres,
Nina S. de Friedemann y Robert Friedemann,
maestros y amigos

Contents

List of Figures

List of Tables

List of Maps

Foreword

Stephen Gudeman

Colombia has cornered one-third of the fresh cut flower market in the United States measured in dollars. This assembly line business brings foreign currency into the country, generates employment, and provides a peaceful sector in an otherwise unstable political environment. But wages are low, the work is labor intensive, and the workforce is primarily female. Anthropologists, feminists, and many others have argued that gender exploitation provides the competitive edge for this "third world" form of production.

Greta Friedemann-Sánchez insightfully challenges this common wisdom in her study of the flower industry that is located north of Bogotá. Women, she finds, seek work in the flower companies, find satisfaction in their jobs, and use their monetary power to refashion gender relations. Work in a global industry provides them with bargaining tools for confronting male power in villages and at home. Friedemann-Sánchez counters as well a current divide in the social sciences that particularly afflicts anthropology. According to some commentators anthropology is a humanistic discipline focused on the meaning and interpretation of language and practices; according to others, anthropologists generate and apply theories to explain behavior and the details of cultures. Is anthropology like literary criticism or political science and psychology? Should anthropology emphasize grand theories or local voices that express the contingencies of life? Friedemann-Sánchez maneuvers through these shoals by showing how the contrary approaches can be brought together. She illuminates her field materials by placing them in the context of formal models and global conditions, and she creatively joins quantitative information and individual voices by relating "hard" data, such as land ownership, to "soft" data, such as social capital. The result is a balanced and convincing assessment of the local situation.

The flower companies are like assembly plants. Friedemann-Sánchez describes the steps, dangers, and discipline involved in the industry. The work is skilled, closely watched, and brings new discipline to the women employees. Friedemann-Sánchez underscores the irony brought by these exacting working conditions, for they have become a source of change in domestic life. In the flower industry men largely oversee women. Workers, supervisors, and professionals wear color coded outfits: in their green clothes the overseers blend in with the foliage, whereas the workers stand out in their red uniforms. But this bureaucratic discipline, reinforced through patriarchal language, provides women with skills and knowledge for contesting patriarchy at home. The flower companies, keenly aware of domestic abuse that affects their workers (and may buttress violence within the nation), also offer workshops through which women are gaining a greater sense of self-value and independence.

On turning to domestic life, Friedemann-Sánchez demonstrates how the new working conditions empower women. Here she employs Nash game theory and a bargaining model to understand household relationships. At home, women use their new financial and social assets as leverage, and they enhance their economic positions by using the cognitive skills of planning, acting responsibly, and managing money, which are learned in the flower farms. As their relative wealth increases, women bargain with men about whose money should be used to meet household needs, who should undertake domestic chores, and who should be financially responsible for children. The male "bargaining chip" of physical abuse appears to be disappearing with the expansion of the flower industry.

Women's bargaining strength is principally determined by their wage income and property ownership, but social networks help determine these economic factors, and network strength is related to a person's time of residence in the area which is coded through local categories, such as "roots," "old," and "migrants." Women's self-affirmation gained through work and training in the flower industry also aids their bargaining position by contributing to their sense of having a "foundation." A man's foundation, in contrast, starts with land ownership and agricultural work, and though males still have an edge in acquiring landed property, women are slowly "debasing" traditional male positions through their economic activities. Overall, through their increased empowerment that is created by wage work, property ownership, and social relationships, women are exercising new domestic rights through the strategies of "exit," "voice," and "loyalty," to use Hirschman's terms (1970). But the entirety remains in flux, because female flower workers also are subject to the older notion, reinforced by the church, that flower workers are promiscuous!

Whether the current balance of global forces and gender empowerment will remain stable is uncertain, for female wages are low, one transnational has entered the scene, and other nations are expanding their production of flowers. Regardless, Friedemann-Sánchez ingeniously blends different methodologies and theoretical approaches with feminist economics and ethnography to illuminate the contemporary situation to the benefit of the reader.

Reference

Hirschman, Albert O. *Exit, Voice, and Loyalty*. Cambridge: Harvard University Press, 1970.

Acknowledgments

One of the threads woven throughout this book is the idea that social communities, institutions included, are essential to an individual's life. Without them life at home and at work is not possible. I am fortunate to have had at one time or another, both in Colombia and in the United States, the support, guidance, teaching, encouragement, affirmation, and love of colleagues, teachers, mentors, family, and friends. This book has emerged only because of their support. I would like to thank each and every one.

The research on which this book is based has been supported by various individuals and institutions. In the United States, fieldwork was funded by the MacArthur Interdisciplinary Program on Global Change, Sustainability and Justice at the University of Minnesota. The preparation of the manuscript was possible with the generosity in time and resources from the Center for Chronic Disease and Outcomes Research, CCDOR, at the VA Medical Center in Minneapolis, and the support of my mentor, Melissa Partin. Stephen Gudeman, my advisor in the department of anthropology at the University of Minnesota, where I completed the doctorate in anthropology, introduced me to the field of household economics and guided me through a stimulating intellectual journey. Ragui Assaad and Ed Schuh, my advisors at the Hubert Humphrey Institute of Public Affairs at the University of Minnesota, introduced me to development studies and international rural development policy. The MacArthur Interdisciplinary Program on Global Change, Sustainability and Justice and its affiliated faculty and scholars were formative and provided an immense source of intellectual stimulation. In particular I would like to thank Ragui Assaad, Raymond Duvall, Allen Isaacman, Karen Brown-Thompson, Jim Johnson, and Vernon Ruttan. In addition, I am grateful to the Graduate School Minority Fellowship Program; the MacArthur Interdisciplinary Program on Global Change, Sustainability and Justice where I was a fellow; and Graduate Assistant Fellowships and Tuition Fellowships from the department of anthropology.

I would like to express my immense gratitude to the individuals in Colombia, many of whom requested anonymity, who welcomed me into their lives and generously shared their thoughts, their emotions, and the details of their private lives. This group includes the owners of the flower farms who shared their knowledge and gave me access to their farms and the farms' workers. Their support made my research possible as accessing flower farms in Colombia is difficult. Anthropologist Jaime Arocha, my *licenciatura* advisor and mentor, provided critical methodological advice during fieldwork as well as theoretical feedback. Anthropologist Pedro Sánchez Baracaldo conducted some of the interviews with male floriculture workers. Thank you to all the executives at Asocolflores and Aflonordes who took time to be interviewed.

Andrea Cutting and Lynn Nordquist made preparing for and conducting fieldwork possible. They supplied countless hours and days of care for my two sons, stepping in to fulfill my household role, often without prior notice and for extended periods of time. I would like to acknowledge Andrea Cutting in particular who traveled to Colombia to care for both children and traveled back to Minneapolis with the oldest, further taking care of him and my household in my absence! I am indebted to both for offering me unconditional and spontaneous logistical, intellectual, and emotional support. Through a surprising turn in life, I have the fortune of having Andrea Cutting as my research assistant at CCDOR. She has made possible the timely delivery of the manuscript, re-entering all the survey data into a statistical package after my first dataset was lost. She has analyzed the data, made the tables, and read the manuscript.

I have had the benefit of teachers, family members, and friends who read my work and offered feedback in its first version as a dissertation, including Professors Stephen Gudeman, Ragui Assaad, Ed Schuh, Daphne Berdhal, Kathleen Barlow, Bernard M. Levinson, Ronald J. Duncan, Jaime Arocha, Robert Cowle, Nancy Friedemann, Amy Porter, and Andrea Nightingale. Bernard M. Levinson in addition provided critical lessons on writing in the English language. Colleagues at CCDOR, where this manuscript was finalized, have provided a welcoming and vibrant intellectual environment. Joan Griffin, Nina Sayer, and Diana Burgess at CCDOR read one chapter of this manuscript and offered their sharp minds at crucial moments. Carmen Diana

Deere and Cheryl Doss offered analytical guidance on the land and housing property data analysis. Jason Hallman and my editors at Lexington Books, brought my research to light. Constructive critiques by Lexington's anonymous reviewer are gratefully acknowledged.

I am grateful to family and friends who have provided energy and an ear to this study. In particular, I would like to acknowledge the work of a lifetime done by my parents. My mother, Nina S. de Friedemann, also an anthropologist, instilled in me the passion for understanding people through anthropology. Through the years she provided many lessons on theory as well as examples of how to conduct fieldwork, the last taking place in September 1998. Her guidance and ethical behavior as a scholar and a teacher are embedded in me. Her death in October that year prevents her from seeing the completion of this project. Robert Friedemann, my father, has offered me a vibrant aesthetic view of the world, which I hope to have carried through in this book. Izak León and Lukas Uri Kelsey-Friedemann, my sons, came with me to conduct fieldwork. They have brightened every day, filling them with the roaring laughter of their lives.

A *todos, muchas gracias*.

CHAPTER ONE

Introduction

By 5:40 in the morning the yellow dirt roads of the rural areas in the Sabana de Bogotá in Colombia are filled with women and men riding bicycles to work at one of several hundred fresh-cut flower farms. They are due at their workplace by 6:00 A.M. when their supervisors check attendance. By 8:00 A.M. people in red, green, and blue uniforms are hard at work, scattered over the flower farms cutting roses, gerberas, and gypsophila, among many other flower varieties, most of which will be in supermarkets and florist shops in the United States in forty-eight hours, and the rest in a few other countries like Canada, Japan, and Germany. By 10:00 A.M. all flower cutting is done, and cultivation, classification, and packing begins. Between 12:00 and 3:00 P.M. the trucks arrive and load up the cardboard boxes that will fly, via Bogotá's international airport, to airports worldwide. Meanwhile at the farms, as the day goes by, the temperature in the greenhouses increases. Workers who came to work wearing sweaters, jackets, and *ruanas* are now sweating under the intense heat of the greenhouses. The lively conversation that starts the day can be heard again at lunch and yet again at 2:30 when workers break to go home. Some women will pick up their children before proceeding home to their domestic work as homemakers, mothers, wives, daughters, grandmothers, and sisters. At home, they wash the family's clothing by hand, make and serve dinner, wash dishes, and care for the children, among many other tasks. Other women and most men will run errands in town or head to the local store to socialize. At around 6:00 P.M. the men arrive home, have dinner, and sit down to watch television while the children play and the women wash dishes and get the household ready for the following workday.

In another home in the northern hemisphere, flowers on a dining room table become one more piece in the global mosaic of household goods and services: cars and garage door openers assembled in Mexico from parts that may have come from anywhere in South East Asia; clothes woven somewhere in Central or South America, Turkey, Israel, or Malaysia; United States credit card and health care bills processed anywhere from Barbados to India; Indian telephone-based computer technical support for the United States; and even domestic service provided by individuals from the Philippines or South America.

Cut Flowers in a Global Perspective

Around the world, the increasing flexibility of production and distribution of goods and services underlies the expansion and adjustment of capitalism to new forms of production, labor, accumulation of capital, and consumption patterns. Fresh-cut flowers embody all aspects of this complex and fast expansion, now called globalization. Initially located in the United States, the cut-flower industry moved south, to Colombia, in 1965 in search of lower production costs. Roses, carnations, pompons, chrysanthemums, alstroemerias, statice, gypsophilas, gerberas, calla lilies, and limonium are among the fifty types of flowers produced. Today, 95 percent of its production is shipped to wealthier nations, principally the United States, Germany, and Canada. In fact, almost two-thirds (59 percent) of all the flowers sold in supermarkets and florist shops in the United States are Colombian (Asocolflores 2004b, USDA ERS 2003). Women constitute close to 70 percent of Colombia's floriculture workforce, a percentage similar to those of other global assembly line industries as the majority of the world's global assembly lines rely heavily on female labor.

The gendered global economy of which floriculture is a part has been studied with great interest since the 1980s, fueled by the realization that poverty is gendered.[1] The studies, which have in common the examination of gender and labor, may be clustered according to the types of production associated to the global assembly line. Most influential are those that study specific factory settings, some of which are located in free trade zones (Cravey 1998; Freeman 1993, 1998, and 2000; Fuentes and Ehrenreich 1983; Fussell 2000; Kim 1997; Louie 2001; Mills 1999; Safa 1995a; Tiano 1994; Wolf 1992; and Wright 2001). Of particular importance among this group are the ethnographies of María Patricia Fernández-Kelly (1983) and Aiwa Ong (1987) and the research of Helen Safa (1986) and Jorge Carrillo and Alberto Hernández (1985), all pioneers of the study of gender inequalities on the factory floor.

Research has also examined subcontracting and the home-based global assembly line composed, for the most part, of women who do piecework at home (Benería and Roldán 1987; Gringeri 1994; Mies 1982; Peña 1989; Wilkinson-Weber 1999).

Studies of gender and labor go beyond what is known as the global assembly line. Scholars have recently turned their attention to the links between gender, transnational migration, and the home service sector demonstrating that the trends of globalization are not contained within industrial production (Anderson 2000; Chang 2000; Colen 1995; Constable 1997; Ehrenreich and Hochschild 2003; Gamburd 2000; Hondagneu-Sotelo 1994 and 2001; Parreñas 2001; Romero 1992). As an extension of examining the informal sector (Babb 1989; Clark 1994; Ehrenreich and Hochschild 2003; Seligman 2001) and craft production (Ronald J. Duncan 1998 and 2000; Grimes and Milgram 2000), recent studies explore the microenterprise (Ehlers 1990; Grasmuck and Espinal 2000; Milgram 2001; Rozario 1997). From a theoretical perspective, this formidable body of research explores the production and reproduction of gender inequalities and the ways in which the global economy has used local gender ideologies to aid their capital accumulation in turn shaping local constructions of gender and reinforcing patriarchal social relations (Elson 1995; Enloe 1989; Leacock and Safa 1986; McCann and Kim 2003; Nash and Fernández-Kelly 1983; Stichter and Parpart 1990).

What is striking about studies of gender and labor is that this apparent consensus on the production of inequality is actually quite varied cross-culturally as it hinges on local contexts. Most research has analyzed women workers as passive victims of gendered globalization and the industries as exploitative of women (Benería et al. 2000; Díaz and Sierra 1995; Fussell 2000; Kaufman and Gonzalez 2001; Mascia-Lees and Black 2000). However, as Linda Lim (1990) pointed out, a few studies have revealed that women actually use their working status and their labor to forge independence, delay marriage and childbearing, contest male domination in households and communities, and shape new identities (Amin and Al Bassusi 2003; Amin et al. 1998; Feldman 2001; Freeman 2000; Hondagneu-Sotelo 1994; Mills 1999; Tiano 1994; Yelvington 1995). The industries might even help integrate women into the economy (Freeman 1998; Lim 1990; Safa 1995a and 1999; Tiano 1994). Does the expansion of the market economy exploit women, liberate them, or something in between (Meier 1999; Tiano 1994, 2001)? These differing views on women and development share an interest in the constraints the market economy places on the individual. The industries, the political economy of the export business, and the effects of international policies are the focus points of this dominant debate on the integration or the exploitation of women. Such an analysis, however, centers on issues of structure instead of the agency of individuals, seeing women not as active participants in the process of industrialization but more often as victims.

Because the global assembly line, such as the cut-flower industry, has as much to do with capital accumulation and labor as it does with identity (Freeman 2000), I explore the links between the structure of the cut-flower industry in Colombia and the exercise of women workers' agency. What from a global perspective, analyzing issues of structure, might be perceived as exploitation, from a local and individual perspective, analyzing issues of individual agency, may be seen as an opportunity—one that often presents itself at the household level. Thus, as this study will demonstrate, by assembling flowers women are able to cultivate homes.

Probably because gender ideology associates women with the private sphere, the household is precisely where women first contest gender inequality. As we shall see, access to a steady income can provide women the means to challenge the patriarchal definition of the marriage contract—that is, the expectations of male and female roles—within their personal relationships and households. As they do so, women gain a larger margin of ideological mobility in society at large, gradually re-writing the gendered role expectations in the marriage contract. In order to fully examine the effects on workers of the global assembly line, in this case the floriculture industry, one must go beyond the factory floor and examine how intrahousehold dynamics shape women's participation and experience in the factory. In short, one must ask what happens when people leave work and arrive home.

In this study I intend to answer a seemingly simple question, but one that still hovers over most research done on the floriculture industry and applicable to other global assembly lines. That is, why do women workers in the fresh-cut flower industry in Colombia remain employed for ten years or more if the working conditions are as deplorable, the pay as terrible, and the overall employment as exploitative as most research has claimed (Maharaj and Dorren 1995; Medrano 1982; Medrano and Villar 1983; Reis et al. 1995; Silva 1982; Velez 1995)? Broader questions inform this study: Does employment in the non-traditional export oriented sector reinforce patriarchal relations of reproduction? How has rural women's entry into formal rural employment changed rural household dynamics and specifically intrahousehold bargaining? Does formal employment in the agricultural sector improve women's lives? If so, what role do wages and cultural attitudes toward women play in women's empowerment? What are the implications of gendered agency for development policies? This ethnographic study explores the ways in which women floriculture workers in Colombia challenge male domination in households enabled by wage income, property ownership, social networks, and improved self-esteem. In particular, this research fills a gap that previous research has not explored: understanding how domestic violence affects women's experiences and perceptions of wage labor in the formal sector as well as their intrahousehold bargaining processes and outcomes.

From a theoretical perspective, this ethnography explores the links between factory assembly line industries that have flourished under structural adjustment programs and the ways in which people experience the changes brought on by the programs and the factories at a household level.[2] This study analyzes the ways in which global economic processes articulate with local household processes to produce, in specific cultural contexts, a more gender equitable society. My research challenges the consensus that global assembly line industries reinforce patriarchal relations of reproduction.

I situate my study within the research field of women and development, focusing on global assembly line industries, because several characteristics of the fresh-cut cut flower industry in Colombia are similar to those in transnational industries. The floriculture industry may at one level seem to be significantly different from assembly line industries in that it is not a conventional manufacturing industry using machinery but is instead, at its base, agricultural. However, the flowers are mass produced in a series of standardized steps, the fundamental principle of factory assembly. The manner in which the workers and the work itself are organized and the export marketing of the product are characteristic of those found in manufacturing processes in global assembly line industries, regardless of the type of product involved.

To begin to answer the questions posed above, I did research among fresh-cut flower workers in Cajicá and Chía, two towns located in the Sabana de Bogotá (see figure 1.1).[3] The name Sabana ("savannah") was originally simply descriptive of the high-altitude flat grassland in which Bogotá is located. However, it has come to be used as a proper noun referring to the political and cultural entity of the central high plain rather than simply describing the geography of the area. As such I use the Spanish name throughout this text rather than translating it to English.

In Cajicá and Chía I examined the effects of working in floriculture upon individual's identities and household dynamics. From this perspective, my research questions the dominant exploitation model by demonstrating that the floriculture industry improves women's lives through promoting gender equity and fulfilling a quasi-governmental role in the region. The fresh-cut flower industry is in fact a catalyst for social change and female empowerment. The flower farms are modifying the cultural

Figure 1.1. The Sabana de Bogotá

definition of who is a formal worker, thus promoting cultural change. By hiring primarily women, who previously had been restricted to the informal sector and proscribed by peasant culture from becoming factory workers, the industry is affirming the value of women. By giving women a secure and permanent source of employment that provides a steady income, women are allowed to change the patterns of decision making inside the household as a result of having more bargaining power on matters ranging from purchases, physical mobility, and amount of domestic abuse they will withstand.

Women perceive themselves, their bodies, their capacity to work, and their social networks as the new base, defined as the elements necessary to make a living socially and materially (Gudeman 2001). The industry also empowers and affirms women both directly and indirectly by providing the scaffolding from which to build a base. Directly, flower farms provide workshops to the workers on domestic abuse and self-esteem, among other topics. Indirectly, flower farms empower women by providing a community where social networks are created. In turn, these elements propel women to challenge gender inequality. Although, women do not resist the authoritarian structure of the industry, they do oppose male dominance outside of the industry, particularly in their homes. Women are forging new identities while challenging and resisting male domination within the household.

This challenge is presented in both overt and subtle ways as well as in between. On one end of the spectrum many women are overtly opting out of the bargaining process in the household by establishing households without male partners, in effect guaranteeing themselves the role of head of household and sole decision maker. On the other end of the spectrum, women who do have male partners but do not acquiesce to male domination employ the threat of abandoning the home temporarily, using their income, job stability, and housing ownership, if they have it, along with household and child-rearing work as leverage for better treatment and more control. The industry also has an indirect role in shaping a more gender equitable society in Cajicá and Chía because the cultural changes occurring among fresh-cut flower workers permeate the culture of the region at large. Women who are not workers in the industry recognize the improved self-perception of the fresh-cut flower workers and emulate them.

That the choices women make are so dramatic and at times confrontational attests to the level and pervasiveness of violence and domestic abuse in Colombia. My study shows that in the region where this research was conducted, intrahousehold bargaining includes items such as women's freedom of movement, women's right to work for pay, and women's right to live free of dometic abuse. In fact, I argue that domestic abuse is so prevalent it constitutes a critical element in intrahousehold negotiations and should be incorporated into quantitative and qualitative studies of intrahousehold bargaining, as its absence may bias study results.

Local Models

This research is oriented by the understanding that "the processes of making a livelihood are culturally modeled" (Gudeman 1986, vii). Flower workers construct and traverse bridges between cultural realms: between the flower companies and their households, between their jobs and their position in their communities, between the flower industry economy and the economy of the community, and between the global economy and the household economy (Gudeman 2001). Like an individual with two cultures and two languages, the flower workers navigate constantly between worlds that intersect at some points and separate at others. They live simultaneously within various realities and speak several social languages: the languages of the flower industry, the community, and the household.

This differs from the neoclassical economic approach, which would focus on how the flower industry makes a profit by using land, capital, and labor to create flowers for export in a globalized economy. In such a framework, the women would be seen mostly as workers who sell their time, labor, and skill for a salary. In turn, these earnings will enable them to buy food and other consumption goods to distribute in their households. However, an economy also involves social relations, their development and maintenance as investments, and the construction of social networks, which may be called social capital. Economic anthropology addresses areas that, even economists agree, neoclassical economics struggles to incorporate into their modeling as endogenous variables (Agarwal 1997; Hart 1997) and generally leaves out as externalities. While constructing and traversing cultural bridges between various realms, flower workers are exercising agency, not merely resisting, in the world of global capitalism.

This study strives to focus on the benefits evaluated according to the workers' own measures of benefit and value. Individual and communal relationships imply the creation and maintenance of a social base that will yield returns that are hard to measure monetarily, and yet are full of value (Gudeman 2001).[4] Looking only at individual income and the amount of exports and foreign exchange generated would be subsuming value to the constraints of economic models. Benefits and value are qualitative as well as quantitative. Yet it is impossible to say that the influence of the flower industry is either all bad or all good. I consider that the positive effects of the industry should be highlighted, however, particularly for women, for three main reasons. First, sociocultural conditions are context specific. It is not possible, for example, to make labor standards in northern European countries the normative model for labor standards in Colombia, and on that basis to state that floriculture is an exploitative industry. I echo Lim's (1990) critique on export industry research: by evaluating worker's experience with the experience of workers in richer countries, the conclusions are not relevant to the contexts in which the export industries are actually located. Employment alternatives, labor standards, and quality of life *in Colombia* must be the basis for comparison to determine whether or not the flower sector is beneficial. Unarguably, in Colombia as in most parts of the world, the United States included, labor standards have much room for improvement, and the ideal would be the establishment of international labor standards that would be exercised and overseen worldwide. In practice, we are left with local alternatives and realities. In addition, the importance of local household contexts is of paramount importance. The opportunities that a woman, who suffers at the hands of her husband, sees in Colombia's flower industry might be different from those of other women living in less violent and more gender equitable societies.

Second, the negative view of the flower industry is based on data acquired during the early years of the industry. Floriculture has matured and, while there remains room for improvement especially with regard to occupational health and the environment, the advances that the industry has made in the last ten years need to be acknowledged. The floriculture industry plays a positive role in many women's lives, a role that is embedded in the ways they talk about their possibilities and options in life. Women power the engines of their own destiny in Cajicá and Chía, and they do it with a positive attitude.

Third, in spite of the obstacles the flower companies have had to overcome for over two decades,[5] they continue to provide jobs and to interact daily with the women who seek employment at their door. It could be argued that floriculture workers only earn minimum salaries, yet the industry has a large profit margin. Nonetheless, for many women the alternative is to have no employment at all or be employed in the informal sector with lower wages, without benefits, and in positions that offer lower status. This study provides an alternative perspective on this conundrum. Of course, this positive perspective does not intend to deny that the industry and its workers face numerous and enormous challenges. These challenges include occupational health, as I shall address later on, and the uncertainty that workers, not unlike most people in Colombia, face with respect to retirement and insufficient pension funds.

Political and Economic Context

An examination of the floriculture industry cannot be undertaken without an understanding of the national context. In a country that suffers from an intense economic recession, the flower companies offer hope. Not only do they provide jobs and community for many families, they employ one of the most disadvantaged groups in central Colombia: rural women. In addition, they provide a sense of order and opportunity in the midst of chaos and poverty. In the following sketch of Colombia's current political situation, I will provide a context for the reality of the people who work in the flower farms, as well as their alternatives, which we must consider in evaluating the relative value of floriculture work and the industry. My intention is not to provide an analysis of Colombia's recent history, already accomplished by many brilliant scholars (Ardila Galvis 2000; Arocha 2004; Bergquist and Peñaranda 1992; Duncan 2000; Jaramillo Agudelo 1976; Leal Buitrago 1994; Llorente and Deas 1999; Palacios 1995, 2001; Safford and Palacios 2002; Tirado Mejía 1998; Vélez R. 2000), but, rather, to present an ethnographic description of the current climate for those who live in the rural areas.

Some regions of Colombia have experienced political and social unrest since the 1930s (Duncan 2000). High altitude areas in the province of

Cundinamarca, where the Sabana de Bogotá is located, have enjoyed relative peace. Chía and Cajicá are among those towns that have been politically stable from the 1990s until today.

The turmoil that envelops the country has its origins in the unequal distribution of wealth, particularly of land. Current (Fuerzas Armadas Revolucionarias de Colombia-FARC and Ejercito de Liberación Nacional-ELN) and former (M-19) guerrilla groups first formed in the late 1960s and early 1970s and initially had as a main objective the redistribution of land. In the mid 1980s, in response to the guerrilla's systematic extortions and incursions into land, large landowners organized paramilitary organizations (Autodefensas Unidas de Colombia-AUC). The involvement by both guerrillas and paramilitary organizations in the illegal drug industry, which supplies the drug demand of northern markets like that of the United States, has made a complex military and political picture even more intricate. Recently, as Alejandro Reyes documents, the land ownership conflicts have been replaced by conflicts over territorial control; the state is one of several players using force instead of politics to achieve its goals (1988 as cited by Cubides 1999, 162).

In the late 1980s and early 1990s, the political and economic situation of Colombia dramatically declined as a result of this conflict for territorial control. Large numbers of wealthy or prominent individuals have left the country seeking greater economic and political stability. Over the decade of the 1990s, 2 percent of Colombia's population emigrated, predominantly the educated class (Price 2004). The net international migration rate for Colombia is estimated at –0.31 per 1,000 citizens in 2004, or approximately thirteen thousand leaving per year (US CIA 2004).

Even so, migration has been, for the majority of Colombian residents, within Colombia's national borders. While the upper classes left the country, many peasants in affected regions fled to urban centers in safer regions, such as the highlands of Cundinamarca, in search for employment. More than two million persons were internally displaced during the second half of the 1990s (Sarmiento Gomez et al. 2003, 5). Human Rights Watch estimates that 300,000 individuals were displaced throughout the country in 2001 alone (2002).[6] Colombia's National Administrative Department of Statistics (DANE) estimates that at the beginning of 2003, 8.5 million people were living permanently in a locality other than the one where they were born (2003). The issue of migration is difficult to tackle. What percentage of migrants are voluntary, and what percentage are forced migrants (displaced individuals)? Future researchers might find this question interesting and relevant given Colombia's context as migration is fairly substantial and common in developing countries (Massey 1988).

While the topic of migration lies beyond the scope of this study, I can note that the internal migration has largely been one of long distance displacement, migrants moving not simply from one town to another or even from one province to another, but actually relocating from one region to another (Sarmiento Gómez et al. 2003, 10). A striking 19.8 percent of all Colombian citizens are permanent internal migrants, primarily peasants who moved from rural to urban areas. Of these internal migrants, 31.2 percent have settled in the capital city of Bogotá (Sarmiento Gómez et al. 2003, 5). Thus, 2.65 million individuals, just over 6 percent of the nation's population, have migrated to the capital city within their lifetimes.

In the past couple of years, the situation in Colombia has shown signs of improvement. However, the massive internal migrations of the previous decades continue to have a major impact on the economic structure of the country. This exodus of vast numbers of Colombians to Spain, the United States, Costa Rica, Venezuela, and Ecuador, along with massive internal displacement, has intensified the country's economic recession. The economic crisis is so severe that in 2000 the official unemployment rate was 20.1 percent in urban areas and 13.3 percent in rural areas (Sarmiento Gomez et al 2003, 20). In 2004 the number of individuals living off *el rebusque*, or selling trinkets, rose to 800,000 (*Cambio* 2004). The streets of Bogotá are still filled with refugees standing under streetlights *rebuscando*: selling trinkets, cigarettes, discarded flowers, phone cards, or holding cardboard signs offering their labor in exchange for food. Over 50 percent of floriculture workers in the Sabana de Bogotá are also migrants.

While other regions experienced social and economic upheavals, the region of Chía and Cajicá has remained an oasis of calm. It enjoyed the high levels of human development characteristic of Bogotá and the rest of the Sabana. For instance, life expectancy, a general measure of welfare affected by a wide variety of social conditions, is high in the region. In 2001 the life expectancy at birth in Bogotá was 72.9 years (Sarmiento Gomez et al. 2003, 6). This rate is comparable to that of Venezuela (73.1 years) and Mexico (71.5 years) and substantially better than that of many Latin American countries, including Peru (70.0 years), Bolivia (63.7 years), and Brazil (62.9 years) (United States Census Bureau 2004). In addition, though throughout the years turmoil affected much of the rest of the country, the region remained an important source of employment, many of those jobs in the flower industry. Others come from the restaurants, clubs, small industries, and houses located in the region. As one walks in the villages and the region as a whole, there is a sense of peace and stability.

Labor Context: *Haciendas*

The Sabana de Bogotá, located in the province of Cundinamarca (see map 1.1) has three somewhat distinct floriculture sections with different sociocultural environments. The southern part of the Sabana is where floriculture started and has the oldest farms in the industry. This section includes the municipalities of Soacha, Madrid, Mosquera, Bojacá, and Facatativá (see map 1.2). Some of these municipalities have become more urban because of

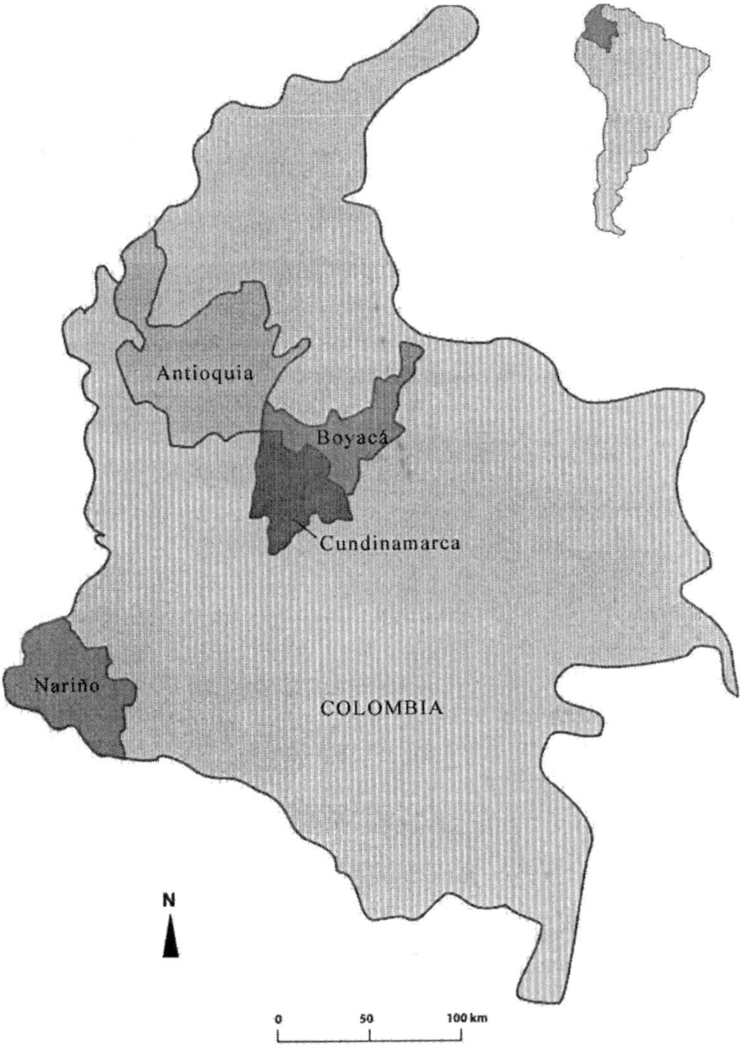

Map 1.1. Colombia and Four of Its Provinces (*Departamentos*)

Map 1.2. Villages with Floriculture Production in the Province of Cundinamarca

their proximity to Bogotá. Their population is more proletarian, and there are guerrillas in the region. Upper-class families and a few foreign firms own the majority of the farms in this region. Subcontracting has been observed in this region, which has union activity.[7]

To the north and beyond the Sabana includes the municipalities of Tocancipá, Gachancipá, Chocontá, and Villapinzón where the most recent flower farms have been established. Probably due to labor scarcity in that area of the Sabana there are contractors who find individuals to work at the flower farms and get paid a fee for each worker they bring.

In the northern area, still contained within the limits of the Sabana and where I chose to do fieldwork, flower companies are characteristically owned by landowners who have possessed the land for several generations. Municipalities in this section include Chía, Cajicá, Sopó, La Calera, Cota, Tenjo, and Tabio. In these towns the social relations of production date back to the colonial period and the *hacienda* system where permanent contracts are the norm.

Understanding the history of *haciendas* is important because the social interactions between the landed upper class and the landless lower class are based on the socioeconomic system established within the *hacienda*.[8] Even though *haciendas* as economic entities have for the most part disappeared, the social structure of labor relations they created persists and permeates labor interactions throughout the region. Thus labor interactions in the *haciendas* are replicated in the economic and social relationships between floriculture workers and flower industry owners and managers.

In general terms a *hacienda* is a large estate dedicated to agriculture, raising cattle, or both. Landed estates have existed in Latin America since the seventeenth century. The definition of *hacienda* that best encompasses most of its characteristic elements comes from Eric Wolf and Sidney Mintz (1957a): "An agricultural estate, operated by a dominant landowner and a dependent labor force, organized to supply a small market by means of scarce capital, in which the factors of production are employed not only for capital accumulation but also to support the status aspirations of the owner" (Wolf and Mintz 1957a, translated by Duncan and Rutledge 1977, 5). This definition highlights two interrelated structural elements of *haciendas*, one economic (capital accumulation) and the other social (status aspirations).[9] For the most part, *haciendas* have been replaced by agro-industries such as floriculture largely to become more profitable, or else their lands have been divided and sold. There are still a few *haciendas* left in Colombia, however, such as Hacienda Fagua in Cajicá, where a portion of this study was conducted.

Haciendas in Nueva Granada had wage workers called *jornaleros* and tenant laborers called *concertados*.[10] The tenant laborers were men who received the right to live within the *hacienda*, to cultivate a small plot, and to receive a small salary in exchange for their labor.[11] Even though the literature almost never mentions these laborers' families, it is assumed that they also lived on the *hacienda*; however, it was the males who held the labor contracts.[12] The family contributed labor for cultivating the plot and performed small menial jobs for the *hacienda* owner's family. Once a tenant laborer found a *hacienda* to work for, he usually stayed. In fact, the descendants of the tenant worker also often received jobs in the *hacienda* and eventually inherited the father's position. This patron-client relationship between landowners and employees is common today in Chía and Cajicá, regardless of the size of the landholding and whether the land is a *hacienda*, a large landholding known as a *latifundio*, or a secondary house for urban dwellers. Labor relations have continued to be based upon similar rights and obligations for landowners and tenant workers and their families, although today they are hired to *cuidar* (watch, take care of) a property and they and their jobs are called *cuidanderos* (caretakers). Flower companies commonly employ former tenant workers or their family members as *cuidanderos* in particular to keep watch at night. While the *cuidanderos* do not have any land to cultivate, they are provided with housing and guaranteed salaried jobs at the flower farm. Another less common name for these workers is *mayordomos*, whose jobs are called *mayordomías*.

As will be examined, an intergenerational association with the landowner is common practice among the flower farms located in former *haciendas*. Children and grandchildren (both women and men) of workers who were tenant laborers four and five decades ago currently work at the flower farms.

Field Site: Cajicá and Chía

I conducted my research in the northern section of the Sabana in two neighboring towns called Chía and Cajicá, in the province of Cundinamarca, central Colombia.[13] Specifically, I did fieldwork in the *veredas* of Fagua and Canelón, political subdivisions of the towns.[14] Fagua belongs to the town of Chía, while Canelón belongs to Cajicá. The villages of Chía and Cajicá are located 40 kilometers (25 miles) at the northern end of the Sabana (see maps 1.2 and 1.3).[15] According to the most recent national census, done in 1993, Chía has a population of 45,696 people and Cajicá of 29,504 (DANE 1993, 45).[16] However, given the massive rate of internal migration discussed above, these figures are outdated and probably greatly underestimate the actual current populations of the two towns. The capital Bogotá, a city of seven million people, is surrounded by an impressive chain of mountains on both the eastern and western sides, naturally limiting the growth of the city in those directions. Thus Bogotá grows toward the south and the north. The south is recognizably low income, destitute, and industrial while the north is wealthier. In recent years Chía and Cajicá have begun to be populated by the upper class, which has traditionally moved northward as the city has expanded. The land here is coveted and expensive, and the prices of land and housing have been driven up further by the drug cartel that, in an effort to launder money and to ascend socially, has bought extensive land, accomplishing, in effect, a land reform (Deere and León 2000; Reyes 1997).[17]

The *veredas* of Canelón and Fagua are located next to each other and on the west end of the towns of Cajicá and Chía (see map 1.3). Mountains on the west provide a beautiful and majestic view, as well as the geopolitical limits of Cajicá and Chía. A highway running parallel to the chain of mountains marks the eastern border of Fagua and Canelón. The yellow dirt roads of Fagua and Canelón are flanked on both sides by *vallados*, an old water repository system that was fed by natural water and protected by native *aliso*, *sauco*, and *sauce* trees (see figure 1.2). Twenty years ago children would catch frogs

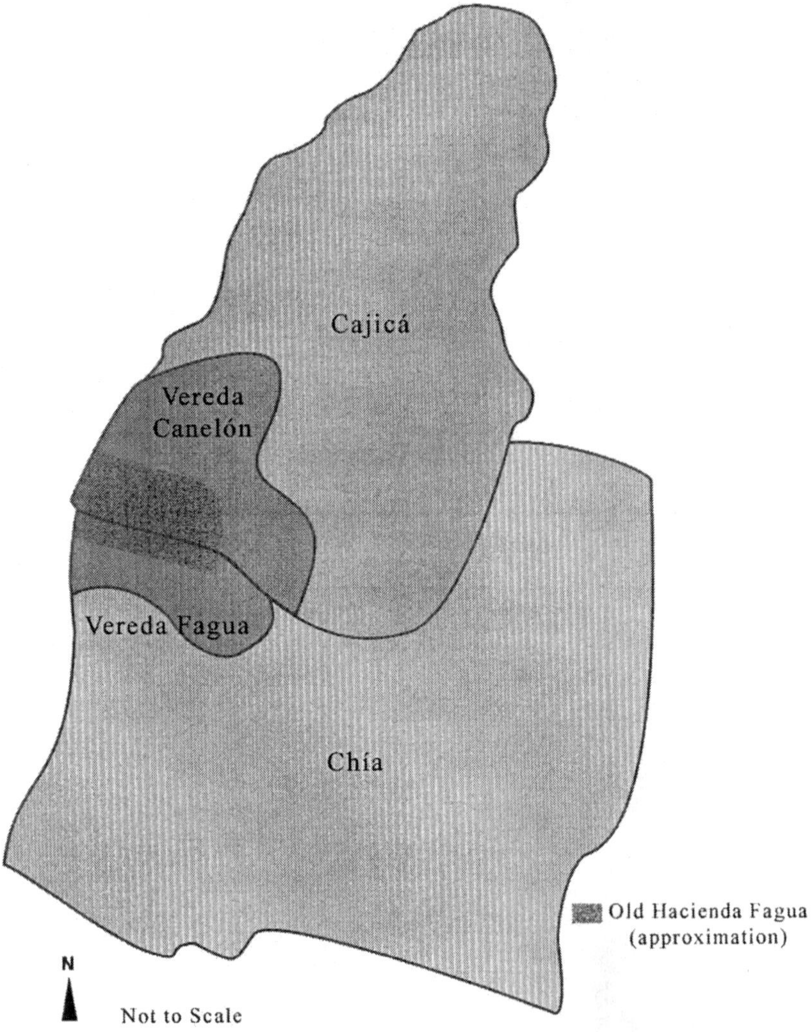

Map 1.3. Veredas Fagua and Canelón. *Note:* Fagua and Canelón are located in the municipalities of Chía and Cajicá, respectively.

there that thrived among the floating *buchones* (water plants) in the unpolluted water. Now, the trees have been cut, and the *vallados*, partially filled with dirt, are used by the region's inhabitants in part to dispose of sewage. Walking by, one might see an old woman wearing a black felt hat, wide grey skirt, and rubber boots dumping dirty liquid from a bucket into the *vallado*. A few meters ahead there is a machine pumping water from the *vallado* to irrigate a small plot of beets. In some areas, roads are lined by houses made in brick and cement instead of the traditional *tapia pisada* or *adobe* (dirt and straw bricks), in others by plastic greenhouses filled with flower plants. Scattered through the region, a few small pieces of land are used for intensive agriculture, and on the side of the roads one will see a few cows, calves, and sheep.

Wealthy families have also resided in the region since the colonial period, which, as stated above, defined the history of the land and its people and continues to shape inter-class and intra-class social patterns in Fagua and Canelón. In fact, while the economic structure of the region has changed dramatically, the social structure has not. One hundred years ago the *hacienda* system was so predominant in the Sabana that current neighborhoods in the city of Bogotá and *veredas* in towns are often named after the original *haciendas*. Vereda Fagua, for instance, is named after Hacienda Fagua.

Vereda Canelón and part of Vereda Fagua were included in an Indian reservation, called Cajicá, from 1593 to 1834. At the time of its dissolution

Figure 1.2. Street in Vereda Fagua with water repository canal (*vallado*) on the right

in 1834, the Cajicá reservation consisted of a total land area of 2,277 *fanegadas* (3,620 acres) and 1,301 surviving Indians. Hacienda Fagua was created in 1838, after the dissolution of both the reservation and the *encomienda*.[18] The *hacienda* comprised 1,231 *fanegadas* (1,957 acres), that is, over 50 percent of the reservation (Umaña 1981, 60–62). The more than 1,000 people who then found themselves landless became the available labor force around the *hacienda*. (It is not known what happened to the rest of the reservation land. It is assumed that it was acquired by different individuals for subsistence agriculture and some cattle grazing.) The original owners of Hacienda Fagua were Don Antonio Castro and Doña Juliana Uricochea (Umaña 1981, 60–70).

From 1917 to 1941, Hacienda Fagua was in the hands of the Umaña family. In 1941 it was split between two disputing brothers, sons of Don José Antonio Umaña, with 350 *fanegadas* (557 acres) each (Umaña 1981, 68). One half of the *hacienda* continues to be called Hacienda Fagua and continues to be operated as a *hacienda* under the ownership of a prominent upper class family who acquired it from Enrique Umaña Valenzuela sometime in the mid-1940s (Umaña 1981).[19]

The owners of the other half divided the land between eight siblings in 1974. One of those tracts of land has since been held by a line of men who have all shared the same first and last name. They sold some of the land to upper-class individuals who have built homes on one hectare (2.47 acres) each and commute one hour to Bogotá every day for work. Another tract of the land in this second half remains a cattle pasture. In the last fifteen years, the rest of this section of the original Hacienda Fagua has been cultivated with flowers for export by several companies and under varied ownership. One farm is managed by a descendant of the original *hacienda* owners on the inherited property. Other farms produce flowers on land that was sold after 1974. Somewhat ironically, this section of the original Hacienda Fagua, which has developed in a way that has removed it far from its *hacienda* economic origins and incorporated it into global commerce, is named Vereda Fagua. The remnant of Hacienda Fagua that remains in operation as a *hacienda* is associated with Vereda Canelón.

The specific labor relationships within Hacienda Fagua, at least for the twentieth century, have been described in the ethnography of Laura Umaña (1981). From 1917 to 1941 Hacienda Fagua employed both temporary wage workers called *jornaleros temporales* and tenant laborers. The specific terms used for tenant laborers in Fagua are *arrendatario* and *aparcero* rather than *concertado*. The tenant arrangement, according to Umaña, was a strategy of the *hacendado* to provide the *hacienda* with a stable labor force. The tenant laborers were compensated for their work with a minimal salary and with the right to cultivate a piece of land around the small houses that the *hacendado* provided for them. The wage laborers arrived for the harvest and were usually hired in *cuadrillas* or groups of thirty to forty individuals. The *hacendado* was obliged to feed and house them until the work season was over.

Even though the economic characteristics of the region are different today than in the first half of the twentieth century, the social patron-clientship ties between worker and boss have remained the same. The cultural patterns people have followed in the last one hundred years to secure land tenure and economic security exhibit such relationships. Through purchases of small plots of land in the first half of the twentieth century, temporary workers in *haciendas* or other large landholdings turned Vereda Canelón into a region of small subsistence farms known as *minifundios*. In this way, the neighboring areas to the *hacienda* became repositories of available wage labor.

Hacienda Fagua not only had tenant laborers but also temporary workers. The *hacendado* in Hacienda Fagua would impose the stipulations of the work contract with both types of workers. The *caporal*, *mayordomo*, or *capataz* (manager) was in charge of the management of the *hacienda* and would hire temporary laborers by giving them an advance and then transport them to the *hacienda*. This still holds true in areas north of Cajicá and Chía. In Tocancipá, Gachancipá, and Chocontá, people are hired on the spot to work in flower farms and are taken to the farm by busload.

The flower farms where I did my fieldwork are located on large landholdings in this general region. The flower farm where I conducted lage portions of my fieldwork and which I will call Muisca Flowers, has roughly 120 *fanegadas* (191 acres). Although its owner comes from a wealthy rural family, he is adamant that his family did not own a *hacienda* and that they have never been *hacendados*; "my family was not an aristocratic family." His insistence on the distinction between being wealthy and being *hacendado* is subtle yet piercing and demonstrates the rigidity of the class system in Colombia. As Ronald Duncan notes "Colombia's rigid social-class system functions as a semi-caste system that locks certain people into their birth status. A person's caste status is determined first by their family name, with a few Spanish and other European names constituting the small elite group. The elite functions as a closed caste, rarely admitting new members, and when they do, they are wealthy people of Western European Christian origin" (2000, 21). Today as two centuries ago the elite owners of *haciendas* control politics and finances. Following the elite in this social hierarchy, according to Duncan, are professionals in traditional careers like medicine and law, as well as artists and intellectuals. The working class is divided into those in service, clerical, and technical occupations and below them those in manual work. Upward social mobility is possible for people in the first category who have more opportunities for education and mobility. The manual workers, at the bottom of the class system have a social position that, like that of the elite, is ascribed and difficult to move out of. *Campesinos* (peasants) belong to this class, and *campesinos* of Afro-Colombian and indigenous descent are more rigidly locked into their status than *campesinos* of European descent (Ronald Duncan, 22). While *hacienda* families may be less wealthy than other individuals, they still have the social standing that they have enjoyed for generations. Their last name evokes a halo of aristocracy around them.[20]

The region where the towns of Chía and Cajicá are located is known as the *altiplano Cundi-Boyacense,* which includes two provinces with cultural and historical associations to one another: Cundinamarca and Boyacá. The peasant population of the *altiplano*, as this vast region is commonly called in Colombia, is at the bottom of the rigid class system because of its indigenous ancestry. Fagua and Canelón are populated today by the top and the bottom tiers of the class system. They are just 40 miles from Bogotá, the seat of government since colonial times, giving the elite of the area access to the center of political power. In the second half of the twentieth century, the region also began to be populated by the middle range of the class system. It is this middle class, the working class in service, clerical, and technical jobs, that is emulated by the peasant population (Bourdieu 1984). This rigid class system is a model that lives in people's minds. When people of the region talk about their dreams, their wants, their life in the future, they often state that they want to *superarse*: to become better, superior, more educated. The yardstick, the standard of what they hope to achieve, is the social group immediately above them.

The class system also determines the regional characteristics of land ownership and economic organization. The cultural patterns established by the *hacienda* system extend beyond the physical boundaries of the *hacienda* into the *veredas* and towns. Indeed, the cultural context of *hacienda*, including social relations, permeates the culture of the region as a whole. Although contemporary Fagua and Canelón have a diverse pattern of land ownership, social ties between the workers and owners are very similar to those from the early twentieth century. The vision and the specific possibilities, however, have changed in the last twenty years. Previously, people hoped to buy enough land to cultivate and build a house. Today, their hope is to buy a big enough lot on which to place a prefabricated house and not have to pay rent, without the accompanying desire or the possibility to cultivate a subsistence plot. The change reflects the reality of exorbitant housing prices, scarcity of land, and urbanization. Regardless of the size of the land individuals struggle to buy, the strategy of using worker-boss labor relations to achieve property ownership has remained the same. Such struggle is demonstrated in the testimony collected by Umaña: "About forty years ago we bought this small piece of land with money from temporary work at the [*hacienda*] . . . , with that we gathered some money, and before it was cheap, we bought a *fanegada*, and then a quarter. We kept on doing temporary work there (*jornaleando*), *they lent us money, and we ended up owing them*" (1981, 76, emphasis added, my translation). The testimony exemplifies the patron-client link through social assets between the *hacendado* and the peasant, one that both parties struggle to maintain through social practices and loans. I am using Guyer's concept of asset in the widest sense considering social networks and relations as assets (1997). Loans guarantee workers for the *hacendado*, for while workers owe money, they cannot leave the *hacienda*. In addition, by lending them money, the *hacendado* establishes a social debt with the workers, as the workers and their families are obligated to reciprocate in some fashion. That social debt then becomes an asset to the *hacendado*, which can be "cashed in" in services rendered by the workers' spouses or children. In turn, as the peasants and their families are aware, their debt becomes a social bond. For the peasants and their families the financial protection of the *hacendado* provides them with social capital in times of need. The *hacienda's* owner, known as *el patrón* (the boss), was seen as a benefactor because he granted people the favor of jobs.

This perceived patron-client relationship still holds true in Chía and Cajicá and specifically in Fagua and Canelón. In a few of the flowers farms of the region, including the farm where I conducted fieldwork, many workers talk about the owner in these terms. Their deferential attitude was evidenced by their calling him *patrón*. Social reciprocity across class lines exists in the same way as between *hacendado* and tenant laborer. For example, the flower farm Muisca Flowers employs a psychologist, Victoria Rondón, who works as the human resource manager for the company. In her forties and divorced, mother of a ten-year-old daughter, Rondón has been working for Muisca Flowers since it started twenty years ago. She is treated with respect but not as deferentially as the owner. She is called *Señora* Victoria, a step down from usages of *Don* (with first name) or *Señor* (with last name) employed for the owner, as a member of the upper class. This despite the fact that, for the most part, Victoria decides who gets hired or fired and thus for people working in Muisca Flowers it is she, not the owner, who is at the top of the social/work pyramid. She has close social networks to certain individuals who work at the farm through which she guarantees a steady supply of people who work for the company and have allegiance to it. As in *hacienda* times, workers know that Muisca Flowers can be a source of jobs for relatives through Rondón. In addition, because Rondón has access to networks they do not, she might be able to find them jobs in other flower farms. Certain provinces and towns are more represented among the workers in the company than others, reflecting Rondón's particular preferences and the alliances she has forged with certain workers. For instance, Rondón prefers to hire people from Chía rather than from than Cajicá who, according to her, like to fight too much. She also favors people from Nariño and Boyacá (also regions where *haciendas* existed). There are entire families from these two regions working in Muisca Flowers.

Clearly, not all individuals benefit from *hacienda*-like labor relations. In fact, distinctions can be analyzed examining the emic or local categories of social differentiation. Among rural inhabitants and their descendants, who would not characterize themselves as *campesinos* or peasants unless they are old or live off of subsistence agriculture, but rather think of themselves as workers, social distinctions are drawn between three distinct categories: *raizales*, *antiguos*, and *migrantes* (defined below). As emic categories, the terms *raizal*, *antiguo*, and *migrante* are labels that have arisen locally to describe the residents' own perspective on and analysis of important social divisions. These differentiations are based on people's length of time living in the region, but the most important distinction, the yardstick, is based on an individual's association to the *hacienda* or other large tract of land, its owner, and the length of such association. In this way *raizal* refers to those who have been in the region for several generations and who worked for Hacienda Fagua or for other large landowners in the first half of the twentieth century. The metaphor people use is one of plants: *raizal* comes from the Spanish word *raiz* (root) and means "rooted in the region." It acknowledges the connection of the people to the land in a historical sense, and also suggests permanence and affirms people's ongoing connections to the land.[21]

In contrast, those referred to as *antiguos*, meaning "old" or "antique," are people who migrated to the region roughly fifteen to sixty years ago and have been associated with the region for at least two generations. While they have extended family in the region, their families usually are not as large as the *raizal* families and their patterns of property acquisition, as we shall see, are different from those of *raizal* individuals.

Finally, new families and individuals have migrated to the area in search of jobs in the flower industry.[22] Most individuals arrive in the region alone, and after securing a job, some bring their immediate family as well. With time, the extended families of the original migrants also begin to arrive to the area, usually finding jobs in the same flower companies where the initial migrants work. One finds entire families, whether *raizal*, *antiguo*, or migrant, working for one flower company where their jobs are secured through a social network of worker-*patrón* relations.

The local or emic classifications of *raizal*, *antiguo*, and migrant have been conceptualized and maintained by *raizal* people. In their view, even if a person's parents were born in the region, if the parent's parents were not, they are considered *antiguo* rather than *raizal* individuals. Newcomers to the region do not realize that there is a distinction between *raizal* and *antiguo* but rather see everybody in the region who was not born there as "not an old resident," "not from the region," or "not from here." For the *antiguo* or old families, the distinction between the three sets of groups is accepted and used as a way to mark and differentiate the population. One can see from this how employment at the flower farms has penetrated the region and is defining rhythms of life.

Table 1.1 shows the percentage of survey respondents from Muisca Flowers who belong to each of these three social categories. Approximately one-third of women (33 percent) and one-fourth of men (27 percent) reported being *raizal*, that is, being native to the region and potentially having *hacienda* social relations. Almost half of women (47 percent) and three-fifths of men (59 percent) have migrated into the region within the past fifteen years. (This table describes the 74 percent of all workers who completed the survey at Muisca Flowers, the flower farm where this fieldwork took place. The full description of survey methodology is found below.)

Although *raizal* families conceptualize the status of people in the region in exclusionary terms—either *raizal* or not *raizal*, that is, new to the land—it is the immigrant population that is most responsible for setting the newly proletarian tone of region. There is a give and take dynamic between these two communities. The people of Fagua and Canelón are becoming increasingly proletarian, with an urban style of living within a rural setting. Most people no longer produce any of their own food, and most people under thirty do not have food-related agricultural knowledge. Rather, they buy milk, produce, potatoes, fruit, and meat products at the market once a week. A few families have a milk cow, some chickens, or a big enough plot of land to grow

Table 1.1. Emic Categories of Residential Status

	Women		Men		All	
n =	231	64%	129	36%	360	100%
Migrant	108	47%	76	59%	184	51%
Antiguo	46	20%	18	14%	64	18%
Raizal	77	33%	35	27%	112	31%

cilantro, mint, and chives. Older *raizal* women do use trees and plants of the region for medicinal purposes, but even this is becoming more difficult. For example, the region has become so devoid of vegetation that when Josefina Puentes wished to make *sauco* tea for respiratory ailments, she had to send her grandson Jairo Cáica to gather leaves from a tree on the side of the road about half a mile from her house.

Most people native to Canelón and Fagua do not describe themselves as peasants but rather as rural workers, though they recognize themselves as being of peasant descent. Most recent immigrants state they are *campesinos* (peasants) or that they come from *el campo* (the rural area). This distinction is important given the social structure in Colombia, described in the previous section, as *rural worker* is a step above *peasant*.

People in the region make a living in diverse ways. They might own a *cantina* (bar) or *tienda* (store and bar) where mostly men, and recently a few women, congregate on Sundays to drink alcohol and play *tejo* or *turmequé*, a game indigenous to the region's pre-Colombian Muisca culture. The purpose of the game is to place the *tejo*, a thick iron disk, inside a brass ring hidden under clay. The *tejo* is thrown from one end of the court to the other. Each end has a wooden box filled with clay. If the disk falls inside the ring, a few firecrackers explode. The game is traditionally played by men and is filled with sexual metaphors and connotations. In the last few years, however, women have begun to play, which is in fact a sign of the type of cultural change described in this book. The *cantina* or *tienda* where *tejo* is played is a type of store, but store sounds too sophisticated to describe what the business really is, as all that is necessary to have a *tienda* is enough space to place a set of *tejo*. Both Fagua and Canelón have six *tiendas* that sell basic groceries like sugar, flour, oil, coffee, eggs, and soda pop and also have sets of *tejo*. There are several houses that sell beer, and all that is needed for that business is a few stools or benches where people can sit and someone to be home on a permanent basis to give out the bottles of beer and take the money. Not even space is necessary, since the bench or the stools can be placed on the side of the road. Fagua has one bakery that is operated by a husband and wife, and Canelón has a family-owned mini-market. Men who do not own a business work in construction, car repair, floriculture, baking, truck driving, day labor in agriculture, and retailing. Others are factory workers, guards, gardeners, and workers at a local egg farm. Women are employed as house servants, retail employees, gasoline dispensers, flower workers, cooks at restaurants in Cajicá and Chía, and childcare providers. Some people hold two jobs. Some supplement their salaries by cooking and selling meals, selling cosmetics, working as night guards, and washing clothes. In this respect, the people from

Fagua and Canelón have a life in which "occupational multiplicity" (Weil 1995, 2) is the norm.

Fieldwork

I chose the northern section of the Sabana, where Chía and Cajicá are located, as my field site with two criteria in mind, representativeness and physical security. First, I was looking for a representative area, one that has had flower farms since the industry was established in 1965 because it would have a population of workers associated with the industry since its inception. Chía and Cajicá have had flower farms since the 1970s. I also considered the region representative because it has flower farms associated with the Asociación Colombiana de Exportadores de Flores (Asocolflores, Colombian Association of Flower Growers) as well as those that are not, a distinction that is important because Asocolflores establishes social and environmental guidelines for associated farms. Affiliation is optional, however, and thus the differences in the overall quality of the flower farms can be large, as other researchers have noted (Meier 1999). My observations of the farms themselves were done mainly in a single flower farm, Muisca Flowers, where I spent the majority of my time. I also visited a few flower farms in the towns Bojacá and Mosquera located in the south and one in Gachancipá in the north. In these farms I mainly observed their physical and organizational structure. The people I interviewed worked in a variety of farms in the area of Chía and Cajicá.

Second, I was looking for a region that was politically stable for the safety of myself, my children who accompanied me, and the people I interviewed. I chose this region in part because it has no guerrilla or paramilitary presence.

I did fieldwork in several stages that included one visit each year between 1991 and 2000 to develop and maintain a network. The initial information regarding the industry itself I obtained while doing fieldwork in 1996 and 1998 to complete a master's degree at the Humphrey Institute of Public Affairs at the University of Minnesota. The majority of the ethnographic information was gathered during four months of field time in each of 1999 and 2000. Developing my network over an extended period of time allowed me to develop rapport with flower industrialists who are suspicious about researchers and others who want to gain access to the flower farms. I was also able to follow up with a certain number of people who work at the flower farms and understand how their lives changed over time.

I am from Bogotá, and I belong to a family that has ties both to Colombia and the United States. Spanish is my native language. I am culturally fluent in the urban context of Bogotá and relatively so in the specifics of rural culture of the region. I have had close connections to the region through family and life-long friends. As a result, I did not have to acquire the language and cultural learning necessary to navigate the region.

My bicultural experience is embedded in my name and in the identities I negotiate. I did not encounter the standard social obstacles to talking with people and developing rapport that an outsider would face. Most importantly for developing rapport, my given name and first family name are foreign, placing me immediately outside of the elite and aristocracy and inside the intellectual class, allowing, I believe, for easier access while talking to elites. My second family name is common in Colombia allowing me an easier approach among the people that live and work in the region. Thus, my very name allowed me to negotiate my identity depending on the context. Doing fieldwork with my two children, who were between the ages of two and six years, while challenging was advantageous too. Mothers, grandmothers, and mothers-to-be were happy to talk with me, perhaps thinking that I shared some of the same challenges they faced in coordinating motherhood with work.

Being native to Colombia was also helpful in knowing how to navigate the political arena and to avoid bringing up sensitive topics that have forced previous national and foreign researchers to abandon their research. The topic of households and women seemed harmless and irrelevant to politically charged issues in the industry because they are "women's issues." This made my fieldwork less difficult and risky, both for me and for the people I interviewed.

Muisca Flowers, Fagua, and Canelón

Gaining access to a community, a major endeavor and key for any anthropological fieldwork, is something I developed through the years beginning with my first independent research project. I conducted fieldwork in 1988 and 1989 in the Vereda Saucío in the town of Chocontá, located just north of the Sabana, which ultimately led me to focus my public affairs and anthropology dissertation research, on which this book is based, in the cut-flower industry. At the time I was studying mass communication and development in the same area previously studied by Colombian sociologist Orlando Fals Borda. In the process, I became interested in the workers lining up at 5:00 A.M. in the central plaza of Chocontá to take company buses to work at flower farms located in nearby towns. Being aware of the difficulty of doing fieldwork in Colombia in general and in the flower industry in particular, I planned in advance my meeting with Leonardo Cárdenas, owner of Flores Amazonas. I had contacted him during previous trips, developed a rapport with him, and received his permission to do interviews and conduct a questionnaire at his flower farm as a springboard to getting to know many people in the region. In June of 1999, however, I was told upon arriving at the farm that Leonardo Cárdenas was very ill. Thus, there was no possibility of doing research there. Fortunately, a friend and colleague then offered to put me in contact with the uncle of a friend, owner of a flower company in the region.

The owner of Muisca Flowers was the contact my friend provided. He was a kind man in his fifties. It appeared from his attitude when I first arrived at his office at the flower farm that other researchers had approached him before. He slouched down on the leather couch and said, "Speak." As I told him about the project and what I wanted to do, he sat straight up and began to show interest. We had a two-hour in-depth conversation. In addition to the information he gave me in the interview, at the end of the visit he stated, "I am going to help you, but I am going to tell you why I am going to help you." He had been writing a doctoral dissertation in the 1970s in the United States on education in Colombia.When he returned to Colombia to do fieldwork, however, the government suspected him of working for the CIA, and education leaders suspected him of working for the government. He was never able to finish his doctorate. To this he added, "You will do what I was not able to do," and proceeded to call all the administrative personnel and asked them to help me in whatever ways I needed. After this, he took me on a tour of the farm, introduced me to the managers and supervisors, and described the farm's general procedures.

Muisca Flowers has 40 *fanegadas* (64 acres) dedicated to production of flowers or flower plants. The property is lined with large eucalyptus and pine trees. A guard in uniform is posted at the large red entrance gate. He lets workers in and stops visitors, calling the main office to get permission to allow them in. On the left of the tree-lined road is a big artificial water reservoir that was under construction when I was there. Beyond the "lake," as the water reservoir is called, are pastures for cattle where a dozen or so Holstein cows eat grass. The cows are a "leftover" of what once was the dominant mode of production in this large piece of land. At about 40 meters into the farm, on the right, is the first block of flowers. Another 50 meters into the farm, workers and visitors are greeted by geese in a fenced pond. From this point on, one can smell the roses. There are two red brick buildings where the administrative staff works and, at the end of the corridor, there is a large doorway leading to the classification area where the flowers, mainly roses, are classified, packed, and put into trucks. This area is where the wonderful aroma comes from.

I spent approximately one-third of my time in Muisca Flowers and the other two-thirds outside of Muisca Flowers in the *veredas* of Fagua and Canelón and in other flower farms. Access to individuals in the community was logistically more difficult than my previous experience in Chocontá among peasants engaged in subsistence agriculture. I quickly realized in the *veredas* of Fagua and Canelón that people, particularly women cut-flower workers, could not find time to talk to me once they got home because both the children and the house needed tending and few men went home directly from work. In addition, women were eager to talk to me while they were at work. By interviewing at the flower farm, I was providing women with a break from the routine and a period of recess or slow work.

I was prepared to encounter some resistance as I had in Chocontá. To my surprise not only was there no timidity, women, particularly the cut-flower workers, *wanted* to be interviewed and demanded that I give them an appointment and even expressed feelings of rejection when I did not. Although men were generally not as forthcoming, I was able to develop excellent rapport with four men and their families. In total, I conducted around sixty individual interviews. Forty-eight of those were in-depth individual interviews with male and female floriculture workers (see table 6.1). In addition, I conducted multiple informal conversations and interviews with workers from other farms as well as with people not engaged in cut-flower work. Individuals for the in-depth interviews were both men and women workers chosen from the same flower farm where the survey, described below, was administered. These forty-eight individuals were chosen using a stratified random sample from the following subgroups: men or women who had been working with the company from one month to two years, from three years to five years, from six to ten, from eleven to fifteen, and from fifteen on. All interviews were conducted using interview guides covering topics relevant to household economics and the life history, including work history, of each individual and their family members. I observed people in households, flower farms, and public places such as the market, streets, and shops off the street and conducted participant observation as possible in people's houses and the market. I followed up with eight of those individuals using extensive interviews and participant observation in their homes and in the *veredas*. In addition to the individual interviews in Fagua and Canelón, I observed and engaged in conversation with people in Cajicá and Chía's markets, Chía's shopping center, and other public places.[23]

I performed a survey of all 488 employees in Muisca Flowers. All female and male floriculture workers at Muisca Flowers, the largest flower farm in Chía and Cajicá, participated. I designed two largely identical surveys with sixty-eight questions each, one for women and one for men. I trained three assistants to administer the survey and record responses; all respondents were interviewed by one of them or by myself. The difference between the surveys was the wording for three questions in relation to children and to their financial and emotional support. The survey included basic demographic questions: age, marital status, number of children, level of education, town of origin, years living in Chía or Cajicá, years working in flowers, years working at Muisca Flowers, previous occupation, and occupation of parents. The survey also included questions related to household chores and expenditures and household decision making.

In addition, the survey included questions on land and housing ownership. Until twenty years ago, the region was dedicated to intensive agriculture and extensive cattle farming with most families owning their own homes, modest as they may have been. Since then, however, high fertility rates and bilateral inheritance patterns that divide property in equal portions among siblings have contributed to intense subdivision of the land. The resulting plots, called *minifundios*, have become so small that agriculture is near impossible and they are used mostly for housing. Since an individual may inherit such a lot with or without a house, the survey gave people the opportunity to state how they had acquired ownership of their lot and house in separate questions, questions that agricultural censuses do not ask (Deere and León 2003). Finally the survey had questions related to attitudes with respect to the flower farms and other types of work, what people do on their free time, and what they would like to see their children do.

Of the 488 survey participants, 360 (74 percent) consented to complete the entire survey. The reasons why individuals did not consent to some questions vary. These included having very low literacy skills and not being able to verify the content of the questionnaire and regarding the research as a nuisance. Most importantly, some individuals, following the cultural parameters of Andean peasants, were suspicious of any written document, especially one containing personal information, despite reassurance that surveys were anonymous.

Representativeness of My Survey

After I administered my survey at Muisca Flowers, a consortium of ten flower farms including Muisca Flowers took the opportunity to learn more about their workforce by using my survey questions to gather data in the year 2000 on all of their 2,068 employees. Those ten farms represent a large proportion of floriculture for the northern section of the Sabana of Bogotá. This consortium survey thus creates a picture of the broad population of flower workers within which Muisca Flowers employees, the focus of my survey, are situated. An analysis of the demographic characteristics of consortium employees shows that my survey respondents are similar to the region's floriculture workers as a whole and thus are representative. (All consortium data presented here was obtained directly from the Consortium on January 3, 2001.)

The demographic characteristics upon which my household decision-making analysis rests are gender and residential status. Throughout the region as in my survey at Muisca Flowers, women constitute a majority of floriculture workers. Among consortium employees, 61 percent are female, compared to 64 percent of my sample of survey respondents.

Half of floriculture workers are migrants; 51 percent of my sample and 48 percent of consortium employees have moved to the region within the past fifteen years. At the other extreme, three-tenths of floriculture workers are *raizales*, that is, native to the region. In my sample, 31 percent of the workforce is *raizal*, compared to 28 percent throughout the region's flower farms. The greatest difference between my survey and the consortium survey is found among *antiguos*, those who migrated to the region fifteen or more years ago. In my survey, 18 percent of respondents reported *antiguo* status while 24 percent of workers as a whole fall into this category.

Data on age, education, and marital status also show that my sample is representative of floriculture workers in the region. Muisca Flowers employees are slightly younger than cut-flower workers in general. More than half (54 percent) of my survey respondents are under age thirty, compared to 42 percent of the region's cut-flower workers. On average, Muisca Flowers employees in my sample have completed 6.5 years of education compared to 6.2 among consortium floriculture workers as a whole. Almost two-thirds of cut-flower employees are married (civil, religious, or de facto); 65 percent of Muisca Flowers employees in my survey reported being married, compared to 64 percent of floriculture workers in the consortium. Conversely, 34 percent of Muisca Flowers workers are single (never married or separated), compared to 35 percent of the region's cut-flower workers generally. When all of these data are disaggregated by gender, the similarity between the participants in my research and in the northern section of the Sabana cut-flower workers generally is borne out.

Organization of the Chapters

Given the amount of data collected during fieldwork, one difficulty an anthropologist often must face in the process of presenting the data is deciding which topics to include and which to leave for later analysis. In this book I have not included politics among the municipalities, civic leaders, and the flower industry owners. Such a topic is more appropriate to an analysis of the role of institutions in rural development. Another topic is the development of the industry itself. While my results show that the industry has been beneficial for women and that it is a catalyst for social change, undeniably not every effect of the industry is positive. Negative impacts include the resulting environmental degradation, which, although generally outside of the focus of this research, needs to be briefly addressed regarding two main issues: water use and the chemical contamination of water and soil. The use of exorbitant amounts of water by the floriculture industry is of concern to many municipalities. The Sabana de Bogotá, in geological terms, is a great sponge of clay. Most flower farms have their own water wells that pump water from 200 meters and deeper underground aquifers. Such large quantities of water are used that the water table is dropping, in turn making the soil collapse in certain areas and roads and buildings crack. In effect, Colombia is exporting water in the form of flowers, and the bulk of the floriculture industry does not pay the state in any way for the use of this resource. This may be one of the reasons costs are lower for Colombian flower production. In addition to the uncontrolled use of water, pesticides and fertilizers may be contaminating the ground water. Although studies on the health hazards to female workers have been conducted (Medrano and Villar 1983), which include the effects of chemical use on fetuses and babies as well as dermatological and respiratory problems, new studies on occupational health are needed. This is especially true since Asocolflores designed new guidelines for chemical use and application in the mid 1990s and many associated flower farms have since implemented the guidelines. However, despite the new guidelines, I did observe a couple of farms in Chía and Cajicá that did not follow safety rules for the use of pesticides. All these issues are outside of the scope of this research but clearly need to be independently researched.

In chapter 2 I present a theoretical overview of the global assembly line, which includes the labor debates regarding the exploitation or integration of women and how such debates relate to the flower industry. I address the ways in which labor conditions have improved in the last ten years in the industry, including the topic of labor security. An ethnographic description of the Muisca Flowers flower farm is presented in chapter 3. In it I describe the organization of most flower farms, the segmentation of tasks, and the management of labor. By examining schedules, tasks, and organization, my aim is to explain how such routines and discipline transfer to people's larger lives and identities. Chapter 4 focuses on the ways in which the flower farms have heightened a sense of identity and empowerment for women, which in turn affects internal household dynamics and social structure. In this chapter I explain the social component of the Florverde program, which includes workshops on self-esteem, domestic violence, and literacy. In chapter 5, I shift from looking at the farms to looking at the relationship between floriculture wage work, the emic categories of residence and social assets, and women's and men's property ownership. To analyze these data I introduce the chapter with the theoretical underpinnings of household economics and intrahousehold bargaining. In chapter 6 I pick up immediately with the data and results presented in chapter 5 and examine the gendered ownership of land and housing and the differential effect that wages and property ownership have on intrahousehold bargaining, including patterns of decision making on household expenditures. I provide four case studies that exemplify changes in social structure as well as challenges to cultural patterns of male domination by people in Fagua and Canelón. In the epilogue I take a step back and look at the effects of the industry at a regional level as the industry has replaced the absent state by taking responsibility for the quality of life of its workers.

Notes

1. See Naila Kabeer (1997) for an analysis of the links between gender and poverty.

2. The International Monetary Fund and the World Bank have instituted structural adjustment policies, also known as restructuring and neoliberalism, since the mid-1980s in response to the 1980s economic crisis. In general, the policies call for a greater role of the market economy and a reduced role of government, thus shifting the burden of the crisis from the government to individuals. Under structural adjustment, export-development strategies have replaced import-substitution development strategies. Non-traditional manufacturing sectors, such as cut flowers and fruits, have benefited from the policies, however literature on female labor and the formal agricultural sector is scant. One study that focuses on non-traditional exports is Barrientos et al. (1999). For an excellent analysis of structural adjustment in the Latin American context see Safa (1995a and 1999).

3. Geographical names are not pseudonyms; all individuals' names and flower company names are pseudonyms.

4. While trying to understand the world of Chía and Cajicá outside the framework of neoclassical economics, it might seem inconsistent to use terms like *assets* and *social capital*. However, the intent is to highlight that in this research these concepts are broader than those used in neoclassical economics. While I agree with Jane Guyer (1997), who asserts that anthropology has to engage the capitalist and vernacular vocabulary, I think that this engagement should go hand in hand with an analysis of local cultural constructions of economics (Gudeman 1986). In this way, terms that are

redundant in Western culture such as *social capital* and *cultural investment* are easy to grasp yet are imbued with new meaning.

5. The Colombian fresh-cut flower industry was sued by producers in the United States several times for selling flowers in the United States market at lower than cost, called "dumping," thus competing unfairly with United States flower producers. See J. Michael Finger and Nellie T. Artis (1993) on dumping worldwide and José Mendez (1993) and Irwin A. Douglas (1994) for the specifics to the Colombian cut-flower industry.

6. Note by way of comparison that the Croatian Serb refugee population totals an estimated 280,000 to 330,000 people (Human Rights Watch 1998), yet Colombia's continuing refugee problem cannot be addressed by the United Nations because it is not an international issue.

7. Subcontracting in floriculture means an individual or an agency hires workers to sell their labor to the flower farms (Reis, Sierra, and Rangel 1995). Subcontracting often lowers the working conditions, thus driving the workforce to organize for their improvement.

8. Wolf and Mintz discuss at length the personalized relation between *hacendado* and worker. They assert that it served not a personal function, but an impersonal one, which was to secure labor (1957a). Literature on *hacienda* tends to focus on the economics; only a few, like Wolf and Mintz, allude to such a relationship.

9. Some scholars stress the nature of the *hacienda* as a profit seeking enterprise (e.g., Bauer and Hagerman Johnson 1977; Deas 1977; Florescano 1977; Kay 1977). Yet others emphasize the *hacienda's* objective to be a social one: augmenting the landlords social position within society at large (Branding 1977a and 1977b; Chevalier 1966; Tord and Lazo 1981; Wolf and Mintz 1957a). Others have examined differences between *haciendas* held by religious orders and those held by lay people (Polo y La Borda 1981; Tord and Lazo 1981). Hacienda Fagua, in Cajicá, falls in the latter category. As the only residence of the *hacienda* family, the *hacienda* was both a way to maintain their social status as aristocrats and descendants of Spaniards and a way to make a living and to accumulate capital and land.

10. The same type of labor force has different names in the central Andean region: *mitayos*, *yanaconas*, and *huaccilleros* in Peru and *huasipungueros* in Quito (Mörner 1984).

11. There is a question of whether members of the labor force, both tenant laborers and wage workers, were truly free to leave the *hacienda* (Bauer 1971; Martínez Alier 1977) or if they were bondage workers (Borah 1951; Bracamonte y Sosa 1988; Chevalier 1952; Knight 1986; Mörner 1973, 1984; Polo y la Borda 1981; and Wolf and Mintz 1957b). Wolf and Mintz suggest that at least some element of coercion was involved by noting the *hacienda*'s need for land, not necessarily for cultivation but to force the landless population to work for the *hacienda*. *Haciendas* needed to control large extensions of land not only for production, but to secure a constant labor supply by providing workers with subsistence lots and other benefits like firewood, that compensated for the low salaries paid due to the *hacienda*'s lack of capital (Wolf and

Mintz 1957a, 504). This argument is supported by the voices of Colombian rural people who explain that by supplying people with money or in-kind advances, the *hacienda* kept people in "slavery" (Gudeman and Rivera 1990, 90). An opposing line of argument states that *hacienda* peons had the liberty of leaving the *hacienda*, but they did not because they lived better than landless workers (Bauer 1971; Martínez Alier 1977). I would argue that this discussion should not be either/or, but one of degrees of freedom or bondage in different areas of Colombia according to different demands for labor.

12. Mörner, referring to the *yanaconas* in Peru, states that they not only constituted a permanent resident labor force but in fact they were tied to the estate (1984, 198).

13. Since pre-Columbian times, the region has been a major agricultural center dominated by the Muisca people, who belonged to the Chibcha linguistic family. Both Chía, which means "moon," and Cajicá, which means "stone fortress," were organized into chiefdoms called *cacicazgos*. The Muiscas had two rival chiefs who dominated different but bordering regions in the country. Both Chía and Cajicá belonged to the chiefdom of Bacatá, whose chief was named the *Zipa*, and in turn each village had a local chief called a *cacique*. The rival chiefdom of Hunza was headed by a chief named *Zaque* (Falchetti and Plazas 1973; Suescún-Monroy 1987). After the arrival of the Spaniard Gonzalo Jiménez de Quesada in 1537, the *encomienda* system and Indian reservations were established by the Spanish crown. The *encomiendas* were grants of Indian labor, Indian-produced goods, and/or Indian taxes given by the Spanish crown to Spanish individuals called *encomenderos*. In exchange for this labor and these commodities, the Indians were given religious instruction and protection (Cushner 1980; Keith 1976; MacLeod 1984; Mörner 1984). With the rapid decline of the Indian population due to epidemics, the *encomienda* began to weaken by the mid-sixteenth century (MacLeod 1984, 224; Mörner 1984, 192).

14. Municipalities or towns are divided politically into several *veredas*. The municipality of Chía is composed of the *veredas* of Yerbabuena, Bojacá, Fonquetá, La Balsa, and Fagua. Cajicá has four *veredas*: Canelón, Chuntame, Calahorra, and Puente Torres. People in the region consider themselves as belonging to a *vereda*. They might say, "I am from La Balsa but I live in Fagua." For this book I follow the local usage of using the names Vereda Fagua, Fagua, or simply *vereda* interchangeably.

15. The Sabana de Bogotá extends 1,100 square kilometers (425 square miles).

16. Almost half of Cajicá's population lives in the urban core (15,687 people), while in Chía more than two-thirds live in the urban core (41,632 people). These percentages indicate Chía is a small urban commuter city, in spite of being called a town.

17. The process by which the drug class socially legitimates itself can be called *social laundering*.

18. The dissolution of the reservation and the *encomienda* in Cajicá and the appearance shortly after of Hacienda Fagua supports the links scholars have made between the *hacienda* and the *encomienda*. While they are different institutions that operate at different historical moments there is a connection—if not economic then

social—between the two. Both *encomiendas* and *haciendas* were institutions designed to support the Spanish population and thus were based on socioeconomic structures that had in principle the same objective. While the *encomienda* operated on an economy of extraction (*extracción*), the *hacienda* was based on an economy of production. Thus their views and treatment of land, capital, and labor were different. Nonetheless, because the social structures in which they were embedded were very much the same, historians debate the links between the two institutions (Lockhart 1969; Mörner 1973; Villamarín 1975). According to Mörner the consensus among historians is that although the two institutions had different legal standing, people who had *encomiendas* found it easier to buy or have land grants (1973, 188). Villamarín states that indeed being an *encomendero* facilitated the acquisition of land in Nueva Granada, the area now called Colombia (1975, 332). In fact, in the Sabana of Nueva Granada, in the same region where Hacienda Fagua is located, the *encomenderos* played a major role in the land appropriation process after conquest because they were in control of the town councils and could allocate themselves land within their *encomiendas* (Mörner 1984, 199).

19. Vereda Canelón has remained more rural because Hacienda Fagua sits in the middle of it. In contrast, Vereda Fagua is more densely populated and has more construction and rural planning problems including slum-like construction.

20. Among supervisors and managers, *hacienda* owners who own floriculture farms are known to treat the workforce in a *capataz* (foreman) style.

21. *Raizal* in Fagua and Canelón has the connotation that *base* and *fundamento* has for people of the altiplano, as examined by Gudeman and Rivera (1990). I do not refer in this section to the *base*, however, because it is not a distinction that *raizal* people make themselves. As I will discuss in chapter 4, only male migrants referred to *la base*.

22. Migration patterns in the Sabana de Bogotá are examined in an excellent study that includes fresh-cut flower migrant workers in Chía (Hoyos 1996).

23. *Mercado* in Colombian towns is not just an enclosed place where you simply buy groceries and leave. Mercado is a weekly event that takes place during *el día del mercado* (the market day), a remnant of the Indian tradition. Different towns have market on different days, and people bring and place on the ground produce, baskets, dairy products, meat, aluminum pots, and trinkets to sell. In addition, there is usually a section that has ten to twenty *almorzaderos* (from the verb *to have lunch*), food stands serving breakfast and lunch. Some towns have portable fairs where children can go on rides, enjoy cotton candy, and have their picture taken.

CHAPTER TWO

Flowers in the Global Assembly Line

In general, global assembly line industries are those that produce goods in third world countries for first world markets. Initially, global assembly line industries produced hard consumer goods such as apparel, computers and computer parts, automobiles and auto parts, electrical appliances, and so on. In recent years global assembly line industries have included agricultural products such as flowers, fruits, vegetables, and wood. Electronic data processing and phone customer service are the newest forms of global assembly line industries. The evolution of the global assembly line can be explained by the shift, during the 1970s and 1980s, of manufacturing processes worldwide from center to periphery and specifically to free trade zones. The shift was possible due to advances in communications and the fragmentation of the production process. A majority of the workers that filled up the new transnational factories in the periphery were and continue to be women.

The history of the fresh-cut flower industry illustrates this shift from center to periphery. The production of flowers moved from the United States to Colombia during this period. To be able to compete in international markets with low prices, transnational corporations have to reduce costs which they achieve, in part, by employing low cost labor. Global assembly line industries are located mainly in countries with low wages, high unemployment, limited natural resources, low levels of unionization, and stable governments (Safa 1982, 1986). Countries that host global assembly line industries hope to generate foreign exchange and employment. The companies involved hope to increase their profit margins. In this chapter, I will focus on studies that examine export-oriented transnational companies in order to highlight the similarities and differences between Colombian floriculture and other global assembly line industries. To do this, I will draw mainly on global assembly line literature, that is, the body of research that examines factory-based work, as opposed to home-based work, performed for the most part by women who participate in the export network.

Factory Global Assembly Line

The Field of Global Assembly Line

The extensive global assembly line literature is divided into two subfields. One portion of the literature analyzes workers who are subcontracted, are paid on a piece-rate basis, and work out of their homes (Acevedo 1995; Gladden 1993; Mies 1982, 1986; P. Peña 1989; Truelove 1990; Ward and Pyle 1995). Studies that focus on women in agribusiness (Barrientos et al. 1999; Newman et al. 2002) are almost non-existent (Tiano 2001); thus I draw mainly on another portion of the literature, that which examines work perfomed in factories located in free trade zones and non-free trade zones (Fernández-Kelly 1983; Freeman 2000; Ong 1987; Tiano 1994; among others).[1] For Latin America, this field is known as *maquila* literature, named for the assembly line factories in Mexico, *maquiladoras*. It is useful to keep in mind that the theoretical discussions such as why women enter the workforce, or the underlying patriarchal ideologies of labor and gender, are applicable to all research on gender and labor, including the literature that examines home-based work and factory work. Specific to factory work are studies that look at labor conditions, labor issues, factory discipline, and resistance.

The study of export-oriented industries is shaped by development studies and political economics research on transnational industries. Since the 1980s international financial institutions, such as the International Monetary Fund and the World Bank, have heralded global assembly line industries as instruments for development.[2] The new model of development, known in Latin America as neoliberalism and worldwide as structural adjustment, includes the promotion of export industries, reduction of government intervention, privatization of firms, deregulation of labor, and the integration of national economies to global markets (Oman and Wignaraja 1991). While structural adjustment programs have brought an increase in income inequalities and poverty (Gwynne and Kay 2000; Safa 1999), some economies have also experienced an increase in their exports and formal labor employment. Export processing zones with assembly industries have multiplied as a result of neoliberal policies.

Export-oriented industries, like floriculture, have replaced import substitution industrialization. Import substitution industrialization policies, known in the English-speaking world as ISI, were designed in the 1950s by the Economic Commission for Latin America, better known in Spanish-speaking Latin America as the CEPAL. The central idea of ISI was to replace importation of goods with domestic production, in effect trying to make nations self-provisioning and autonomous. Hallmark strategies were to erect tariffs on imports in order to protect infant industries, to restrict foreign direct investment in domestic industries, and to control foreign exchange. At the same time that ISI sought to guide development so that a nation would spend less of its currency in foreign markets for products needed at home, it also aimed to foster industries in which the nation held a comparative advantage. It was hoped that these comparative advantage industries would eventually provide a source of foreign exchange, believed to be a key component of economic growth and development (Escobar 1995; Kay 1989; Prebisch 1987).[3] In direct contrast to the ISI focus on self-sufficiency and relative economic isolation, structural adjustment programs guide national economies toward integration in the global economy. Structural adjustment policies remove protectionist barriers, welcome foreign investment, and relinquish control of exchange rates.

Thus, in alignment with structural adjustment policies, many industries in poorer countries come from wealthier countries. They move, usually south, in search of the lower labor costs that will allow them to compete successfully in international markets. Many non-traditional export products, such as flowers, have been introduced to countries specifically for their export value (Barham et al. 1992).

In the 1980s and early 1990s the key component defining a global assembly line was the national origin of the capital used to set up the industry; the assembly line had to be located in a third world country, and the capital invested had to be at least in part foreign.[4] Given today's fluidity of capital, goods, and people, this initial definition is not very useful. In fact, Colombia's floriculture industry shows the inverse pattern of capital flow. Colombia's floriculture industry was initially set up with an overwhelming majority of national capital and a few individuals. Only in 1998, when the industry was mature and established, did the multinational corporation Dole invest heavily in the industry. In my judgment, rather than the source of investment capital, four other characteristics are more useful to describe a global assembly line industry, all of which are applicable to the floriculture industry. First, a large quantity of product is created for export to first world countries. Second, the organization of the industries, the work schedules, and the breakdown of the work into small tasks are geared to managing workers and creating a uniform product. Third, the industries are exempt from local taxation. Fourth and most importantly, the workforce is predominantly female.

As described in the previous chapter, the global assembly line literature is a part of a larger body of research on gender and labor. Given the expansion of capitalism, the concept of globalization has become the underlying factor unifying research on gender and labor. This is no coincidence, however, as export industries were promoted as instruments of development at the same time that international organizations were demanding the integration of women into the development process (Escobar 1995).[5]

Development theory has produced three different positions with respect to women and capitalism. One considers women to be marginalized from economic processes and unable to participate in the paid workforce (Bosé and Acosta-Belén 1995). The second considers women to be exploited workers. The third and most recent theory argues that women are neither marginalized nor exploited, but that they become integrated into the economy when they work for pay outside of the house. The second and third positions have replaced the initial characterization of women's marginalization. The research of the last decade has been made more complex by the examination of the feminization of the labor force and the patriarchal structures that underlie this feminization.

Critiques to Global Assembly Line

Supporters of the exploitation thesis view global assembly line industries as exploiting women and taking advantage of women's gender-related vulnerability in the labor market. They argue that women work in global assembly industries out of financial need. Furthermore, the supporters of this thesis state that the industries use the patriarchal structure to subjugate women further. They specifically criticize the industries for poor and hazardous working conditions (Bolaños and Rodríguez 1988; Carrillo and Hernández 1985; Ehrenreich and Fuentes 1981; Mies 1986; Mitter 1986). Diana Medrano and Rodrigo Villar (1983) and Norma Mena (1999) document comparable poor conditions within the floriculture industry in Colombia and in Ecuador, respectively, highlighting occupational health risks. Another criticism is that workers are often denied insurance and disability support (Abraham-Van der Mark 1983; Fuentes and Ehrenreich 1983). Many workers have low job security and are prevented from forming or joining unions (Abraham-Van der Mark 1983; Ehrenreich and Fuentes 1981; Enloe 1983; Mitter 1986). In Colombia's floriculture industry, unions have been present since 1976, but have been ineffective due to the unequal power relations between them and the industrialists (Reis, Sierra, and Rangel 1995). Apparently the same is true for Ecuador's industry (Korovkin 2003; Mena 1999).

The most incisive criticisms based on the exploitation model revolve around the reasons women are hired, the short duration of their jobs, and how little they are paid. These issues are linked because, according to critics of global assembly line industries, women are hired because they can be paid lower wages than men. In addition, they have short labor contracts to circumvent additional long-term labor costs. The industries tend to portray women as docile workers and claim that they hire more women than men because of women's supposed greater dexterity and patience with delicate and repetitive tasks (Enloe 1983, 412; Mitter 1986; Safa 1986; Stoddard 1987). The justifications for the use of female labor in the flower industry in Colombia (Friedemann-Sánchez 1990; Medrano 1981, 12; Reis, Sierra, and Rangel 1995; Silva 1982), Costa Rica (Bolaños and Rodríguez 1988), and Ecuador (Korovkin 2003) are very similar: women are said to be better at the delicate treatment that flowers require and at routine and repetitive tasks. However, it is important to take into account that in rural communities, such as in Colombia and Ecuador, women are socialized in harvest and pot-harvest activities and thus may indeed be better at delicate, repetitive tasks (Friedemann-Sánchez 2002; Silva 1982) and are associated with those tasks (Newman 2002). Safa states that management usually relies on sexual stereotypes to defend its use of female labor; it depicts women as patient with tedious jobs, having nimble fingers, and exerting good visual acuity (1986). However critics argue that, despite industry claims, women are actually preferred over men because they are more easily controlled and can be paid less.

According to various scholars, the industries exploit women by taking advantage of their vulnerability in the labor market due to their gender (Abraham-Van der Mark 1983; Benería and Roldán 1987; Carrillo and Hernández 1985; Fernández-Kelly 1983; Mitter 1986; Nash and Fernández-Kelly 1983; Ong 1987; Safa 1986; Standing 1989; Kathryn Ward 1990). Cheaper labor means higher profits, and, since women have been traditionally paid less, they are hired more often than men. Such lower wages are seen as a reflection of women's subordinate position in society and of the belief that women's income is supplementary to men's, despite growing evidence of the exact opposite (Safa 1995a, 1999; Tiano 1994). Carrillo and Hernández (1985) agree with Safa (1986), stating that the majority of the workers are young women not because they have more dexterity and are more delicate, as *maquila* owners claim, but because their labor is cheaper than that of any other group. These theorists maintain that women are forced to work in global assembly industries to survive financially but that they receive no non-economic benefits, such as job satisfaction, self-esteem, or social networks, from their labor. Furthermore, they portray these industries as simply a new arena in which women are subjugated by the same patriarchal relationships.

Scholars who adopt an integration focus for their research (Achío and Mora 1988; Freeman 2000; Lim 1990; Newman 2002; Sen 1990) see the work that women perform in global assembly lines as a way for women to become integrated into the economy. They maintain that women do gain job satisfaction and find that, although women may need the income, they also work because they desire to work. Work in the global assembly line for women represents a way to challenge the patriarchal structures which govern their daily home lives.

While early discussions on the topic of women and development address the exploitation, integration, or marginalization of women (Bosé and Acosta-Belén 1995, for instance), Susan Tiano (1994) establishes the central question with much needed clarity. She argues that research would benefit from questioning whether or not, relatively and absolutely, women are better off working in global assembly line industries. While the integration model minimizes the influence of structure and the exploitation model views workers as passive victims, both ultimately ignore workers' agency. Tiano thus identifies the need for further research on worker identity and culture-specific ideologies of gender. Following this line of critique, research done in the last ten years has focused on the feminization of the labor force and the patriarchal structures that underlie this feminization (Arango 1994; Arango, León, and Viveros 1995; Dombois and López 1993; Freeman 2000; among others).

All global assembly line research, regardless of its orientation, shares the common thread of analyzing the connections between women's subordination and capitalism. In broader terms, the framework of studies using the dominant model has been the analysis of the economic and social structures of capitalism and patriarchy, such as the large body of research examining the rationale behind industrial demand for female labor. In effect, as a result of this institutional focus, such studies continue to view women through the lens of traditional gender roles, characterizing them as passive victims of subordination. They overlook the likelihood that women actively seek such employment. According to Tiano (1994), researchers have studied companies that hire only single women, following the rationale that they will only be available before they have children. Other researchers have examined companies that only hire women who have already had children, claiming that those women have more financial responsibilities and therefore are more committed to work. Both types of studies, I would argue, focus on women as mothers rather than as active agents choosing what is best for themselves and for their families. Given that female subordination is not acceptable or desirable, not surprisingly, the existing research that focuses on the maintenance of female subordination in industry settings is critical of transnational companies and their overall patterns of employment.

In contrast my research focuses on the connections between workers' agency and the structure of capitalism and questions the persistent homogenous and stereotypical view of workers as young, single women who perform unskilled work.[6] My research includes two approaches to analysis. The first approach concerns how new gender conceptions are created as a result of individuals operating within a structure of capital accumulation. The second approach examines how the structure of capitalism, and thus the industrial setting, is used by individual women to further their own agendas. Following a description of the emergence of Colombia's floriculture industry, I will address the claims made by the prevailing research about the way transnational companies function with regard to workers.

Origin of the Colombian Cut-Flower Industry

Shifting North to South

The demand for cut flowers in the United States can be traced back to the late nineteenth century and early twentieth century, which has shaped the organization of the cut-flower industry ever since (Ziegler 2003). In research that follows the commodity chains of fresh-cut flowers produced in Ecuador and the Netherlands and sold in the New York metropolitan area, Catherine Ziegler (2003) notes that, as early as 1916, producers, wholesalers, and retailers had distinct roles in the production and distribution of cut flowers.[7] Between 1949 and 1970, California, Colorado, Florida, upstate New York, and the Long Island region cultivated flowers in the Unites States.[8]

To understand why production shifted south it is necessary to know the nature of the business and production process. The production of flowers varies somewhat from one variety of flower to another. All types of flowers, however, have some production elements in common. All flowers are grown in greenhouses, which permit the control of growing conditions such as humidity, temperature, pests, and diseases. In addition, flowers are an extremely perishable commodity that cannot be transformed into any other product or by-product. Finally, their cultivation is labor intensive and for the most part not mechanized. Almost all aspects of the production process are accomplished manually.

All these conditions were true in the northeastern United States in the 1950s, but they were exacerbated by a climate with variable seasons. In the

Northeast, greenhouses had to be made out of expensive materials, such as glass and metal, to keep the air warm during winter and cool in the summer. The high production season coincided with winter, when light intensity is lower, days are shorter, and more heating is necessary (Méndez 1991).

New York, Philadelphia, Boston, and other cities were the centers for demand, but the land and labor available near those demand centers were expensive. As the air transportation industry developed, flower businesses were able to locate in the west and the south of the United States, where land and labor costs were lower and the climate more favorable. The larger industrial-style production of California, Colorado, and Florida replaced the family businesses of the Northeast (Méndez 1991).[9]

Colombia became a producer of flowers for export in 1965, when an initial seven hectares of carnations and chrysanthemums were planted (Villar 1982, 60–72) by pioneer Edgar Wells, a Colombian of British descent (Fairbanks and Lindsay 1997, 1; Ziegler 2003, 57). This incursion of floriculture producers into Colombia was part of a general shift southward from the United States in search of cheaper land, labor, and infrastructure production costs (Méndez 1991, 6). By 1970 the area cultivated had increased to 27 hectares, by 1980 to 1,100 hectares (Méndez 1991), by 2000 to 5,000 hectares (Asocolflores 2001), and by 2002 there were approximately 5,906 hectares in flower cultivation in the Sabana de Bogotá (Asocolflores 2004a). The first region to begin flower cultivation was the southern section of the Sabana in the towns called Mosquera, Madrid, and Soacha (Friedemann-Sánchez 1990, 128).

In the United States, flower production steadily declined as Colombia entered the industry and gained market strength. The decline in domestic production in dollar terms, shown in table 2.1, masks an even greater decline by quantity or volume. From 1989 to 2002, the dollar value of domestic production fell by 15 percent at the same time that the value of imports rose by 72 percent. For instance, by the year 2000 production of the most common cut flowers had dropped dramatically in the United States, filling only 5 percent of the national demand for carnations and 15 to 20 percent of the national demand for chrysanthemums and roses (Ziegler 2003, 67). As a result, by 2002, imports accounted for 59 percent of consumption in the United States, in dollar terms. At the turn of the millennium, cut-flower producers in the United States faced stiff import competition as well as weak consumer demand due to economic recession. Since 1974 producers in the United States have tried to exclude imported flowers from the United States market, charging Colombian producers with "dumping" and other unfair trade practices.[10] A more effective and recent

Table 2.1. Value of Internationally Traded Cut Flowers by Top Exporting Countries

	1998		1999	
	US $1,000	%	US $1,000	%
Netherlands	2,296,041	56%	2,095,183	56%
Colombia	600,014	15%	546,210	14%
Ecuador	201,883	5%	210,409	6%
Israel	175,196	4%	115,884	3%
Italy	80,158	2%	67,921	2%
Belgium	32,371	1%	33,195	1%
Germany	29,041	1%	25,303	1%
Canada	15,984	0%	15,716	0%
USA	20,569	1%	14,762	0%
Denmark	6,057	0%	4,659	0%
Total	4,084,363	100%	3,769,443	100%

Source: International Floriculture Trade Statistics 2000. Pathfast Publishing, Essex, England. Available at: <www.pathfast.com/ITS20/World%20rank%202000.htm>. Accessed August 25, 2004.

strategy in the United States has been to shift production to higher value varieties such as delphinium, larkspur, gerbera daisy, gladioli, iris, lilies, orchids, and tulips, abandoning the lower value varieties to foreign producers (USDA ERS 2003).

At 53.5 percent of imports by value, in 2002 Colombia alone provided 31.6 percent of total cut-flower consumption in the United States in dollar terms (see table 2.3).[11] In fact, in 2003 Colombia provided 2 billion out of the 3.4 billion flowers on the United States retail market.[12] The difference between the 59.1 percent of consumption by number of stems versus 31.6 percent of consumption by value is due to the fact that production of less expensive varieties has moved to third world farms where costs are lower while domestic production in the United States has shifted its focus to the most expensive varieties.

Colombia's floriculture industry is currently in competition not only with the United States' shift to higher value flowers or with other traditional flower producing countries but also with neighboring Ecuador. Since the 1980s Ecuador too has developed a floriculture industry, owned in part by Colombian as well as U.S. flower companies.[13] The partial relocation of Colombia's industry to Ecuador is due in part to Ecuador's "clean" reputation and Colombia's tarnished reputation, and the European pressure on Colombia regarding labor, human rights, and environmental organizations (Korovkin 2003, 21). Other countries exporting to the United States include the Netherlands, Mexico, Canada, Costa Rica, and Israel, among others.

Table 2.2. Cut Flowers in the U.S. Economy, in US$1,000

1989	482,531	315,654	10,773	787,413
1990	467,720	326,246	29,545	764,421
1991	471,556	322,016	33,699	759,873
1992	458,455	352,366	32,505	778,316
193	423,911	382,182	39,100	766,992
1994	442,297	420,104	37,913	824,488
1995	423,630	511,524	40,314	894,840
1996	412,700	572,550	47,502	937,748
1997	471,569	595,045	48,753	1,017,862
1998	411,595	614,362	44,553	981,404
1999	431,624	592,366	41,726	982,264
2000	429,963	610,461	39,719	1,000,705
2001	418,103	565,468	39,675	943,896
2002	410,015	541,466	36,116	915,364

Source: Floriculture and Nursery Crops Yearbook, June 2004, available at: http://usda.mannlib.cornell.edu/reports/erssor/specialty/flo-bb/flo-2004s.txt>.

Colombia, A Power in Floriculture Worldwide

Consumer demand from the United States for cut flowers rose rapidly from the late 1960s through the mid 1990s. Imports of cut flowers to the United States peaked between 1998 and 2000 at over $600 million dollars, making it the largest importer worldwide of cut flowers. As shown in tables 2.2 and 2.4, the value of cut-flower imports to the United States fell 11 percent to $541 million dollars between 2000 and 2002. For most of the last four decades of the twentieth century, Colombian exports increased faster than United States demand. José Méndez notes that exportation to the United States, Colombia's primary market, expanded very quickly. In 1968 exports grew 78 percent; in 1970, 227 percent; in 1973, 374 percent; and in 1988, 22.8 percent (1991, 31).

Colombia is currently the second largest fresh-cut flower exporter worldwide after the Netherlands, a position that was achieved around 1980 (Bosnak 1993) and has been maintained ever since.[14] In 1999, the fresh-cut flower global trade amounted to about US$3.77 billion (Ziegler 2003, 83). In 1999, Colombia accounted for 14 percent of the value of internationally traded cut flowers (see table 2.1).

Flowers are the leading earner of foreign currency among non-traditional exports in Colombia, with approximately fifty different types of flowers being exported. Close to 98 percent of the current production is destined for foreign markets. According to the Departamento Administrativo Nacional

Table 2.3. Value and Percentage by Country of U.S. Cut-Flower Imports in 2002

Source country	US$1,000	%
Colombia	289,554	54%
Ecuador	87,252	16%
Netherlands	71,256	13%
Mexico	27,495	5%
Canada	17,053	3%
Costa Rica	15,201	3%
Israel	7,332	1%
Rest of the world*	26,323	5%
Total imports	541,466	100%

Note: No other country imports more than 1 percent of total.
Data source: Floriculture and Nursery Crops Yearbook 2004 (Spreadsheet Files). Ithaca: Economic Research Service, United States Department of Agriculture, 2004. Available at: <www.usda.mannlib.cornell.edu/>. Accessed September 22, 2004.

de Estadística (DANE, Colombia's official statistics office) in 2000, 84 percent of the production was exported to the United States and 10 percent to the European Union (Asocolflores 2001). The value of Colombian exports of fresh-cut flowers totaled US$580.6 million in 2000 (Asocolflores 2001) and US$672.7 in 2002 (Asocolflores 2004b).[15] Of several different types of flowers imported by the United States, Colombian flowers represent the following percentages for 2001: alstroemeria, 94 percent; pompons, 91 percent; carnations, 88 percent; chrysanthemums, 71 percent; gerbera, 67 percent; roses, 48 percent; freesia, 12 percent; and gypsophila, 18 percent (Asocolflores 2001).

The industry's rapid and sustained growth in Colombia is due in part to its lack of barriers to entry. The biggest barrier is land ownership. Contrary to assertions by Verena Meier (1999, 273) land in the Sabana is very expensive. Thus, to start a flower farm, an individual mainly needs sufficient land and/or financial capital, both of which are determined by his or her socioeconomic position in Colombian society as a whole. Thus, while entry is selective according to socioeconomic class, among the privileged class it is highly competitive. As was described in chapter 1, many flower farms are located in former *haciendas* and large estates owned by wealthy landowning families. From

Table 2.4. Source of U.S.Cut-Flower Imports, in Nominal US$1,000

Source country	1991	1992	1993	1994	1995	1996	1997	1998	1999	2000	2001	2002
Colombia	202,877	231,397	251,837	270,219	321,273	366,395	359,620	360,626	343,684	347,242	302,450	289,554
Ecuador	12,442	15,244	19,575	26,080	50,498	68,210	83,497	90,119	92,299	89,249	99,722	87,252
Netherlands	49,439	51,080	53,460	57,116	61,162	59,005	61,774	69,200	61,645	71,639	67,070	71,256
Mexico	15,390	11,898	13,930	15,368	23,191	19,522	23,649	25,186	27,224	29,621	29,415	27,495
Canada	3,783	4,133	4,584	5,772	7,455	10,012	14,871	15,554	15,477	17,809	17,959	17,053
Costa Rica	10,180	10,029	11,639	15,060	14,979	16,311	17,974	18,993	19,380	19,427	14,705	15,201
Israel	2,043	1,610	1,828	2,094	3,029	3,350	3,832	4,468	4,345	5,821	6,888	7,332
Rest of the world	25,862	26,975	25,329	28,395	29,937	29,745	29,828	30,216	28,312	29,653	27,259	26,323
Total imports	322,016	352,366	382,182	420,104	511,524	572,550	595,045	614,362	592,366	610,461	565,468	541,466

Notes: Includes fresh, dried, dyed, preserved cut-flower products, and buds for bouquets. Excludes cut decorative greens. No country other than those shown exceeded 1 percent of United States cut-flower imports by value in 2002.

Data source: Floriculture and Nursery Crops Yearbook 2004 (*Spreadsheet Files*). Ithaca: Economic Research Service, United States Department of Agriculture, 2004. Available at: <www.usda.mannlib.cornell.edu/>. Accessed September 22, 2004.

interviews with floriculture executives in Bogotá in 1996 and 1998, I estimate that there were then close to 450 producing and exporting companies controlled by around fifty parent companies.[16] In 1998 the multinational corporation Dole bought four of the largest farms and currently has 800 hectares in production. Noteworthy in an industry dominated by the Netherlands, Colombia is one of the few places where Dutch growers have not established themselves, unlike in Costa Rica, Chile, and Ecuador, among other countries (Ziegler 2003, 104). The average farm size in Colombia is 12 hectares, compared to less than one hectare in the Netherlands. However, as Ziegler points out, despite their larger growing area, productivity is lower. One Dutch hectare produces flowers with an approximate export value eight times that of an Ecuadorian hectare and four times of a Colombian one (Ziegler 2003, 94).

Fresh-cut flowers are produced in plastic greenhouses in two main regions of Colombia. The province of Antioquia produces 12 percent of Colombia's fresh-cut flowers, and the Sabana produces 86 percent, with 2 percent produced in other areas (DANE 2004) (see map 1.1). Regardless of region, production requires the use of greenhouses, a controlled environment, and a labor-intensive production process.

Several environmental conditions give Colombia a competitive edge in relation to other flower producing countries. Because Colombia is in the equatorial zone, its year-round equable climate allows greenhouses to be constructed of cheap materials such as plastic and wood instead of the metal and glass structures used in other parts of the world. Since the Sabana is a plateau at an altitude of 2,650 meters (about 8,660 feet) with an average temperature of 14 degrees Celcius (58 degrees Farenheit), no heating or cooling of the greenhouses is needed, and refrigeration costs are low. In addition, Colombia enjoys twelve-hour days of high intensity light year round, producing high quality flowers without the added cost of artificial lighting (Méndez 1991, 6). The flat, fertile land of the Sabana requires no leveling and minimizes the use of water, fertilizers, and nutrients necessary in the production. Most flower farms are located on existing main highways close to an international airport, critical factors when dealing with perishable goods.

As mentioned, floriculture is very labor intensive. Today in Colombia's cut-flower industry, an estimated average of eighteen permanent workers tend each hectare. The Colombian industry presently generates around 88,300 jobs directly related to production and 75,000 ancillary jobs (Asocolflores 2004a). The latter include truck drivers and delivery, recycling, and packaging companies, among others. To grasp its full economic impact, the jobs the industry generates outside of Colombia should also be taken into account. For instance in the United States flower importers hire approximately

7,000 workers, airlines 2,000, trucking companies around 1,600, supermarket flower departments about 24,000, and florist stores 125,000 (Asocolflores 2001).

In addition to Dole Fresh Flowers, a portion of Colombian flower growers own their own exporting and wholesale distribution companies in Miami. This type of vertical integration cuts out the middle distributors and increases the amount of profit made. A number of Colombian distribution companies grouped together in 1998 to form a public distribution company in Miami called U.S. Floral. The effects of this in Colombia were felt at the time I was conducting fieldwork in 1999. At that time, many flower farms that were not integrated vertically but had had business relationships, built over the years with the distribution companies that restructured into U.S. Floral, lost their distribution counterpart. For these flower farms it meant not having a secure distributor for their flowers. Many flower producing companies collapsed at this time. U.S. Floral was short lived, however, and it too collapsed in 2001 (Ziegler 2003).[17]

The ownership arrangements of flower farms in Cundinamarca are varied. Some companies comprise conglomerates of farms, each having a different name and functioning legally as separate entities but owned by the same individual, group of individuals, or business. This is the reason behind the large number of farms (450) and the smaller number of companies (approximately 50). A few are individual farms with a single owner. As described in chapter 1, some farms are located in former *haciendas* that have become agro-industries. From 1988 to 1996 the flower business was very profitable and expanded into other areas of the Sabana. Even regions such as Chocontá, Villa de Leyva, Chiquinquirá, and La Calera, which are beyond the flat lands of the Sabana and where the terrain is broken and steep, have flower farms. While I did not research the topic, given that each hectare of flower production requires an investment in infrastructure (excluding land) of $300,000, some of these flower farms may be used to launder drug money. The difference, as I observed in 1989 while doing fieldwork in Chocontá, in farms outside and in the northern regions of the Sabana (Tocancipá, Gachancipá, Chocotá, and Villapinzón) was that local labor was not abundant and flower farms hired contractors who in turn hired busloads of people and transported them to the farms every day. In those areas, people were still engaged in subsistence agriculture, so finding laborers for flower work was difficult (Friedemann-Sánchez 1990). Between 1988 and 1996 flower companies in such areas fought over workers. At the bus stops, contractors for different companies would offer 5,000 pesos more per day (approximately US$2.50) to workers who would switch farms. Areas like Chía, Cajicá, and

Sopó have never had to bring in workers by bus as in the northern towns of Tocancipá, Gachancipá, Chocotá, and Villapinzón (see map 1.2). The Sabana, including Cajicá and Chía in particular, have always had an oversupply of labor largely because high population density has made subsistence agriculture increasingly difficult in the last twenty years.

Environment, Health, and Silence

While it has improved in the last few years, the public image of the floriculture industry in Colombia is not a favorable one, and the literature regarding it is scanty. In fact, to those interested in studying it, the industry appears to have put up a wall of silence, and its zeal to ward off researchers has led to much speculation. In part, the bad reputation is based on the poor environmental and labor conditions in the industry during the first two decades of its existence (Friedemann-Sánchez 1990, 1999; Medrano 1982; Medrano and Villar 1983; Reis, Sierra, and Rangel 1995; Safa 1986; Salazar 1995; Silva 1982; Velez 1995; Villar 1982). So successful and persistent was the critique in the early 1990s by national and European non-governmental organizations that the flower industry created a social and environmental program, now called Florverde (Friedemann-Sánchez 1999, 2002). Since then the industry has made positive changes regarding labor conditions and the use of natural resources. In accordance with Meier's (1999) findings in Colombia and Mena's (1999) in Ecuador, I found the industry not homogeneous; wide variations exist between flower farms. Since the industry is self-regulated through its association Asocolflores (Friedemann-Sánchez 1999) and farm affiliation is voluntary, it is up to each owner and management team to follow the association's guidelines. Thus, generalizing about working conditions for the entire industry is not possible.

Environmental and occupational health concerns and the image of the floriculture industry are linked because flower farmers have become suspicious of what they perceive as the slanted views of researchers and journalists (Proyect 1999). In general, such views are situated in a framework holding the flower industry responsible for poor life conditions overall. For example, Ligia Velez notes that flower farms impose a schedule with overtime, but she fails to consider whether or not women desire overtime (1995). Researchers who have studied the flower industry in Colombia argue that the flower industries impose harsh economic conditions and a double workday. They claim that women idealize the family unit as a result of the economic conditions imposed by the flower farms (Díaz and Sierra 1995; Medrano 1982; Velez 1995). Yet these authors do not consider the economic consequences of male abandonment of the home, also present in Ecuador (Newman et al. 2002), which is common, and the inequitable responsibilities for housework and childrearing women want to escape. In fact, in looking at total amount of time dedicated to labor (paid and unpaid) among men and women floriculture workers and non-workers in Ecuador, Constance Newman (2002) concludes that women associated with floriculture do not work more hours than women not associated with floriculture, and that married men who work in floriculture perfom more hours of unpaid household work than men who are employed in other sectors. These findings dispel the notion that export-oriented industries impose an extraordinary burden on women. Furthermore, they point to the urgent need for a gendered analysis of time allocation among all rural inhabitants, not only those associated to the export industry.

Unfortunately, the available information about Colombia's flower industry, a lot of which is dated, regarding labor problems, poor occupational health, and environmental degradation cause industry officials to withhold information that might demonstrate the contributions the industry has made to local life and economy. Although the study of the effects of floriculture on the environment and the workers is beyond the scope of this research, it is undeniable that occupational health needs further attention and enforcement by the floriculture industry. For instance, there are few parameters guiding the protection of workers from chemicals, yet those few are rarely mentioned, much less enforced. Workers are not reminded to wash their hands before eating lunch. In fact, there are not enough bathrooms or washbasins to accomplish this. I did not observe signs providing workers safety guidelines near washbasins or hear any supervisor give reminders. I cannot say whether or not workers are instructed in the safety guidelines when they begin work for the first time at a flower farm. In addition, the farms do not have facilities to launder workers' work clothes; instead workers wash them at home, thereby contaminating their home environments.

Local government also tends to perceive the industry as a necessary but temporary evil. Their negative views have some foundation. They correctly perceive the industry as taking up an overwhelming amount of municipal resources without compensation. In fact, the industry has hidden costs and externalities that it refuses to acknowledge and that shape the dynamics between flower companies and local governments.

The industry does not pay taxes locally because, like global assembly line industries located in export processing zones, it is tax exempt (Carrillo and Hernández 1985; Safa 1982, 1986). This Colombian policy is meant as an incentive to increase exports. Under the *lineamiento* or administrative tax, municipalities have the right to regulate and tax local businesses (articles 287 and 311–14).[18] When municipalities took the issue of the floriculture industry's exemption to court, the Supreme Court ruled that local governments cannot tax it because it is an export industry already taxed via industrial and commercial taxes.

The overuse of the towns' infrastructure is at the core of the municipal government grievances with the industry (Chía 2000, 61). Fifty percent of the people who hold floriculture jobs in the region are recent migrants to the area, and this influx has severely strained the basic infrastructure including education, health services, sewage, electricity, transportation, and services provided by public offices.[19] Local governments have to finance the additional infrastructure without the necessary financial resources, because they cannot tax the industry, and without necessary regulatory tools because they may not license the industry. The *Unidad Municipal de Asistencia Técnica y Agropecuaria*, or UMATA (Municipal Entity for Farming Assistance), is a governmental agency that was created to give technical assistance to peasants and rural inhabitants on farming in order to ensure food security. UMATA has been forced to change its institutional objectives from aiding the rural population to achieve food security to the environmental protection of the rural areas from the flower industry. UMATA, however, is handicapped by its lack of licensing authority over the flower industry and the lack of necessary data on water and chemical use, which the industry is not obligated to provide. The industry's reluctance to offer information on these topics further fuels the animosity between municipal governments and the floriculture industry.

In addition to overuse of infrastructure, lack of compensation to municipalities, and lack of communication, the industry also uses enormous amounts of water, creating a detrimental effect on the environment and constituting an uncosted externality. Flower farms pump water directly from the underground water table rather than using, when available, piped water provided by governmental infrastructure. Because the fresh-cut flower industry uses enormous quantities of water, the subsurface water tables under flower farms are falling, and, as a result, the Sabana is suffering from desecation. A possible solution would be to promote rational water usage and raise public resources by taxing the farms' water use; however, this would require installing meters on the farms' private pumps and enforcing a water tax, measures which the local governments have been unable to enact. An additional problem facing water resources in these regions, as in Ecuador (Mena 1999), the chemicals used by the flower industry and the patterns of plant disposal have increasingly contaminated farm animals, land, and water.

Many non-governmental organizations whose focus has been on labor issues and on the environment are also critical of the industry. So successful and persistent has been their inspection of the Sabana that they have become neogovernmental organizations performing monitoring and advocacy tasks the government should be doing.[20] As a result of the alliance of these neogovernmental organizations and the municipalities, the flower industry came to realize that it had to have social and environmental programs, and their self-regulation in these areas is a result of this joint pressure (Friedemann-Sánchez 1999). Updated research on the environment and occupational health issues would improve the industry's occupational health and environmental regulatory program.

Addressing the Critiques of Floriculture

On Women's Over-Representation in the Informal Sector and on Gender-Based Income Differentials

As stated above, global restructuring and transnational corporations are often critiqued because they increase the participation by women in the informal sector, mainly because corporations use female and home-based labor to cut costs (Ward and Pyle 1995, 45–46). In the region where this research took place and in accordance to finding in Ecuador's flower industry (Mena 1999; Newman 2002), the fresh-cut flower industry shows an opposing pattern: the industry is linked to the formalization of women's labor. In addition in Colombia it is linked to the adoption of standardized labor laws. It is undeniable that transnational companies have moved away from first-world manufacturing locations to those in the third world in search of lower labor costs, as doing so reduces production costs significantly.[21] Because women's wages in these countries are assumed to be lower than men's, the argument also contends that within those third world countries women are preferentially hired (Bolaños and Rodríguez 1988; Friedemann-Sánchez 1990; Safa 1982, 1986; Silva 1982), a disparity that is legitimated by the industries' argument that women's incomes are supplementary to men's and do not constitute the principal income of their households (Safa 1986, 59). In addition, such research assumes that women have been paid less in whatever employment they may have held, as a reflection of their subordinate position in society (Carrillo and Hernández 1985, 105; Safa 1986).

While Silva (1982) reported in the early 1980s that women were paid less than men in Colombia's floriculture industry, my research does not support this argument for the period studied. I found no income disparities between men and women. (Newman et al. 2002 reports similar findings for Ecuador.) Furthermore, the highest paid supervisor was a woman. The majority of the workers are *operarios*, or base workers, who earn the legal minimum salary set annually by the government, which is based on a forty-hour work week.

Workers who monitor plant diseases are exclusively women and earn above the minimum. Supervisors include both men and women and earn between two and three times the minimum salary. Wage differentials among supervisors were distinct, but these differences appear to be based on responsibility and seniority in the company, not gender. All workers get legally mandated employment benefits, such as *prima*, which is half their monthly salary, twice a year at the end of June and December. Another employment benefit is called *cesantía*, a severance payment of one month's salary for every year worked plus the accumulated interest (this money is set aside by the company on an ongoing basis). *Cesantías* are given to the workers when employment ceases, regardless of whether they are fired or quit. In addition, the company contributes to the social security program, which is a pension fund, and to the health care insurance plan, since Colombia has universal health coverage. Companies are obligated by law to contribute half of the health care premium; the worker contributes the other half. Some companies also pay the worker's half if they do not miss any workdays during the month, an incentive for workers to come to work regularly. This highlights the problem of worker absenteeism.

Consistent with Colombian labor legislation and common practice in most industries and formal employment sectors, almost everyone enters the company for a trial period, and most people are offered the security of being hired after this period with permanent contracts. Despite permanent contracts, the flower companies I visited struggle to keep their workers. The high worker turnover is a matter of concern for the owners and managers of Muisca Flowers and for most flower farms in the region where I conducted fieldwork. Most workers who do leave, however, cite personal reasons rather than dissatisfaction with their work or pay. I will come back to this topic in chapter 6.

The topic of wages and wage equity for women must also address gender-specific employment alternatives in the region and women's motivations for working in floriculture. The wages paid by the flower industry are higher than the wages paid in the informal sector, which constitute the majority of jobs available to rural women and include work as domestic servants, cooks, dish and clothes washers, and childcare providers.[22] The wages paid in floriculture are comparable to the wages paid in the few formal employment alternatives rural women have, which include work as retail employees and food manufacturers. Dispensing gasoline has become an employment option for women and is the only type of job other than floriculture that cuts across culturally defined gender lines. All these formal sector jobs, including those in floriculture, pay minimum wage plus benefits such as health insurance and contributions to pension funds. Individuals in the informal sector may receive the equivalent day wage as the minimum wage, although most often it is less, and they never receive benefits.[23]

Men have more formal labor options, all culturally prohibited to women, such as employment as agricultural laborers, construction workers, farm managers, guards, brick makers, bakers, truck drivers, police officers, and poultry and hog farm workers. As others have noted of Colombia's industry, floriculture work has constituted, since its inception, one of the few formal employment opportunities for rural women (Meier 1999; Silva 1982).

Women have fewer employment alternatives due to the cultural definitions of appropriate work, although their employment alternatives increase as their level of education increases. Seniority in the flowers farms of the region is associated with the level of education individuals have. People, for the most part men, who have completed high school think of floriculture as a career option only if they can become supervisors. In contrast, female workers who have low levels of education experience any position in the flower industry as a secure long-term employment opportunity, saying that they see themselves and their children working in the industry all their lives.[24] Among cut-flower workers in my sample, men are slightly less educated than women, particularly among *raizales* and *antiguos*. Among *antiguos*, 46 percent of women but only 33 percent of men have more than a fifth grade education. Similarly, among *raizales*, 55 percent of women but only 43 percent of men have more than a fifth grade education. As we shall see later, this illustrates that men in the cut-flower industry tend to be those with fewer options.

Eighty percent of flower industry workers, including both men and women, have completed the fifth grade, thereby completing elementary school. Seventeen percent have completed high school. Women who work in floriculture have broken down the cultural barriers barring them from agricultural work. Floriculture work is still considered agricultural, involving getting hands dirty, and therefore not desirable. For this reason, people who have completed high school do not want to work in floriculture, claiming that they have not spent all those years studying just *para ir a jalar manguera* (to end up pulling a hose), referring to the water hoses men pull for irrigation. But individuals, particularly men, who have completed high school may continue to work in the flower industry because employment elsewhere is limited. Women who have only completed elementary grades and a few years of middle school actively seek jobs in floriculture and are more likely to become long-term workers than high school graduates. However, since female unemployment rates have been higher for women than for men in Colombia (Meier 1999), it is likely that a larger portion of female than male high school graduates will end up being long-term employees in floriculture.

Table 2.5. Years of Education among Cut-Flower Workers

	Women			
	Migrant	*Antiguo*	*Raizal*	All
n =	108	46	77	231
None	0%	9%	1%	2%
1–2 years	5%	9%	4%	5%
3–4 years	12%	7%	9%	10%
5 years	31%	28%	31%	30%
6–8 years	23%	15%	27%	23%
9–10 years	13%	11%	9%	11%
Graduated	16%	20%	18%	17%
No response	1%	2%	0%	1%
Average	6.7	6.2	6.7	6.6
	Men			
	Migrant	*Antiguo*	*Raizal*	All
n =	76	18	35	129
None	0%	0%	0%	0%
1–2 years	8%	0%	9%	7%
3–4 years	17%	11%	14%	16%
5 years	26%	50%	34%	32%
6–8 years	21%	17%	17%	19%
9–10 years	7%	17%	11%	9%
Graduated	21%	0%	14%	16%
No response	0%	6%	0%	1%
Average	6.5	6	6.2	6.3

Note: Normally in Colombia completion of elementary school occurs after five years of education; graduation from high school occurs after completion of eleven years of education.

Entering Formal Employment: Push and Pull Factors

Although critics of the flower industry state that women work only out of economic need, the women I have studied explain their work in the industry in other ways. The concepts of push and pull factors developed by labor economists are helpful in understanding the motivations behind female employment.[25] Push factors are financial needs the women may have, such as the need to support their family. Pull factors are non-economic rewards that attract women into paid employment, such as personal autonomy and personal fulfillment. As Tiano (1994) points out, both factors work simultaneously and reinforce each other.

In the floriculture industry, in both Colombia and Ecuador, the push factor of economic need is one important motivator for women's employment (Friedemann-Sánchez 2002; Korovkin 2003; Medrano 1982; Meier 1999; Mena 1999; Silva 1982). In the 1970s and 1980s Colombia's floriculture labor force came in large part, as was true in other parts of Latin America, from household members who had to complement poor agricultural earnings with wages (Bolaños and Rodríguez 1988, 81; Silva 1982, 34). Currently, that is the case in Ecuador's industry (Korovkin 2003; Mena 1999). It is worthwhile noting that such combinations of income-generating strategies in subsistence agriculture societies have occurred worldwide and have been studied primarily by scholars under "articulation of modes of production" area studies.

Currently in Colombia, while women, both married and single, enter the flower industry because they have financial need, they also do so for reasons related to their non-financial quality of life. Many stated they get bored at home and with informal labor, like washing clothes or watching babies, and the work in flower industry provides them with personal and social stimulation. Women say they like the challenge of the work, they take ownership of their assigned areas, and they are proud of the work they accomplish. The tasks, while repetitive, require knowledge and skill, as acknowledged by a few researchers (Korovkin 2003, 23; Meier 1999, 277; Mena 1999, 33) and as we shall see in the next chapter. Such work requirements are contrary to the characterization contained in most global assembly line research of labor as unskilled. In fact, floriculture workers need to know why certain tasks are performed and how to exercise judgment to do them well. Women especially take pride in their knowledge about the long-term planning required for production cycles. Women also state that they prefer working for the flower farms because it is higher in the social scale than informal labor, which is at the lowest end of their social options. Such status benefits have been at play since the industry's early years (Medrano 1982, 51). The work as a whole represents a challenge that women meet daily. By accomplishing the work, women see physical results in both income and flowers and emotional results in the encouragement they receive from their supervisors. Therefore, the work can become, as we shall see later, self-empowering, which in turn becomes the ground for success with further challenges.

Another non-monetary benefit of working in flowers is the ready-made community that the flower farms provide to workers and to people that live in the vicinity. This community thus is part of both work life and household life. For women who are single mothers, by choice or not, the community provides logistical and emotional support in the rest of their lives. I will fully explore the role of community as social capital in chapters 5 and 6. In line with the emphasis on context in this research, it is important to note that the social effect of flower farms varies according to local circumstance. In Ecuador, for instance, the social effects in terms of solidarity groups of working in floriculture have been the opposite of that in Colombia. In Ecuador the floriculture labor force is composed mainly of indigenous or *mestizo* peasant communities who base their economy on subsistence agriculture (Korovkin 2003; Mena 1999). The social organization of these communities and economies is the *minga*, solidarity groups that rotate farm labor in a reciprocal manner. Wage work has alleviated the financial difficulties of peasants in the short term. It has also had negative repercussions in the social organization of the family and community as individuals, particularly women, no longer have time to participate in *mingas*, communal activities, or childcare (Korovkin 2003; Mena 1999)

Nonetheless, women state that their primary motivation to work for pay is financial need. Even women living in households with partners who are culturally defined as "the breadwinners in the house" work because of financial need, because they have little or no economic security.[26] Their partners do not always contribute all their income, for example, and women are aware that their partner may leave with another woman; engage in simultaneous relationships, including setting up other housholds with children, as Velez (1995, 27) describes for the town of Suesca in Colombia; or abandon them when they become pregnant, as documented in Ecuador (Newman et al. 2002, 44). However, even women who are married and relatively secure emphasize the freedom they acquire with employment, because they can to choose what they eat and what they buy. Not working for pay means not earning money, having little say in household decisions, and being overly controlled by men. By earning a salary and being out of the house, they are establishing a behavioral pattern of monetary and physical independence, issues which I explore further in chapters 5 and 6. For women who are not married, the decision to work may be to avoid the dependence and submission that marriage represents to them. Working in the flower industry is an easy choice because often the work is a bicycle's ride from their houses. In addition, floriculture jobs are relatively plentiful while informal or other types of formal work *hay que rebuscarlo* (has to be sought). Note that the word used is *rebusque*; the *re* adds emphasis to the action of "seeking," meaning what one is looking for is harder to find, a hassle. The added emphasis also implies that such work has to be found over and over again because there is no job security in the informal sector. Clearly both push and pull factors work simultaneously in Fagua and Canelón in determining whether women look for work in the flower industry and remain there.

The flower industry has provided continual employment to women who would have found it difficult to support themselves in other ways. As such, it has had a profound effect on their lives, both materially and in terms of their capacity to redefine themselves and their futures in a restrictive and often abusive social context. As the women cut-flower workers have renegotiated their roles in the household and their relationships with men, their experiences have influenced the local society, shaping social changes that are now affecting people who have no direct affiliation to the industry. Women who have never worked for the cut-flower industry are now finding themselves resisting domestic violence, renegotiating household roles and expectations, and seeking greater autonomy both within and outside the household.

Job Security

As stated above, global assembly lines generally as well as the floriculture industry in Colombia in particular have been roundly criticized for failing to provide job security to workers. Even though it seems self-evident, I find it necessary to define what job security means given the debates regarding this topic in the literature. Short-term employment entails labor contracts that provide workers employment for indefinite periods or renewable limited time contracts. In Colombia, the norm is to have indefinite-time labor contracts. Long-term job security involves two factors: first, the assurance that the jobs will remain in the region indefinitely and, second, that individual workers can retain their employment in the same line of work for years or even an entire working career. The floriculture industry has been criticized on both counts.

The floriculture industry in Colombia has been criticized by researchers and government officials who argue that the employment it offers is only short term (Díaz et al. 1995, 20; Friedemann-Sánchez 1990, 43–144; Reis, Sierra, and Rangel 1995, 8; Silva 1982, 38).[27] The critiques were well founded in the decade of the 1980s when the flower business experienced its dramatic growth. Until 1990 flower companies rarely hired more than twenty-three employees on a permanent basis, thereby avoiding labor laws regulating companies that hire twenty-four workers or more.[28] The rest of the workers were subcontracted for periods of only two months at a time by subsidiaries that belonged to the same umbrella or parent company but were legally considered independent. After the two probationary months were over, the workers would be legally fired by the first subsidiary and re-hired by another subsidiary, while physically still working in the same flower farm. At the time, the law attempted to protect workers from being continually fired and re-hired by the same company by defining two adjacent contracts as one if they were no more than four months apart. But the sequential hiring by different subsidiaries successfully circumvented this protection (Friedemann-Sánchez 1990, 142–47). Flower companies followed these practices in order to avoid social security expenses for permanent workers and other monetary labor benefits.

My research confirms that since the mid-1990s most flower farms in the area where this fieldwork took place have dramatically improved their labor practices by giving workers permanent contracts, a change resulting from pressure exerted by national and international non-governmental organizations.[29] Almost all of the workers I interviewed or talked with from Muisca Flowers as well as other companies claimed to have permanent and unlimited-time contracts; the few that did not had six-month or one-year contracts. However, due to the extensiveness of the Sabana, this study as well as those of others (Meier 1999) cannot verify that permanent contracts, or subcontracting for that matter, are used by all of the flower companies. In fact Meier reports as recently as 1998 on subcontracting, as allowed by the law, as well as on the existence of permanent contracts. This highlights the need, even in floriculture research within one country, for studies to focus on the social context of the region. As Meier points out, labor conditions can be portrayed "as hell or as paradise" depending on who you talk to and what their stake is in the industry. As Meier (1999, 275) suggests, the examination of the industry within a "situated knowledge" (Geertz 1983) perspective is essential given sociocultural differences by geographical location.

In summary, labor turnover is high in global assembly line industries, including the floriculture industry.[30] In most transnational companies, labor turnover is decided by management, which has control of hiring and firing workers eager to find and keep jobs. In Colombia's floriculture industry, worker turnover is not decided by the flower companies but by the workers themselves. Thus, the issue of employment instability cited by critics of the global assembly line and of the floriculture industry is more complex than it might seem, both in terms of short-term and long-term employment and the role of workers as well as employers.

My research findings overwhelmingly contradict the premise that export industries do not provide long-term employment for individual workers. Unlike many other global assembly line industries which frequently relocate, the floriculture industry in Colombia has stayed put since 1965 and has provided stable employment to two generations of women. Furthermore, even previous to the changes in legislation, when workers had limited time contracts, the same workers were offered new contracts repeatedly for an unlimited number of years. Currently in Muisca Flowers, male *raizal* cut-flower workers have been in the industry an average of seven years, compared to ten years for female *raizales* (see table 2.6). Note also that among *antiguos* and *raizales*, both male and female, 15 percent of workers (approximately one in six employees) have worked in the industry for over fifteen years. (Migrants are not included in this calculation as, by definition, they arrived in the region within the past fifteen years.) In addition, among those surveyed, one in four women (26 percent) and one in five men (19 percent) have worked in the industry for more than ten years. Clearly a large proportion of workers have already benefited from very stable employment in the cut-flower industry.

Workers state that they feel they have long-term job security. Young women, envisioning themselves as flower workers, see older women in the industry as their role models. The few that do not see themselves in this way hold high school diplomas and would like to find different work or pursue more education. Jobs are so stable, in fact, that working in the fresh-cut flower industry is becoming an occupation, a *métier*.

Table 2.6. Years Employed in the Cut-Flower Industry

	Women			
	Migrant	*Antiguo*	*Raizal*	All
n =	108	46	77	231
0–2 years	27%	13%	16%	20%
3–5 years	31%	15%	9%	21%
6–10 years	28%	30%	34%	30%
11–15 years	10%	26%	23%	18%
16+ years	-*	13%	17%	8%
No response	4%	2%	1%	3%
Average	5.3	9.4	10.1	7.7
	Men			
	Migrant	*Antiguo*	*Raizal*	All
n =	76	18	35	129
0–2 years	43%	11%	29%	35%
3–5 years	30%	17%	23%	27%
6–10 years	16%	28%	23%	20%
11–15 years	11%	28%	9%	13%
16+ years	-*	17%	14%	6%
No response	0%	0%	3%	1%
Average	4.4	10.2	7.3	6.0

Note: Migrants have been in region for fifteen years or less and by definition cannot have worked more than fifteen years in the cut-flower industry.

The average age of cut-flower workers is just above thirty years old (see table 2.7). *Raizal* men tend to be younger than *raizal* women. Two-thirds of *raizal* men (69 percent) are age thirty or younger, compared to 47 percent of *raizal* women.

This data show that workers remain for longer than a couple of years in the industry and in one company. Furthermore, it disproves the critique that only young women are workers in the industry.

Marital status characteristics reveal that floriculture farms do not select either single women or married women, as has been claimed for other global assembly line industries (see table 2.8). Single women comprise 36 percent of the female workforce; this includes the 23 percent who are single mothers and the 15 percent who are single and have no children. Among male cut-flower workers, 26 percent are single with no children and 2 percent are single fathers.

A higher percentage of male than female cut-flower workers report being "married," either in de facto marriage-like unions or in de jure civil or religious marriages.[31] Nearly three quarters of men (71 percent) in the cut-flower industry report being married, compared to three-fifths of women (60 percent). The discrepancy is greatest among *antiguos*; sixteen out of eighteen *antiguo* men report being married (88 percent), while only twenty-eight of forty-six *antigua* women are married (61 percent).

Table 2.7. Age of Cut-Flower Workers

	Women			
	Migrant	*Antiguo*	*Raizal*	All
N =	108	46	77	231
17–30 yrs old	61%	41%	47%	52%
31–40 yrs old	30%	30%	27%	29%
41–50 yrs old	6%	24%	21%	15%
51–60 yrs old	3%	4%	5%	4%
Average age	29.1	34.5	33.0	31.5
	Men			
	Migrant	*Antiguo*	*Raizal*	All
n =	76	18	35	129
17–30 yrs old	62%	17%	69%	57%
31–40 yrs old	26%	50%	20%	28%
41–50 yrs old	9%	22%	9%	11%
51–60 yrs old	3%	11%	3%	4%
Average age	30.1	37.7	29.3	30.9

Table 2.8. Marital Status of Cut-Flower Workers

	Women			
	Migrant	*Antiguo*	*Raizal*	All
n =	108	46	77	231
Single, no children	19%	9%	16%	15%
Single mothers	15%	26%	26%	23%
Married, de facto	43%	22%	17%	30%
Married, civil or religious	21%	39%	38%	30%
Widowed	3%	4%	3%	3%
No response	0%	0%	1%	0%
	Men			
	Migrant	*Antiguo*	*Raizal*	All
n =	76	18	35	129
Single, no children	30%	6%	29%	26%
Single fathers	1%	6%	0%	2%
Married, de facto	41%	44%	34%	40%
Married, civil or religious	25%	44%	37%	31%
Widowed	0%	0%	0%	0%
No response	3%	0%	0%	2%

Note: "Single mothers" and "single fathers" include single mothers by choice, and single parents by abandonment and by separation. "Single mothers" and "single fathers" includes only respondents who live with and care for their own children on their own. Respondents who have biological children but do not live with them are included in the "single, no children" category. Percentages do not add up to 100 percent due to rounding.

Marital status alone, without considering children, does not convey the full contrast between men and women's family lives. In chapter 6, I present in-depth data on family composition. Table 6.2 shows the percentages of male and female cut-flower workers who live with their own children ("with children"), who have children but do not live with them ("children elsewhere"), or who do not have biological children ("no children"), as well as whether or not they live with a partner (de facto, de jure, or religious unions). Women's households are characterized by the presence of children, while men's lives are characterized by the presence of female partners. In other words, women are more likely to live with their children than with a partner, while men are more likely to live with a partner than with their children. Chapters 5 and 6 explore this discrepancy and shine light on the decision making inherent in these family configurations. For now, it is sufficient to notice the remarkable disparity between men's and women's lives.

Cut-flower jobs tend to be less desirable for men than for women; women are more likely to see cut-flower employment as a career, while men tend to see it as a stop-gap measure until they find other opportunities. Men, in contrast to women, choose flowers as a last option for employment. With the current economic recession, the construction sector is in crisis, and many men who used to work as construction workers are now in the floriculture sector in what they see as temporary positions. For entry-level male workers who come from other trades, floriculture jobs are considered demeaning, as it is horticultural work based on the land. In addition, after twenty years, the floriculture industry has become culturally associated with women: flower work is female work. Not surprisingly, women tend to have longer work histories in the industry than men. Interestingly, though, men's attitudes in Colombia are the opposite of men's attitudes in Ecuador, who prefer employment in floriculture (Mena 1999, 24).

The industry in Colombia faces a contradiction because those workers who are offered education on floriculture at a technical institution, paid for by the flower companies, do not tend to perceive themselves as long-term flower workers. In contrast, those individuals who have only completed a few grades of elementary school and do not have enough education to acquire technical education wish they had the opportunity to do so and do see themselves as long-term floriculture workers. Companies compromise by providing technical education to some who have completed up to eighth grade.

Conclusions

The fresh-cut flower industry in Colombia functions mostly with Colombian capital but has labor practices and production processes similar to global assembly line industries. However, it differs from some global assembly line industries in that the whole production process takes place in Colombia, while global assembly line industries often make components or parts that are later shipped to assembly factories in other locations. Global assembly line industries have the characteristic of being flexible, meaning that they can be packed up and moved to countries with more favorable conditions. Because of its agricultural basis, the fresh-cut flower industry cannot be moved easily—land is an integral part of the industry.

One main difference between floriculture and global assembly line industries is in ownership. The capital that most transnational industries function with comes from the first world, but most floriculture farms and companies are owned by Colombians and are managed with national capital. The exception is the multinational Dole Corporation. Because of this difference in the source of capital, many flower growers do not consider the land or its opportunity cost when setting the price of a flower. For instance, when I asked the owner of Muisca Flowers if he calculated the opportunity cost of his land into the costs of his business, he started to laugh. He went on to explain the land was an inheritance. The location of the land would make it too expensive either to buy today or even to consider it in his costs. He also stated he was not interested in selling his land. The Dole Corporation, however, must include the price of purchased or rented land among its costs. For many Colombian flower growers, the land is viewed not only as a tool to make money but as a legacy that represents the tradition of the family. According to producers I interviewed, the land in Colombia would never be sold to buy a new piece of land in Ecuador or Kenya, where labor costs are lower, in order to begin a new flower farm. Ancestral land ownership guarantees, to a certain degree, that a portion of the flower industry owners will remain in Colombia. This does not guarantee, however, that the industry itself will remain in Colombia. The Colombian owners could shift the use of their land to another productive purpose. In addition, the multinational company Dole, which apparently rents land, can move to any country where production is cheaper. By moving, they would drive international flower prices down and cut Colombian producers out of the market. This is what Colombian producers did to growers from the United States by having lower infrastructure and overhead costs.

In summary, the floriculture industry may at one level seem to be significantly different from global assembly line industries in that it is not a manufacturing industry with heavy machinery, but rather agricultural. However, floriculture shares elements in common with other global assembly line industries. For example, the products are prepared in a standardized series of steps, work is organized and disciplined, the majority of the workforce is female, the product is destined for export to wealthier nations, the industry has national and international tax incentives, and it does not have to respond to local government. In the chapter that follows I examine one of these elements: the organization of tasks and workforce discipline.

Notes

1. This has become a vast research area, and many researchers have focused their work on factory-type employment (Berik 2000; Carr, Chen, and Tate 2000; Carrillo and Hernández 1985; Ehrenreich and Fuentes 1981; Freeman 1998, 1993; Fuentes and Ehrenreich 1983; Fussell 2000; Lim 1990; Mitter 1986; Devon G. Peña 1997; P. Peña 1989; Safa 1986, 1990; Sklair 1989; South 1990; Standing 1989; Tiano 1990; Villar 1982; Kathryn Ward 1990; Woog 1980; and Yelvington 1995).

2. In the case of Mexico, Tiano (1994) and Carrillo and Hernández (1985) offer a good summary of the emergence of *maquiladoras*. The introduction of companies

from the United States to Mexico began in 1965 with the *Programa de Industrialización Fronteriza* or Border Industrialization Program. Since then, companies from the United States have established themselves on the border between the United States and Mexico to reduce production costs by hiring low cost labor (Carrillo and Hernández 1985). The goal of the Border Industrialization Program was to fix unemployment in Mexico's northern frontier; from 1972 there have been a considerable number of jobs created (Carillo and Hernández, 20). See Tiano for a discussion and analysis of the Mexican paradox: while the Border Industrialization Program or *maquila* program created thousands of jobs, unemployment as of 1983 doubled during the first fifteen years of the *maquila* program (1990, 198). Helen Safa (1986) and Rachel Grossman (1979) state that global assembly line has not diminished male unemployment, and Safa (1986, 65) in particular has proposed that global assembly line has introduced a new category of workers: young women. Various scholars have tried to answer the paradox basing their explanations on the gender component of the *maquila* labor force (Safa 1986, 65). The explanation, which has won general acceptance, is that the *maquiladoras* have not provided jobs for those who needed them most: men. The underlying assumption is that unemployment is a problem faced by men solely and that women do not really "need" wage labor opportunities (Martínez 1978, Fernández 1977, and Woog 1980, all cited in Tiano 1990, 199). See Leslie Sklair (1989) for a summary of this issue.

3. The central proponent of import substitution industrialization (ISI) was Chilean economist Raúl Prebisch. For a detailed history on development theory see Charles Oman and Ganeshan Wignaraja (1991) and Michael Todaro (1977). Arturo Escobar offers a critique (1995).

4. Carrillo and Hernández understand *maquila* industries specifically as industries that (1) are from the United States of America or have been contracted by industries in the United States with both national and foreign capital; (2) are dedicated to the assembly or processing of raw products; (3) are producing either final or intermediate goods that are shipped to the United States; and (4) have labor intensive schedules (1985, 19). Kathryn Ward adds that "global restructuring refers to the emergence of the global assembly line in which research and management are controlled by the core or developed countries while assembly line work is relegated to semi-periphery nations that occupy less privileged positions in the global economy (1990, 1)."

5. For an analysis and critique of the evolution of development and gender see Arturo Escobar (1995).

6. For research that challenges such stereotypes see Susan Tiano (1994), Carla Freeman (2000), and Constance Newman (2002).

7. Ziegler's study looks at the economic and cultural intersections of flower consumption. Specifically, she researches the operations and governance of the commodity chain that supplies flowers to New York City, research that provides an overall view of the cut-flower business from the moment flowers arrive at their northern destination through purchase by consumers. With impressive fieldwork that spans Colombia, Ecuador, the Netherlands, and the New York metropolitan area, Ziegler

explains how distribution chains are heavily dependent on social networks. In addition, she argues that flower consumer tastes change quickly, forcing flower producers to have flexible production processes. She describes how flexible consumption practices have developed, between 1970 and 2000, in correspondence with changes in the organization of producers and distributors, all which imply changes in the organization of capitalism akin to what David Harvey terms "flexible accumulation" (Ziegler 2003, 4).

8. For an extensive description of rise and fall of producers in the United States, see Ziegler's chapter 2 (2003).

9. See M. T. Fossum (1973) cited in Ziegler (2003, 48) for longitudinal data on the geographic shift in production within the Unites States.

10. For an explanation and analysis of antidumping practices and claims worldwide see Michael Finger and Nellie Artis (1993). For the specific accusations by United States producers against Colombian producers, see Méndez (1991, 1993).

11. Data is drawn from tables provided by the United States Department of Agriculture's Economic Research Service. Available at <www.ers.usda.gov/Data/ sdp/>. Select "Specialty," then "Floriculture and Environmental Horticulture." Accessed August 25, 2004.

12. The United States Department of Agriculture Economic Research Service reports the number of cut flowers sold in the United States by domestic producers as well as imported from a variety of countries. In 2003 domestic producers supplied 794 million stems to the market, while 2,617 million stems were imported. Colombia alone contributed 2,016 million stems, or 59.1 percent of the total 3,412 million stems consumed (USDA ERS 2004).

13. See Ziegler (2003) for a description of the development of the cut-flower industry in Ecuador.

14. Others among the sixty-five flower-exporting countries are Kenya, Zimbabwe, Zambia, Tanzania, Uganda, Malawi, Mauritius, Ethiopia, Ivory Coast, Morocco, Israel, Turkey, India, Brazil, Malaysia, Taiwan, New Zealand, and Australia (Maharaj and Dorren 1995, 14–17).

15. Production and exportation data up to 1995 for other producing countries can be found in Naila Maharaj and Gaston Dorren (1995).

16. This number is consistent with findings by Ziegler (2003).

17. Ziegler has an excellent description of the flower distribution mechanisms in the United States as well as a detailed analysis of U.S. Floral and its effects in the distribution system (2003, 267–29).

18. Dairy, beer, and salt are among the big industries in the Sabana that do pay local taxes because the bulk of their production is meant for internal consumption.

19. Velez mentions this issue in her discussion of the town of Suesca (1995).

20. I am indebted to Jaime Arocha for bringing this terminology to my notice.

21. The same is true in the United States with lower and upper income employment. Janitorial, restaurant, and other service sector jobs are performed by recent immigrants who work for lower wages. Similarly, large corporations hire part-time fe-

male employees. While corporations lower their costs by saving on benefits, employees give those up in exchange for flexibility, allowing them to raise children. For more on this topic see Nancy Folbre (1994).

22. According to Meier previous research in Colombia reports that only 0.84 percent of domestic servants receive the equivalent of a minimum wage salary while 72.2 percent receive less than half (1999, 278). Needless to say these women do not receive the employment benefits package.

23. In Ecuador's floriculture industry, the median wages paid to women are twice the wages paid in other industries (Newman 2002, 380).

24. According to Fernández-Kelly (1983, 68) and Safa (1982), most women see their participation in *maquila* industry as temporary, expecting to return to full-time housework. Clearly, this is not the case for floriculture workers in Colombia.

25. See Tiano (1994) for an excellent description of the push and pull arguments. Supporters of the exploitation thesis stress the role of push factors. They assert that capitalism has thrown the third world into economic instability, thus forcing women to work for pay or pushing them into employment. The supporters of the integrationist thesis stress the role of pull factors in motivating women to work outside the home (Tiano 1994, 51–52). According to Amartya Sen (1990, 144), a key issue of women working in paid labor is that it increases their bargaining power inside the household. Irene Tinker (1976, 31) and Rae Lesser Blumberg (1976) point out that paid work enables women to depend less on their male partners and also increases their status in the household and the community at large (Tiano 1994, 52). Safa (1986, 67) does not agree that global assembly line jobs provide women with more leverage.

26. Tiano states that almost half of the women were part of the labor force before entering the *maquila* workforce. She concludes that most women entered the labor force out of necessity. Even women who lived in households with a male breadwinner did not enjoy financial security because of possible separation from or death of partner. Tiano claims her research findings in Mexico disprove that *maquila* women are a new category of workers that would have not entered the labor force if *maquila* industry were not there (Tiano 1994, 143–45).

27. See Lynne Phillips (1998, 41) regarding job security in transnational companies. See also Carrillo and Hernández (1985, 177–78) for labor turnover rates.

28. The labor code changed when Colombia instituted a new constitution in 1991.

29. For additional information on the process see Greta Friedemann-Sánchez (1999).

30. Carrillo and Hernández state that Mexican *maquila* workers get burned out after three years and have to be replaced (1985, 177). In addition, companies ensure turnover through short labor contracts. Another policy is to harass senior employees in various ways, including requiring harder work or shift changes, in order to make them resign. These policies reduce the cost of worker benefits for companies (177–78).

31. In Colombia, a marriage-like permanent union is known as "*unión libre*" or "*unión de hecho*." In it, the partners refer to each other as husband and wife, and these unions can last decades or a lifetime. Since 1990 under Colombian family code, an *unión libre* has all the rights and obligations of any civil or religious marriage after two years of existence. Approximately 19.2 percent of couples in Colombia are in de facto marriages (Deere and León 2000, 75) compared to much higher rates (30 percent of women and 40 percent of men) in my sample (see table 2.8).

CHAPTER THREE

Assembling Flowers

In most ways, all flower farms have the same work arrangements, schedules, and division of tasks, but infrastructure varies dramatically from one farm to another. The quality of the restrooms, dining halls, and recreation areas can differ sharply between farms. The same is true of sanitation facilities (including garbage disposal areas) and even the layout of the farm and the attention paid to its visual beauty.

Muisca Flowers is unusual among flower companies because it has two businesses operating in one single farm. Muisca Flowers produces both fresh-cut flowers, sold to international markets, and flower plants, sold to other flower farms or kept for Muisca Flowers' own use. The area that produces fresh-cut flowers is called *production*, and the area that produces flower plants is called *propagation*. The production area itself is divided into two sections, one called *production* and the other *post-harvest* (see figure 3.1) or *classification*. In addition there is a biotechnology laboratory dedicated to plant sanitation (described below) and an area assigned for waste management.

Production and propagation have distinct work areas and administrations, as well as a separate labor force of both professionals and workers. Each has its own dining hall, bathrooms, locker rooms, and administrative offices. The separation is designed to reduce the risk of contamination between the flower production and plant reproduction areas. If fungus, mold, or insects affect plants in either production or propagation, whole blocks of plants can be ruined within one day.

The organization of the staff at Muisca Flowers takes the form of a squat pyramid, with a very wide base and a narrow top. At the top is the president of the company. Ten professionals report directly to him: a maintenance manager, a post-harvest manager, five agronomists, a director of propagation, a financial manager, and a human relations manager. The agronomists, post-harvest manager, and maintenance manager each manage several supervisors (close to twenty in total). The supervisors manage a total of around 460 *operarios* or base workers, as I will refer to workers in this study. (This is the total number of workers at the flower farm, a higher figure than the 360 who responded to my survey.)

The owner is aware that people deserve promotions, but there are very few advanced spots to fill. The nature of the business is one where most workers (about 94 percent) are base workers. The status of personnel within the organization can be identified by the way they dress. Base workers are dressed in red overalls; supervisors wear green; professionals such as agronomists, biologists, and the human resource manager are in blue. Administrative personnel do not have a uniform, but they rarely leave their offices. In an interview with the human resource manager, she stated she did not recall how she had decided workers would be in red, supervisors in green, and professionals in blue. I noticed, however, that a worker dressed in red overalls can be spotted easily through the thick foliage of rose plants. When I pointed out that supervisors, in green, are hard to spot and therefore could approach an area of work without being seen

Figure 3.1. Post-harvest section: classifying roses

readily, she just smiled. She did offer that base workers in mourning initially objected to wearing red, as it is a bright color, but that they do not anymore.

For the most part, the types of labor done by base workers are divided into female and male and have remained the same as observed by Diana Medrano in the early 1980s (1982). Men are in charge of irrigation, fumigation (pesticide and fungicide spraying), and preparation of the soil in the beds where the plants will grow. Women are in charge of production, including planting the plants, trimming and cutting the flowers, and cleaning the area. Women hold most posts in the classification area, where the flowers are sorted, the stems trimmed, and the flowers packed ready for shipment. One worker may remain in one section anywhere from one to ten years depending on her ability, her willingness to change, openings in other areas, and presence of family members already working in such areas.

Production

Muisca Flowers produces forty varieties of roses, gypsophila (known as baby's breath), asters, and alstroemeria. By far the majority of the farm is cultivated in roses. The greenhouses are structures made of wood and clear plastic. The big greenhouses are called blocks (see figure 3.2). Each block in turn is divided for administrative purposes in *naves*, long sections within a block. Each *nave*

Figure 3.2. Block of roses

has a certain number of *camas* or beds, and each bed has a certain number of *cuadros* or squares. Each block contains approximately 216 beds.

In general, each worker is assigned between thirty and forty beds of roses, depending on the flower variety and the intensity of maintenance it requires. On average, one block of roses will have five base workers, the same five workers who are assigned the same beds. In turn, one agronomer will have seven blocks under his or her management. Rose work, unlike filler work, is lonely. Each worker is given sole responsibility for the care of between 12,000 and 14,000 plants. These workers spend their days alone, tending those plants, and over time each worker's performance is judged based on the health, architecture, and productivity of the rose plants and beds under their care. The agronomer Enrique Isaza manages two male supervisors, twenty and twenty-six years old. In turn the two supervisors manage forty-six rose workers, all women.

Gypsophila, alstroemeria, and asters are *fillers* cultivated to fill in spaces in bouquets between other flowers like roses. Fillers are grown in blocks separate from roses and have their own agronomists and supervisors. The main difference between fillers and roses is that a rose plant is a permanent fixture in the blocks. Once planted, it can produce for up to ten years depending on the variety. It takes a rose plant two years to develop into a mature plant producing export quality roses. With fillers, the plant is grown in a single season, and when harvested the whole plant is cut. Rather than being harvested one by one, as are roses produced on rose plants, fillers are cared for and harvested en masse. As a result, workers are assigned to teams, and they work an area of filler flowers together moving along the field as a group.

María Sánchez, forty-eight, twice divorced and a single mother of four adult children, has been a flower worker for twelve years. She takes side growths off the rose plants as we talk. Workers in roses work alone all day. She is very quick, uses both hands at the same time, lifts up her face to look at me once in a while, and continues her work while she chats and laughs. Aside from cutting roses and sweeping the area clean, done every day, there are twenty maintenance tasks that the rose plants need on a weekly basis. Pruning unnecessary growths and extra buds and trimming are among them.

The performance of each task affects the physical structure of the rose plant, technically known as the plant's architecture. When trimming is done correctly, the stem will be straight and the head of the rose will not be at an angle. The supervisor can tell, by looking at the architecture of the plants, if workers have done the job correctly in the past few days and weeks. This is why the owner asserted that the jobs women perform in flower production are skilled, not unskilled as many claim (see figure 3.3). The owner continued:

> If each woman worker is given from 12,000 to 14,000 plants, and there are on average twenty-eight tasks to be done to each plant, it means that women have

> to perform 352,000 intelligent decisions. Our business is based on the quality of her decision, of where she places that scissor. The worker needs to be alert, intelligent, a good observer, disciplined, and precise for most of her eight hours of work. This type of work that requires such decision making and such responsibility is qualified work.

Unlike other global assembly lines worldwide where workers worry about job security, in the floriculture industry the owners and managers worry about employee retention, critical because it takes about three months for a worker to be trained in one area and to perform the work properly. Unfortunately, annual turnover is approximately 30 percent. In other words, of the 460 base

Figure 3.3. Cutting roses

workers at Muisca Flowers, about 140 quit after one year by their own choice. One of the agronomers was adamant when he stated that "worker turnover is fatal for us." Both the agronomer and the owner voiced their concern over the high turnover of workers. People leave for personal reasons, often emotional. They leave because of gossip that is hurtful personally and detrimental to their household relationships. As the agronomer said, "Here people handle gossip a lot." I will come back to this issue in chapter 6.

Cutting roses begins at 6:00 A.M. and ends at 10 A.M. The work starts early, when the temperature inside the greenhouses is still low and the flowers are still closed up. As the day gets warmer and the temperature increases inside the

Figure 3.4. After roses are cut, they are counted, measured, and placed in a transportation box to be taken by cableway to the classification area

greenhouses, the flower heads open up and they become impossible to pack. Along the production areas is a *cable via* or cableway, a strong cable that holds three hanging carts in which the cut flowers are placed (see figure 3.5). The cableway runs all the way from production areas to the post-harvest room. Many farms still use the *carretilla* or cart, either pulled or pushed by male workers, to take the cut flowers to be classified. Muisca Flowers recognizes that using the cableway is more efficient and also easier on the workforce. This is a good example of technology the firm is putting in place to develop flower growing into a more technology-based business. In this respect, Muisca Flowers contrasts with other local growers who still manage their land and workers in an *hacendado* fashion, with minimal investment in infrastructure.

Figure 3.5. The cableway

Post-Harvest

After the flowers are cut, they are taken to one of the two post-harvest areas. One is exclusively for roses, the other for fillers. These areas, unlike the blocks, are very cool. The roof is designed to deflect the sun's rays. If this area were warm, the flowers would open up and mature faster. The workstations are raised off the floor on wooden platforms to protect workers' feet from the cold floor. In the workstations the flowers are classified by height and quality. Roses with longer stems are priced higher. They are fixed, meaning that petals that suffered mechanical damage during handling are taken off the roses. A rose has between eighteen and forty petals, depending on the variety. Standard practice is to take two petals off the heads of roses regardless of the variety, to assure they leave the farm with no mechanical damage, and take one third of the leaves off the stem from the bottom up. After this, the flowers are placed in buckets with carbohydrates and an antibacterial solution to await packaging. Next they are bunched into packages of six, twelve, or twenty-five flowers. Some flowers are packaged directly into bouquets. These are big sellers because making bouquets in the United States is very expensive due to labor costs.

Up to this point, the post-harvest tasks are all accomplished by women. The remainder of the tasks are performed by men. Colombia, like most Latin American flower producers, dry-ships the flowers, meaning that the flowers are placed in tight bundles in cardboard boxes with no water. This contrasts with the wet-shipping methods used in Europe where flowers are transported by truck in buckets with water (Ziegler 2003, 101). After the packages are bundled by women they are placed by men in cardboard boxes and taken to refrigerated rooms. The size of the box depends on the number of flowers in it and are called *quarter*, *tobacco*, and *full*. Contracted trucks arrive daily and transport the flowers to the Bogotá airport. According to Catherine Ziegler, the value of cut flowers may decrease from 25 to 50 percent with each day that passes after they have been harvested (2003, 98)—thus, the importance of harvesting early in the day before the flowers open up with the day's heat. This insures the buds can be packed tightly without harming the flower, thus maintaining its value.

Margarita López is about forty-five, married and a mother of five grown children. López has been working in the flower industry for sixteen years. She likes it and is grateful for the work in the second post-harvest section where filler flowers are classified and packaged. She is checking that all bundles that were cut are placed in their cellophane bags, as they will appear in U.S. supermarkets, and put in buckets. The buckets contain a solution of water and chemicals, which lengthens the life of a flower. As she suspected, there are some bundles left in the conveyor belt and a few on the classification tables. The day is warm, but that is just fine. Baby's breath (gypsophila) is more resilient and does not have to be placed in cardboard boxes and shipped right away as do roses. I follow her as she checks the work areas after most of the workers have already left.

Propagation

In the propagation area there are two sections: the biotechnology laboratory and the blocks where the mini-plants are put in soil. The laboratory is an amazing place worthy of any science fiction movie. Two big grain silos were converted into the laboratory because they were relatively easy to seal and thus ensure a sterile environment. The purpose of the laboratory is to cultivate in vitro tiny pieces of plants cut from grandmother plants. This process is called micropropagation. All seven workers in this section, including professionals and supervisors, are women.

Claudia Linares, twenty-eight and single mother of a seven-year-old girl, has been working in Muisca Flowers for eleven years, since June 1988. Linares, who comes from a *raizal* family, completed elementary school. She started as a base worker *en campo* or in the field, working beds of carnations. After three months she was promoted to post-harvest. She was there for a few months then promoted to monitor. After five years she was promoted again to work in the laboratory. Here, she worked *en cámara* (in chamber), meaning it was her task to divide plants under the microscope. After a few years she was promoted once more to be a laboratory supervisor. Now she is in charge of mixing up the solutions in which the plants will grow roots and develop in vitro. The base is always agar, to which different solutions are added depending on the species and variety of plant. Linares begins her day at 7:00 A.M. and goes home at 3:30 P.M. When I arrived she was dressed in white, hair covered by a laboratory hat, and she was weighing powdered ingredients to make a solution. She had a book of instructions in front of her on a table.

Linares is very knowledgeable and clearly understands the complicated processes of micropropagation, which is different for each variety of plant. Linares described in detail for me the process for several species of plants. For example, for roses the *yema* or knot is cut out of the grandmother plant. The knot in turn is divided into four parts with the scalpel, and all the pieces are placed in a jar. Each forms a rose plant. If the desired outcome is a rooted plant, then the knot and plant are cut at the apex.

During my visit, Miriam Gallego, nineteen and single mother of two, was retrieving small jars from the industrial size pressure pot where objects are sterilized. She was heading to the second floor to take more jars to Estela Cuero, who was "in chamber" along with five other women. To be in chamber means being in a closed room with white walls and high-intensity lights that shine down on the workers (see figure 3.6). The workstation is partially enclosed by white, metal and glass designed to keep the area as sterile as possible. Like Linares, Cuero was dressed in white, and, looking through a microscope, she was cutting pieces of plants with a scalpel and placing them in the jars of agar. There are two purposes for the division of the plants. Some are placed in a special solution designed to encourage root growth. These will end up in dirt and sold as plants. Others are placed in solutions that command not the creation of roots but of leaves. These plants will see the chamber and scalpel many times since they are placed under the microscope and divided up over and over. Cuero repeatedly sprayed alcohol on her hands to keep the area sterile and complained how dry the alcohol made them. She has been working for Muisca Flowers for six years, three in the field and three in the laboratory doing micro-propagation work in chamber.

The jars containing the plant pieces are taken in metal trays to the second floor of the silo to incubate under white neon lights. It takes four weeks for the complete micro-propagation cycle, that is, for a plant fragment to be ready to once again be divided in chamber. It takes three weeks for a plant to develop roots and be ready to be put in soil in individual plastic containers and in a block. Once the plants are in the greenhouses, they are cared for in

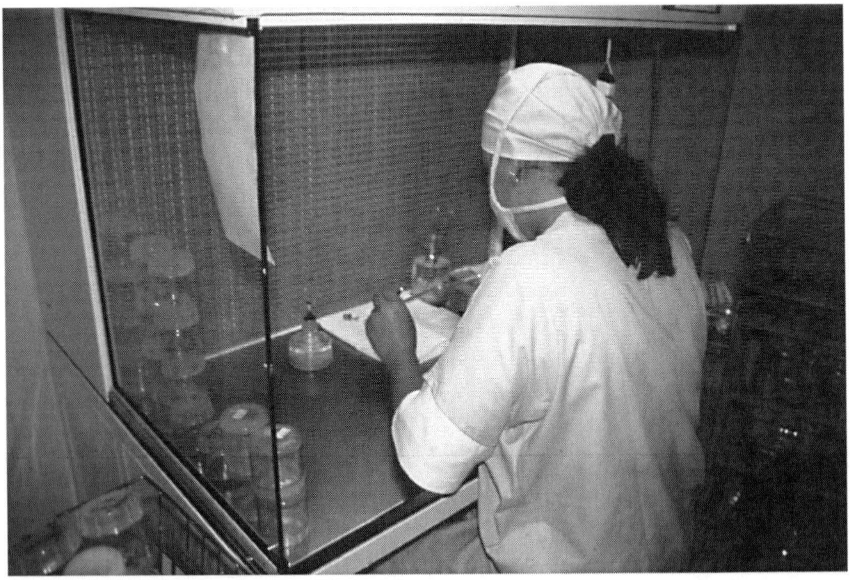

Figure 3.6. Working "in chamber"

a way similar to any nursery. They are separated if they are too close to one another in the same pot. They are watered, sprayed, and transplanted depending on the species and variety and finally packed up in open boxes to be sold to other fresh-cut flower companies.

Plant Sanitation

Maintaining the health of the plants is a tremendous problem in the flower industry. Within a matter of hours plants can be overcome by insects, mold, fungus, or bacteria. Keeping the plant population healthy is so critical that the company has twenty *monitoras* or monitors, all women. Their job is to check square by square, bed by bed, and block by block for any disease. In addition, they take flower samples and place them in a humidity chamber, a bag with high humidity and temperature to reproduce flower packaging conditions and accelerate the decay process. The plant sanitation section was visually shocking: a rose cemetery with rose heads hanging upside down in plastic bags, turning brown and ugly.

By accelerating decay, a monitor can quickly identify whether one area has a mold problem, for example. This is important to protect production from disease infestation. Monitoring through humidity chambers also provides a way to control the quality of flowers already shipped and to double check, when customers complain, if any were indeed diseased when shipped. Each bag is labeled with the date it was cut and from exactly which block, which section, and what square it originated.

The Insectary

The insectary is a laboratory where live insects are bred. The structure is made out of wood, and the walls are fine screen. The insectary was introduced in Muisca Flowers around 1996. Its purpose is to develop biological controls for some of the pests. In another example of using technology to improve production techniques and worker conditions, Muisca Flowers is dedicating resources to the breeding of a parasitic wasp, Diglyphus isaea. The Diglyphus wasp is capable of curbing the destructive 1.5mm leafminer flies (Liriosmyza spp.). The leafminer egg, known in the farms as *el minador*, hatches into a larva that eats through the leaves of plants. The damage to leaves also occurs when the leafminer punctures the leaves to lay its eggs. The biological control works because the Diglyphus wasp finds leafminer larvae and lays its eggs next to larvae. The wasp egg takes its nutrition from the larvae, killing it in the process. The wasps, about a millimeter long in size, are no danger to the plants or workers. Muisca Flowers also sells Diglyphus wasps to other area flower farms. Using Diglyphus wasps along with sticky strips where leafminers flies get stuck are two effective ways the industry as a whole is curbing its use of insecticides and protecting its workforce (see figure 3.7).

The insectary is run by Inés Machado, a twenty-five-year-old *raizal* woman who is married and has two children. She completed high school and has been working at Muisca Flowers for nine years, since 1990. She has never worked as a base worker in the field. She worked in the biotechnology laboratory for three years, three in research, and now three in the insectary. She is fascinated by and proud of her work. Bringing out a microscope, she instructs me to look at the galleries of leafminer larvae. Directing me to look for eggs attached to the larvae, she explains that they use bean plants to "seed" the leafminer pest fly, effective since beans have a large foliage surface.

The plants used as infestation sites are handled in lots. Each lot has twelve trays, each tray has six pots, and each pot has seven bean plants. When the plants are ready to be infested with leafminer, they are introduced to the infestation chamber, a screened room within the larger screened *insectary*, for one day. Once infested with leafminer larvae, the plants are taken out to the breeding area where wasps deposit their eggs on the larvae. Upon emerging from their eggs, the new wasps are collected by a man with a wide-mouth

Figure 3.7. Yellow sticky strips are placed along flower beds to control pests

portable vacuum cleaner. They are either released into the sections of the flower farm that have leafminer or are sold to other flower farms.

Water and Chemicals

Waste management and irrigation (water and chemical) are managed by different supervisors and professionals. The workers under their supervision, however, rotate one month in one place, one month in another. The reason behind this is to not continually expose the same workers to the chemicals in the pesticides and fertilizers that are administered by fumigation. Because women get pregnant, only men do this job. The assumption behind keeping women from this work is that, if they are carrying a fetus, the fetus can absorb the chemicals and be injured. What still needs to be studied, however, are the possible effects of the chemicals on male fertility and the quality of sperm. In my interviews, the men themselves were oblivious to this issue and not even managers had thought about it. The workers are concerned about potential and existing dermatological problems, but there is a sense that life is urgent and is now. Supervisors, as we shall see later, are aware of the health risks associated with floriculture and stated repeatedly that base workers often do not abide by farm rules of staying away from blocks that have just been fumigated. In fact, in order to get in, they often move the wooden tripod structures that block the entrance to sections that have just been sprayed. The long-term effect of chemicals is more a concern among the non-governmental organizations and the developed countries that set the standards for those organizations. As stated before, both research and policies on worker protection need to be performed and implemented.

Every block is fumigated twice a week as a preventive strategy. If there is an outbreak of disease, then the block is fumigated three times a week. I saw men provided with full protective gear to wear during fumigation. The areas being sprayed are clearly marked with roadblocks that inform workers that a specific block is either being or has been fumigated. No one is to be in the blocks during fumigation. The ban remains for twenty-four hours after fumigation.

Andrés Valderrama, thirty-four, is from Tolima and has been working at Muisca Flowers for five years. He fathered a child almost ten years ago but never sees her. Valderrama is the supervisor of fumigation. He began working in the flower industry in 1988 as a base worker in the field. When he started working in Muisca Flowers, he was very excited to see all the technology the farm had. He thought this farm would have fewer pest and mold problems and he would not have to deal so much with the stress of having a whole block disappear in an instant. But it has not been like that. The plagues are in Muisca Flowers as well and because the farm is so large and so intensely cultivated an outbreak has huge repercussions. It is up to Valderrama and his supervisor to do a good job with fumigation. Valderrama has sixteen men working for him, and he feels responsible for their health. With concern showing in his face he states:

> I provide my workers with protection gear. I give them gloves, masks, rubber overalls and jacket, boots. I manage my workers as a supervisor in an industry, unlike in some places where supervisors are *capataces* (foremen) and mistreat their workforce. But people here do not use the gear. I understand; who wants to wear the gear when it is 30°C in a block? Sometimes they don't use it because they are undisciplined, or because they lack the education to understand how important it is to use it. I do not know how much longer I can live with the stress; however, I love the responsibility and I like the company.

Every plant is watered every day. There are fifteen male workers in watering tasks and three ways to water. Roses are watered by drip method. Hoses are dug into the dirt as permanent infrastructure, and once a day the *bomberos* or pump workers turn on the faucet for the exact number of cubic meters of water needed. For propagation, the watering system is also built into the infrastructure; these hoses are not buried under the dirt but instead hang above the plants with a showering head every few meters. Water is also given directly by hose to those plants that need it. This method is hard physical work, as it requires pulling the heavy thick hose, and managers justify hiring men to do this job based on the strength it requires.

Discipline

Most women who work in the flower farms rise by 4:30 in the morning. They make breakfast and lunch for their entire family, get their children ready, and leave their houses by 5:15 A.M. Women who have small children take them on their bicycles to the house where they are cared for. There is one daycare center in the region, owned by one of the flower companies. The vast majority of children are cared for in homes, rather than centers, by female relatives or women who provide childcare as a job. Bicycles often have a metal basket in the front with holes cut in it to fit the legs of a small child. Older children sit on the back of the bicycle holding onto their mothers. This routine goes on year-round regardless of the weather. A few fathers take their children to daycare, but the majority of the parents who transport children are women.

After dropping the children off, women ride their bicycles to work and are at their lockers just in time to change clothes and leave their lunches in the warming ovens. They arrive at 5:55 A.M. sharp at the meeting place where the supervisor is waiting.

With a few exceptions, men who work in the flower industry and live with a spouse and children wake up at between 5:00 A.M. and 5:20 A.M., have breakfast, take the lunch that the wife has prepared and packed, and leave alone on their bikes. Children of school age walk to school on their own and wait there until school starts at 7:00 A.M.

Lunch is between 10:30 and 11:00 A.M. There are three dining halls in Muisca Flowers where the workers have lunch in two shifts. The day is done at 2:30 P.M. A few people stay after hours to complete their labor or when production is high. On the way out of the farm, one can hear the women discussing the household chores they will do when they arrive home. Men are quiet or discuss meeting at a *tienda* or *cantina* or errands they have to run. The atmosphere is one where women dominate the conversation and the space.

The time between leaving home and returning home is full of discipline and precision at various levels. The first type of discipline is technical and depends on the job. Workers are expected to prune, cut, bunch, graft, thread, plant, bag, and weigh with precision. For example, in post-harvest, the rubber bands have to be placed around the bunch of roses at 8 centimeters from the bottom, not more, not less. Gypsophila bunches are packed by weight, which has to be identical in every bunch. Workers comprehend that their task is a part of a whole and understand conceptually the full process. They know that in the laboratory plants are divided and replanted, for instance. While they do not know what agar is or what pH (acidity) of the solution stands for, they appreciate the full picture of flower reproduction. They understand, for example, that roses are grafted to varieties with stronger roots and lots of foliage that feed the plants to create beautiful roses at the top.

A second type of discipline is in human relations. The discipline begins with the work schedule: getting up at early hours in the morning and being at work on time, with the supervisor or professional calling each worker by name and marking whether they are present or absent. One of the workers' organizational responsibilities that demands discipline, for example, is checking off on paper charts their accomplishment of each production task. The supervisor gets these charts every week and compares them with the beds and the development and architecture of the plants, thus being able to check indirectly on work habits and task performance.

Three years pass from the moment a rose variety is chosen to the moment when it is first harvested and sold in the international market. A rose plant can remain in production for many years. If the plantation loses a harvest of roses, it has also lost many years of planning and investment. Losing a harvest of filler flowers is disastrous, but to lose a harvest or, worse, a plantation of roses is catastrophic. This is why there is so much control. Women chart daily the number and variety of roses cut and even the time they were cut. The charts are entered into computers by the post-harvest supervisors, who print out the production of each worker at the end of each week.

Clearly, the retention of trained and productive workers is critical. In order to retain workers, the company has dramatically improved its physical structure. For example, it provides comfortable and appealing dining halls and dispenses mandatory work clothing and tools on schedule (every three months), which not every farm does. It also administers an employee loan fund for workers, as we shall see later.

All the controls described in this chapter allow the industry to manage the workforce carefully. Workers are required to have discipline. The implications of close management, strict controls, and discipline will be analyzed in the next chapter.

CHAPTER FOUR

Disciplined Labor, Identity, and Gender

That women are still associated with the household but have actively entered the public sphere and work arena in export industries requires an analysis of gender ideologies and how they are either being reinforced or challenged by global assembly line industries in their own factory floors as well as in the communities where they are located. Such analysis has mainly looked at the construction and use of gender ideologies on the factory floor as a way to justify the employment of either young, single, childless women (Drori 2000; Fernández-Kelly 1983; Kim 1997; Ong 1987) or older women who are possibly mothers (Lee 1998; Roberts 1994; Tiano 1994). Few studies have looked at the construction or deconstruction, by corporations, of the ideologies of gender exercised *outside* the industry and its effects on local culture. This chapter intends to do so by examining in what ways cut-flower workers bridge their work culture with their household culture. It describes the floriculture industry's construction of a gendered ideology of household equality and its effects on women's identity and self-esteem. It also examines the ways in which the fresh-cut flower industry in Colombia couples two remarkably different objectives: it reinforces the social class system of domination at the same time that it promotes gender equality in the community and provides female workers with instruments for contesting the patriarchal structure of power in the household. By analyzing the role of the people and the industry as well as the interaction between them, this chapter will show some of the ways in which flower farms are becoming catalysts of cultural change in the region in both direct, purposeful ways and incidental ways.

The Public Transcript of Flower Farms

As James Scott (1990) argues, power, resistance, and subordination are articulated in public and hidden transcripts expressed through characteristic patterns of speech, practices, and gestures. A public transcript is the symbolization of domination and the enactment of power in a public way, while a hidden transcript speaks about uneven power relations. The existence of a public transcript of domination in turn creates a hidden transcript that critiques that domination.

In applying Scott's concept to this research, I add the element of gender. Colombia's society is a class pyramid, a steep one, but it is also a gendered one: women have lower status than the men in their class. Bosses and owners of flower companies have public transcripts about their status and power over their employees, and husbands, fathers, and other males in families have transcripts with regard to their spouses and female relatives. In turn, while all workers may have hidden transcripts referring to their relations to the boss, women also have hidden transcripts with regards to their relations toward male members of the household. These hidden transcripts have their public counterparts as well.

The organization of the flower farm, described in the previous chapter, sets the parameters of consistent behavior and performance for workers to ensure that the flowers are produced within a set schedule, at the lowest cost possible, and with the highest quality. But at the same time the parameters are a public transcript of domination that ensures that power relations between workers and management are maintained and reinforced. As Scott put it, "Every visible outward use of power—each command, each act of deference, each list and ranking . . . is a symbolic gesture of domination that serves to manifest and reinforce a hierarchical order" (1990, 45). The hierarchical order maintained in Fagua and Canelón is a patriarchal and class system of social domination. In fact, class relations are not merely maintained by but are engraved in the social structure by the public transcript of domination and power that flower farms create. The discourse of domination and power is enacted symbolically in the color of the uniforms of all the personnel: red for base workers, green for supervisors and monitors, blue for professionals. Upper management, even though they have blue uniforms, never wear them, which sets them apart as overseers, using Michel Foucault's concept, of the color-coded panopticum (1977).

Rank within the flower farm is reinforced by the way supervisors organize oversight of workers. The colors of the uniforms denote the rank a certain person has within the company, while at the same time they signal social class in terms of who supervises whom: workers dressed in red are supervised by workers dressed in green, who in turn are supervised by workers dressed in blue. Those dressed in blue report to and are supervised by those who do not wear uniforms. Rank and class are also reinforced by the content of the supervision. Supervision spans everything from setting schedules, such as times of arrival to and departure from work, to controlling the specific amount of time a worker spends at a given chore. In addition to controlling time, the supervisors keep the chores themselves under surveillance. For example, supervisors ensure that roses are bundled at 3 inches from the bottom up of the stems, and workers are required to record the different chores they do and their progress on forms. Each worker is approached by her supervisor once a week, and her performance reviewed.

The public transcript of domination is also evident in the terms of address used among workers, and the way workers are addressed is a subtle way in which class stratification is not only displayed, but maintained as well. In Muisca Flowers the professionals, dressed in blue and all male but one, address the base female workers as *niña* (girl), regardless of the worker's age; one might, for instance, hear a supervisor say to a worker "*Niña, venga para acá*" (girl, come here). In fact, the terms of address with relation to age also reinforce class relations, as the convention of showing deference toward someone older is reserved for same-class interactions. Supervisors who are closer in class to base workers than the group of professionals address workers most of the time by name, though there are a few who use *niña*. The workers, however, cannot reciprocate with the same form of address, but respond with deference, using *señor* (mister) or *señora* (ma'am), with or without adding the name of the person after the term of address. The wider the difference in class between worker and boss, the more deference the worker will show in his or her address. For example, the owner of the farm is always referred to by base workers using the Spanish honorific *Don*. The human resource manager, who has a lot of contact with the owner, addresses him instead as *Señor*, reflecting her middle-class and his upper-class status. While she still shows deference to him, she shows less deference than do the base workers. In turn, the owner of the company calls the human resource manager simply by her name, Claudia, while workers call her Señora Claudia. She is called only *Señora*, not *Doña*, because the status differential is less between her and the worker than between the owner of the flower farm and the worker.

In contrast, male base workers are not called *niños* (boys), but are addressed by name. The fact that men are not called *niños* denotes their higher status with respect to women. This difference shows that in spite of the industry's clear goal of greater gender equality among the lower class, there is a lack of consistency.

Although upper-level management of farms and the officials of Asocolflores and Aflonordes are conscious of the subtleties involved in the gender equality change they are trying to implement, these and their ultimate goal have not always been clearly communicated to and equally instilled in field managers and supervisors who still treat male base workers with more respect and dignity than they do the female ones. I will return to this point below.

Identity Changes and Style Transfers

While class relations are reinforced at the flower farms, the behavior and discipline required in order to complete the work has taught workers new skills and has unleashed a transformation in their sense of identity. Women have entered the paid labor force, and a few women and men have become middle- and upper-level workers in the floriculture industry. Women enter the floriculture industry aware that there are limited possibilities of moving up in the company, given its structure as described in the previous chapter. Thus women's objectives are not career oriented in terms of climbing to upper level jobs within the flower farms. In contrast, they view their work as a way to become, in their words, "better people, to rise above the place where we came from," meaning to become more educated and to raise their social status. Women also express the belief that their work in and affiliation with the flower industry affirm their intrinsic value.

Instead of setting their own schedule and rhythm of life and work as women did prior to entering these jobs, female workers in the floriculture industry have a fixed schedule. For women, the change is more dramatic than it is for men: they have a set schedule on the job, but when they get home from work they still face the same amount of housework but compressed into a lesser amount of time in which to perform it. As construction workers or farm laborers, men had and still have a schedule from 7 or 8 A.M. to 4 or 5 P.M. After work, men still have beers, run errands, visit friends, or go home, but do not have unscheduled work waiting for them. For the majority of women, having a schedule set by someone else is totally new, even for those who worked as maids or servants in other households. As women's labor patterns outside the home have changed, the change has been in addition to their household responsibilities.

The changes in work for everyone require segmenting labor in ways that are not applicable in housework, child rearing, subsistence agriculture, or construction. But again, the change has been more radical for women than for men. Women in the floriculture industry perform parts of a job, and have no control over the process as a whole. In contrast, the tasks of housework are performed from beginning to end: choosing the food to cook, cooking the meal, apportioning it, washing the dishes, planning meals, and calculating the amount of food available in the house in relation to the numbers of people and of meals that have to be served until the next market visit. Similarly, men doing subsistence agriculture choose the seed, the time to plant, and the type of crop. They have control over plowing, planting, harvesting, selling, negotiating the price, and letting go of the product.

People transfer what they see and how they behave on the farm during their eight hours of work to their lives in general. In other words, at the flower farm people have acquired a cognitive style that carries over and is transferred to other areas of life (Berger, Berger, and Kellner 1973). The discipline involved at the job has changed people's organizational skills—task planning, job completion, time management, and creativity. In turn, by having acquired these skills the self-esteem of the workers has improved.

Andrés Valderrama, the fumigation supervisor, talked about this transfer of skills like this:

> Working in flowers has helped me become more responsible. There are tasks that need to be done and cannot wait. The flowers have helped me become what I had always wanted to be. They have helped me *surgir* [rise]. As a manager, I need to be creative. And being creative does not stop at the farm door.

While this feeling is strong among male and female supervisors such as Valderrama, who feel affirmed by the company, statements that "the company saw my potential" and "the company believed in me and gave me an opportunity" are common and frequent among all workers. These are indications of the opportunities people have at the flower farms for personal accomplishment.

People have transferred the principles of respect, discipline, and understanding of tasks they have learned at work to the household and to childrearing. Nubia Fuentes, a base worker in the field, was explicit about how she incorporated her experience at the flower farm into her household:

> Working in flowers has helped me with the economy in the house. I am more orderly and disciplined now. At home there are certain tasks that also need to get done just like here at the farm. But they have to get done in a short amount of time. Now I plan ahead, and I know how to plan ahead. Here I am needed, I have friends. I maintain my self-esteem high. At home I know that it is important to transfer that high self-esteem to my children. Children need explanations. In the old days it was thought that a child learned through pain. Before it was *coge y tome*: "You don't understand the homework? Bring me my belt [*coge*], and we will see if you don't understand the homework [*tome*]." No, at home, like here, children need to understand why things are the way they are, how things can be done and why.

The transfer of cognitive style to their domestic life, however, is also gendered. The majority of women go back and forth in conversation between the house, their children, and work. Although some men state that working in floriculture has made them better managers with household budgets, and some men with wives working in the flower industry have stated that working in the same industry has made them realize that women should not have to do all the housework alone, the majority of men do not make the connection between house, family, and work that women do. While Andrés Valderrama states that he is more responsible now, what he means is he is more responsible at work. Valderrama has not transferred his new sense of responsibility to his home. He still has yet to contribute financially or emotionally to the upbringing of his daughter. His new wife is pregnant, and he laughs when asked how much time and money he contributes to the household. He pays for the household utilities and no more. In fact, when looking at his monetary budget, a smaller amount of money is spent on his household than on entertainment, and his time budget is not very different. Women do not see their lives as sharply segmented between home and work as men do, which might explain the gendered mechanism of cognitive transference. My point here is not as much on work and cognition, better left for psychologists to study, but rather on its effects on self-esteem.

The Cut-Flower Industry and Gender Equality

At the same time that the flower industry reinforces the steep social class system in Colombian society, it has also explicitly facilitated positive gendered identity changes. In 1995 the presidential administration of Ernesto Samper created the National Office for Women's Equity (*Dirección Nacional de Equidad para las Mujeres*) as a response to the 1979 United Nation's Convention on the Elimination of All Forms of Discrimination against Women. It launched major programs around the country with the ideology that the country cannot find peace at large if there is no peace at home. The Colombian Association of Flower Growers (Asocolflores) and its regional administrative divisions like the Association of Flower Growers of the Northern Region (Aflonordes) have developed programs called "Florverde," which reflect the goals of the presidential office by providing its floriculture farm members with guidelines for promoting gender equality within rural communities (Friedemann-Sánchez 1999). In turn, flower farms that are associated with Asocolflores or any of the regional associations, address certain themes designated by Florverde: (1) *Cultivemos la Paz* (let us cultivate peace) deals with conflict and violence inside and outside the household; (2) child care;

(3) housing; (4) women's equity inside the household; and (5) literacy. The Florverde program, as stated in chapter 2, also has an environmental and occupational health component, key to the green label that European countries require for purchasing flowers.

Each flower company's human resource manager is responsible for implementing the larger social component of the Florverde program on the farms. This is accomplished by developing a series of workshops addressing the themes. It is difficult to assess what percentage of farms have followed through with the workshops, since, as stated before and by other researchers (Meier 1999), affiliation to Asocolflores or any of the regional subdivisions of the association is optional. In the case of Muisca Flowers and the other farms that form part of a consortium of farms located in the same region and which employ close to two thousand workers, the managers have planned and implemented the workshops for all workers. Every farm but one in the consortium has female human resource managers. In Muisca Flowers, the human resource manager conducts some of the workshops herself and trains the supervisors to develop the topics for other farms, giving them guidelines to follow. For purposes of this book I focus on two of the five themes identified by Florverde: violence prevention and gender equity. In addition, I examine the issue of self-esteem, which is related to both violence prevention and gender equity.

Given the level of violence that Colombia is experiencing, the set of workshops on violence addresses violence in a holistic way by operating under the assumption that peace begins in the home. These workshops tackle the difficult issues of domestic physical abuse against women and provide an accompanying booklet of ideas for handling anger and achieving conflict resolution within the home. The tools provided encourage dialogue between spouses, and between parents and children and develop an awareness, among both men and women, that domestic abuse against wifes, female partners, and daughters is not acceptable nor desirable. The awareness on violence that they intend to develop is gendered.

Only women participate in the workshops on self-esteem. The workshops directly address self-esteem by talking in detail about the value of women as people and stressing that women's rights are equal to those of men. In the workshops women learn about their bodies and sexuality in a positive and affirming manner, and learn, for the first time for many women, about their reproductive system, contraception, and sexuality. One of the goals is for women to realize that they should not feel obligated to have sex with their partners or co-workers and that they can have control over their bodies, including with respect to becoming pregnant and preventing sexually transmitted diseases.

The workshops are also thought of as a way to empower women within the household by addressing self-esteem and domestic abuse from a woman's perspective. In the workshops women are encouraged to understand that men do not have the right to hit them and that such behavior should not be the norm. In addition, the workshops speak about women as mothers and how to better their parenting skills. The information provided includes ways to communicate with children and classes on nutrition, health, and sexual abuse. Finally, the workshops available to all talk about *compañerismo* (comradeship, friendship), the need for co-workers to be civil and good to each other.

In effect, the flower industry is disassembling the public transcript of male power within the lower-class rural community, and it is doing so in a public way. In fact, it is using its dominant power relations to change the gender status quo within the community itself. This intent does not mean that inconsistencies do not exist in the industry's actions. One such inconsistency, mentioned earlier, is the fact that base male workers are not called *niños*, while base female workers are consistently called *niñas*. Another inconsistency is that, despite the fact that there are female supervisors and professionals, the majority of these positions are held by men, while the majority of base workers are women.[1]

Regardless of whether a farm has workshops on equity or self-esteem, the flower farms and their workers constitute a community reinforcing a set of values and beliefs. The flower farms foster relationships that have become the basis for people to trade services like childcare, goods like a cup of sugar, and stories. Flower companies also provide women an arena in which to resist the domination of men over women: this arena is the physical farm, the work place. While men have always had the *cantina* or *tienda* where beer is consumed, as a socially sanctioned meeting place to voice grievances and create discourse at predictable times, women have not traditionally had a socially affirmed place to meet because the local view has been that women belong to the home: each one *in* her own home. The flower farms, therefore, have become such a new arena for women, reinforcing the discourse for female support.

Affirmation and Submission

Most theory on factory work and modernity addresses the issue of worker identity by claiming that workers in assembly plants experience the self in a segmented way, experiencing their identity as workers as being less real than their identity as private people (Berger, Berger, and Kellner 1973). The transference of tasks, of cognitive style, that has occurred for the case of women in the floriculture industry has had the opposite effect than the one claimed by the model on factory work. Women in the floriculture industry have not become alienated from themselves, nor have they experienced the self in a segmented way. On the contrary, the alienation they felt at home has been replaced by an awareness of their paid and unpaid work.

Many elements influence the way people feel and act, and one cannot say that in Fagua and Canelón the workshops have had more influence on women's self image and behavior than the income they earn. Neither can one say that the discipline involved in the work weighs more in terms of the way people change their behavior than the flower industry as a community has had. It is probably a combination of all factors. The work people perform in the flower industry feeds into the experience of the workshops that address self-esteem. Simultaneously, the organization of work and the feedback people get from their work go hand in hand with the experiences they have at home. The experience of working in the industry in general, the job in particular, the self as worker, the individual as mother, and the relationships with other workers are processed in the mind and feed into each other to validate women as individuals.[2]

Women and men participate in different activities, and in doing so, they create different worlds and their experience of society is different. Despite their paid employment in the formal sector, and in accordance with Safa's findings in the Caribbean (1999), women continue to be identified, and to strongly identify themselves, with the chores associated with motherhood and the house. By working in the floriculture industry, they have also claimed a sense of self and of dignity that they did not receive, for the most part, from their families, particularly, from their male relatives. Women's awareness of this contrast has led to a questioning of their lives at home: if their work and their beings as individuals are valued at the flower farms, should they not also be valued at home? The workshops directly address this issue by talking about family violence.

In conversation women will bridge the themes of their households, jobs, family, and community through the concept of *valoración* (valuing) and autonomy. Women feel that their individuality, their humanity, and their identities as women are erased or do not count when the space they occupy day and night is exclusively the household. Young women have seen their mothers and grandmothers alienated at home, responsible for all the housework, taking exclusive care of the young and old people, and tending the cattle pastured on the side of the roads. Middle-aged women with children received no help with any of these responsibilities from their husbands if they had set up traditional households, or from the fathers of their children if they had been abandoned. In addition, physical domestic abuse was common until the women were older and the children had left the home. Men had decision-making power over household finances and purchases, including those in the market.

The women I interviewed who work on the flower farms did not feel alienated, but exactly the opposite. Work at the flower farms makes them feel integrated into a community and as complete individuals. They say that their individuality is recognized by their supervisors and that their work is valued. They see value in their own work and feel that their self-worth is affirmed and recognized by others. As Carmen Ramírez stated:

> Before I worked in flowers I cooked and cleaned for everyone. But after dinner when all the dishes had to be washed, who noticed that the kitchen was clean before dinner? No one. And who noticed that the dishes were now dirty? Everyone. In the house the work only counts when it is not done. But no one notices when it is done. Of course, only dirt shows. Housework is very ungrateful, and who gives a thank you afterward? But here [the flower farm] I count my roses and they [supervisors] count my roses. The work shows. I still have to cook and clean, but at least in the *floristerías* [flower farms] I get a thank you and the satisfaction of my work.

The social aspects of flower farms' operations has provided women a worldview that did not exist for them before, one in which they are valued both by themselves and by others. The word people constantly use to describe this change is *valoración*. In Spanish it is a versatile word that denotes a wide range of concepts including valuing something monetarily; giving someone or something a value, not necessarily in terms of currency; having a high regard for or thinking highly of someone; and valuing the self. People have not acquired the language of *auto-estima* (self-esteem) used by the floriculture industry in their policies and workshops, but women have acquired the concept and transposed it to their own cultural notions of value.

Women state that they get from the flower companies what they do not get at home: being *valoradas* (valued). Most women recognize, although not in necessarily the same conversation where they mention being *valoradas*, that the flower companies have played a role, by discussing self-esteem and domestic abuse in the workshops, and by valuing the work that women perform at the farms. In essence, women feel recognized for their work by their superiors in the farms, and often state that they should be *valoradas en la casa* (valued at home) just as they are at work. Some of the few women who do not feel valued at work have completed their high school education and feel that their potential is far greater than the company is willing or able to recognize by promoting them to upper-level positions. They also tend to feel that the workshops are too basic, not taking into account that the majority of the workforce has not completed the same level of education they have.

Individuals' experiences in one part of their lives provide a basis for and tools of critique of experiences in another. Statements such as "*me dí cuenta que*" (I came to the realization that) are common among women who compare their work at home and at the flower farms. The realizations are also framed in the present tense—"*me doy cuenta que*" (I realize that)—as openers for a discussion of an array of different life possibilities that women express according to their particularities of age, household composition, education, and experience. In effect, when women state that they "came to the realization," they are questioning the cultural rules under which they live. So, the full statements often include "I came to the realization that other people treated me better," "that I could be a better person," "that I was bored at home," "that I would not let him hit me again," "that the children feared him," "that I can make my own money," "that I count as a person," or "that I should be valued."

The self-realization arising from the work situation occurs in different ways for women and men as they engage in different occupations, which are associated with different social class positions. Agricultural work, which has to do with *la tierra* (the earth) and getting the hands and the body soiled, is at the lower levels of the social structure.[3] Being an agricultural worker is not a profession valued by middle and upper classes in Colombia's social structure. Thus it is no surprise that *operarios*, men working in the field as base workers getting the flower beds ready, do not express any of these same feelings of validation that many women feel. For men who have worked in construction, working as base workers in the flower farms is socially a step down: it is going back to the earth. For men who are sprayers or supervisors their jobs are one and two social steps above being rural workers. The few men between eighteen and twenty-two years old who work in the field doing flower work alongside women see their jobs in the industry as having more status than the purely agricultural work of preparing the beds. The difference between the group of men who prepare the beds and these workers is subtle but forceful: the few men who work alongside women handle flowers, not soil. Their work has to do with the dirt, but is not with the dirt.

For the women who are in the field as base workers working inside the plastic greenhouses, the job is higher in status than anything they have done before, and the majority perceive their jobs positively.[4] This difference in the way female and male base workers experience their jobs is explained by the lower position women have in relation to men in Colombia generally. *Trabajar la tierra* (working the land) is below most other professions, but the chores women perform in a household like raising children, cooking, cleaning, and watching animals, have lower social status even than the chores men perform working the land. Thus, for women, flower work, even if it implies getting dirty and being associated with the earth, is socially above any position they have held before. In addition, for women, flower work, even working under plastic inside the greenhouses, implies being out of the house and experiencing a new freedom of mobility.

Floriculture work is socially stratified. Monitors and laboratory personnel are above base workers in status but below supervisors. Women who are monitors, supervisors, or laboratory personnel have increased their social status in the community as a whole. Most women recognize that in the floriculture industry they have learned an occupation and acquired a variety of skills, but also realize that promotion can also mean a loss of the social fellowship shared with other base workers. Women who ascend partially lose their network of social and emotional support among peers; they lose their social base. Thus there is a public discourse or transcript among women that discourages them from ascending the work ladder by ostracizing and creating gossip about the person who breaks the canon of conformity. It is not surprising, then, that when asked, most women will respond that they do not wish to be supervisors or monitors, but that they wish to move laterally within the farm as a base worker and learn other skills.

There is no parallel for men regarding this issue of *valoración*. The work of men has always been valued in Colombian culture. Even male agricultural work has value within its own social class: it is above women's paid work and unpaid housework. Therefore men do not experience the work at the flower farms the same way as women do in that they do not see it as a step up socially or emotionally. In fact, they state it is all the same whether they are planting potatoes or working at the flower farms. For men, it is almost like any other work available—*almost*, because construction, driving a truck or a tractor, or any activity that involves machinery or that is not associated with the land, is socially superior to agricultural work even if the income earned is the same. In other words, while all of these jobs are in the same pay range, the social rewards are different. In my interviews, the statements by men about this issue are consistent, expressed similarly to the response of Tulio Romero: "It is all the same, all the jobs pay the same: the minimum salary. It does not matter where one works as long as one gets paid." But men, including Tulio Romero, consistently state that they would rather have a job in *la rusa* (construction) as *obreros* (construction laborers). Working in flowers is a step down socially in prestige.

In terms of actual earning, women and men earn the same salaries in the flower industry. There are slight variations depending on seniority, but as a rule as stated in chapter 2, an entry-level worker, whether man or woman, starts with the minimum salary set by the gorvernment based on a forty-hour work week. An entry-level construction worker also earns the minimum salary, but men consider work as *operarios*, base field workers in the flower industry, demeaning to their social status and their persons because flower jobs are considered women's jobs. It is not the job itself but the fact that women perform it that lowers the status of the job.

Men express feelings of physical confinement in the closed up environment of the greenhouses made of plastic. The experience of confinement for men, in opposition to the experience of freedom for women, may seem surprising. However, women feel confined at home and liberated in the flower farms, in contrast to men who express feeling free when working *en el campo* (in the open countryside). On the flower farms men describe themselves as feeling *sometidos*, a word that translates as submission and obedience, although that translation does not grasp the concept as a whole. *Sometimiento* also entails feelings of being, not only under someone's control, but subjugated and humiliated. José Rodríguez describes the experience as follows:

> The change in work [from traditional agriculture] has been the *sometimiento*. In the countryside [*campo*] there is freedom, here there is *sometimiento*. In the countryside there is also a person who controls you. But here, the *sometimiento* comes with demands. In the countryside, I manage my own time. Here, each task has a time limit, and if you go over it, then you have problems with the supervisor.

José Rodríguez voices the loss of control in pacing the work that men experience going from subsistence agriculture, construction, or other manual labor to flower work and in the amount of discipline embedded in the operation of the farms. Young men who come from Chía and Cajicá do not express this feeling as strongly as older men who come from rural areas located far away from Bogotá and who have had less education and experience with urban life. Some men stop working at flower farms because they cannot handle the discipline. Of course, the *sometimiento* is more poignant if their supervisor is a woman, because men are used to women being submissive toward them, not the other way around. Men are used to giving orders to women, not receiving orders from them. This hidden transcript became more explicit when I asked a male friend, also an anthropologist and a colleague, to do a few interviews with men because they did not seem as comfortable talking to me as women did. Given these attitudes, it is especially notable that the generally accepted transcript of male domination outside the farms is not acceptable anymore inside the farms when the male is of lower rank in the company structure than the women with whom he is interacting. This unacceptability stands even when both the man and woman belong to the same social class outside the work setting. So men have had to learn new ways to relate to women, at least when they are dealing with female supervisors and managers inside the flower farms.

In addition, José Rodriguez, like other men, describes the change of work setting in the floriculture industry as a change from being *jornaleros* (rural laborers) and *campesinos* (peasants) to *obreros* (proletarian laborers). This change is true for them even though the flower farms are located in the countryside and the work is agricultural, connected to dirt; it is not considered work in *el campo*, the countryside. As a sideline, this further supports my view that floriculture work is global assembly-line work instead of traditional agriculture.

Women do not express either feelings of *sometimiento*, confinement, or lack of control in their work. Such feelings are expressed with regard to their positions in their households, which the women speak of in terms of enslavement. Women actively voice their opinion that flower farms have provided them with an opportunity to create and expand social networks, even for workers who are alone most of the day tending their rose beds. Many workers are happy to have the group of flower workers as a community of friends to talk with and with whom they can build a sense of camaraderie. Numerous women stated they "could not wait" to work on the flower farms, earn some money, and be out of the house. At the farms they have company, while at home they feel *solas* (alone, lonely) and bored.

Polyphony of Voices

According to Stephen Gudeman and Alberto Rivera (1990), the objective of the house in the *altiplano*, the region where Fagua and Canelón are located, is to keep or maintain itself. The local language calls this maintaining the base, *la base* or *fundamento*. As they point out, the base is the platform on which the household is built; it is the basic element necessary for it to work and includes land, tools, animals, seed, and medicine for the animals. In this metaphor the foundation can expand and contract according to the size and affluence of the household: a better-off house is one that has a larger base. The building and maintenance of assets by individuals is done not only to increase leverage and power within households, but as a strategy by individuals and family members to further their possibilities in the future, to maintain their standard of living, to support their household, to keep their base.

The region of Fagua and Canelón has changed culturally at a very fast pace in the last twenty years, due in large part to the fresh-cut flower industry. When Fagua and Canelón's economy was a peasant economy, based on subsistence agriculture, every part of the production process came from within the household, and every effort was made to keep it inside the household in order to preserve *el fundamento* or the foundation, the base. In such a local economic model, Gudeman and Rivera point out, the house produced and dealt mainly with circulating capital, through which it was connected to the market (1990). People cultivated certain crops for sale outside the house to be able to get cash and to buy other items that entered the house and replaced the base that had previously gone "outdoors." For example, people might have cultivated onions not to consume but to sell in the market in exchange for rice.

Although there is no census data regarding the percentage of the population in both municipalities dedicated to agriculture, a simple walk in Fagua and Canelón tells the visitor that there is very little. Borrowing Gudeman's theoretical model in which the base "refers to anything that contributes to the material and social sustenance of a people with a shared identity: land, buildings, seed stock, knowledge of practices, a transportation network, an education system, or ritual" (2001, 27), I would like to address some questions that arise given the dramatic and sudden cultural change in the region. What happens to the base when property itself has been reduced physically to the point that there is no additional land around it and people, using Gudeman's concept, are debased? How has thinking about the base changed now that almost no one lives off subsistence agriculture and few own their houses? Do men and women think about these matters in different ways? I would argue that the changes in Fagua and Canelón reflect the adaptations individuals have made to make and keep their base. The base has been reconceptualized by local people to include no longer seeds or agricultural land, but bodies, energy to earn a wage income, and violence-free homes.

There is a sense of urgency and immediacy to people's lives in the region. Many individuals plan how they are going to pay for food and rent not in the long run but in the next two months. Life in the region is about physical and emotional survival; even Colombia's civil conflict takes second place. What people do have, as I will explore in the next two chapters, is their selves and the social networks they build. Their new base comprises their bodies and their social relations, rather than the concept of material holdings as assets that their grandparents might have held as central. That is why individuals invest diligently in social networking. As Gudeman states, "Making and keeping the base is a central concern of community, for the base makes a community as it is made" (2001, 36). People create and cultivate their social capital because those who do not develop relationships go from poor to destitute (Guyer 1997, 121).

The cultural atmosphere in Fagua and Canelón is in flux; a mix of migrants, locals, and urban people live in the region. Most migrants have traditional cultural views anchored in subsistence agriculture, while local people have a proletarian work ethic and a mixture of urban and rural culture. As will be described in detail in chapter 5, the majority of the people who own property in the region own enough land to place a prefabricated house on it or to build the house themselves, but not enough land to live by doing subsistence agriculture. My survey data shows that close to 47 percent of women and 59 percent of men in my sample have come from other towns in the last fifteen years. The majority of the people who migrate bring a culture of subsistence agriculture and patriarchal household arrangements.

Not surprisingly, therefore, the differences in the way people approach life and perceive the household are stark. There is a sense of disjointedness in the polyphony of cultural voices. There are the women described in chapter 6, who are forging new identities, a new conception of household and family, while at the same time there are entire families who migrate together and hold on to their ideas based on subsistence agriculture while working at the flower farms. The most conservative in their views about gender division of labor and household arrangements are single male migrants. It is necessary to hear all these voices in order to understand the variety in household arrangements and the way they reflect gendered visions of life and, hence, of household arrangements.

From the Base to the Body

Men who come from Boyacá and Cundinamarca (areas dedicated primarily to subsistence agriculture) are very alarmed about the treatment of the soil in the flower farms. Before working in the flower farms, these men had been agricultural workers, mostly cultivating potatoes and onions. They voiced dismay with the way flower beds are prepared for cultivation, which includes the sterilization of the soil with hot steam to control pests, fungus, and mold (see figure 4.1). The men see this practice as contrary to the natural order. God—as they argued to Gudeman and Rivera (1990)—has given life to the soil, and sterilizing it is going contrary to the way God has meant the earth to be. These men expressed that by forcing the soil to do what it is not meant to do, the companies are pushing it beyond its limit. The men, too, referred to the soil as *la base* (the base), documented as well by Gudeman and Rivera (1990). By sterilizing it, according to these men, they are killing the base. The men talked about the sadness the *pena* (grief, sorrow) they felt for the soil, the base.

Thus *la base* or the base for rural individuals who have lived off agriculture is a vision that in Fagua and Canelón becomes intangible and impossible to fulfill. There is no land, there is no subsistence agriculture, and in this sense people, using Gudeman's concept, are debased (2001). There are only salaried jobs. Alirio Casas, forty-seven, a migrant from the Tolima region, voices his vision of *la base* saying, "My salary is not enough to live with *fundamento*; it is enough only to live. The best would be to have a small house and not have to pay rent." His salary does not stretch to living with *fundamento*, by which he means to own a small house and not to have to pay rent. Alirio is voicing with the term *fundamento* the same concept developed by raizal people: he cannot put down roots. He lives with his wife, Margarita Rodríguez, in meager living conditions in which all three sleep in a rented room, their possessions a bed, a table, several stools, and a radio tape player. Margarita cooks in a makeshift kitchen outside of the house. The two-burner stove is placed on a wooden

Figure 4.1. Getting the ground ready for flower production

table outside the house against one of its walls with a tin roof above it to protect her from getting wet when it is raining. She washes the dishes in the *lavadero*, the same place where she washes the clothes.

Unlike the men, rural migrant women did not talk in terms of the base, and few people originally from Fagua and Canelón spoke of the base or *fundamento*. Wherever they are from, people in Fagua and Canelón do not live the same lifestyle they had fifteen or twenty years ago, and because of the scant living circumstances described above, less thought is given to the future than to immediate needs. For most, life is survival from one pay period to the next. The way *raizal* and old households established with children, parents, and grandparents (if they live with them) extend themselves into the future is through their children. But among the younger people, those between eighteen and thirty-two years of age, their focus and goal is to *superarse*, which means to overcome, to surmount. The transcript here is to overcome a lack of education and lack of material and financial stability, while the subtext includes bettering one's self in terms of social class position. Young people who do not come from a culture of subsistence agriculture are better able to bridge the cultural gap. For them the base does not consist of land, because there is none. Rather they themselves are the new base: their minds, their bodies, and their capacity to work are what is needed to *superarse*—to improve themselves, to become better than they were before. This is their purpose in life and what keeps them going. For most *superarse* is something to be done personally. Among this group of young people, women argued that *superarse* is done also through the children, in contrast to men who do not include their children. Thus, women talk about *mis hijos* (my children) and *los hijos* (the children) as part of the base, though often absent from women's conversation was the mention of family as a unit. Interestingly, men mention *la familia* (the family) more often, without specifying what members that entails. Also, their language denotes a bit less of a personal connection, since what they say is *la* (the) familia, not *mi* (my) familia.

As noted, single male migrants are among the most conservative and traditional. They come from rural areas where little or no education is available. The majority of them had been peasants, working the land for subsistence agriculture or as paid laborers. A few who come from the western plains or the Atlantic coast instead took care of cattle. These men want to set up traditional households where they will provide the income and women will stay home, raise the children, and do all the household chores. They are sensitive to the environment in Fagua and Canelón and at the flower farms, however. They realize that the family they envision might be possible "there," meaning where they came from, but not "here" in Fagua and Canelón.

In contrast, single female migrants are among the most liberal and non-traditional. They are struggling against the cultural ideals that permeate the region and that are exhibited by single male migrants, families of migrants, and other traditional local families and individuals. Migrants have usually been men, not women, and thus a woman who migrates alone constitutes someone apart from the group where she comes from. These women are pushing cultural change forward, forcing change by setting a different standard of behavior that does not conform to traditional culture. As we shall see, they are choosing to lead lives without male partners because men are regarded as a drain. In effect, by withdrawing their unconditional housework, women are taking away men's base or *fundamento*, keeping it within their bodies, literally, by expending less energy in the housework that men require. Local men and society as a whole have not caught up with the cultural change. On the contrary, women's choices have created a backlash that I will explore in chapter 6.

Motherhood and Fatherhood

Most women have not replaced their identities of motherhood with identities as workers, but have combined them. Such women have acquired an intense sense of being in this world alone, without partners or potentially without partners, and of having two life purposes: to work and to raise their children. This process has been gradual. There are already three generations of flower workers in the region, and the young have observed the old, learned from their experience, and adapted. By taking control over their own households many women have turned around what was often their source of their subordination—their association with domestic life—to empower them.

While women who have children present themselves to the world as mothers, the equivalent is not true for men, who do not volunteer that they are fathers but simply state that they are single. Men only present themselves to the world as fathers when they are the only parent available to the child. Single mothers refer to themselves and are referred to by others as *madres solteras*, which refers to a lack of partner or father for the children and to *el estado civil* (marital status) of being single. In the case of men, however, they do not call themselves *padres solteros* (single fathers) but rather *padres solos* (fathers alone). The term *padre solo*, which can be translated as lonely father, instead refers to an emotional and individual state rather than a social one. Thus, the terms themselves denote a different conceptualization of self and parenthood.

For a large portion of the individuals I talked with, men are perceived as and see themselves as transient. Hernán Rocha, thirty-four, is an immigrant from Pasto, in the southwest of Colombia, and an absentee father of one child. He does not remember how old the child is. Hernán has transported flowers on the cableway for two years. His thoughts on parenthood echoed those of many of the men I interviewed:

> Children belong more to their mothers than to men. A mother does whatever is needed for her children, never leaves them. Us men, well, we can be responsible, but it is never the same. We are alone in life. Women always have their children.

Note that Hernán Rocha speaks of men as men, even when they are fathers, and of women always as mothers. Even the terms he uses—mothers and men—reveal his thinking. His categorization of men and women is not parallel.

Hernán Rocha, like Antonio Yepes and other men, had a sheepish smile on his face when he answered whether he had children, where they were, and whether he was responsible for them. Men realize they should be responsible, at least financially, for the children they produce, and the smile denotes a realization that this responsibility is not being fulfilled. It denotes a sense that they are getting away with something. Fatherhood is a responsibility that is optional for men.

It is interesting that, culturally, women workers in the flower industry are being pejoratively called *las floristeras* (the florists), a derogatory allusion to their supposedly being loose sexually. This reputation, as I will explain later, is a result of their autonomy and illustrates how those with traditional values are threatened by the change heralded by the independence of female workers. The allegations of promiscuity are an attempt to invalidate the choices women are making and to maintain the status quo that is determined by a patriarchal ideology. In general men and women's perceptions of the world are not in sync. As much as women are driving the cultural change, men are resisting it. Some men feel caught between traditions that they disagree with, because they are *machista* (male chauvinist) and they have a standing in society as men who should be able to control their wives. However, the deeper meaning behind the transcript of women being called *floristeras* is not understood by men in general who have not caught up with the rapid changes. Women, on the other hand, are aware of the meaning that lies behind it. Women who work in the flower farms are outside the realm of the house on a daily basis breaking traditional gender conventions. When asked about their reputation as being loose sexually, workers laugh and say "*Y qué, que les duela. Yo recibo mi depósito cada quincena.*" This translates to "So what? I get my direct deposit every two weeks." The *qué les duela* phrase, difficult to translate, is the recognition that people might be annoyed at their being out of the house and earning a wage income.

Dignity and Autonomy

Because women in the global assembly line literature have largely been depicted as passive victims of the industries, scholars trying to provide women with agency and portraying them as resisting the industries have broadened the definition of resistance to include symbolic acts that provide psychological relief without actually challenging the existing authority structure in work settings.[5] More helpful in understanding the case of women in this study is Scott's (1990) definition of resistance as a way to voice dissent behind the scene, to voice uneven power relations in hidden transcripts that nonetheless transform public transcripts as well.[6] In this light women in Colombia can be seen as not resisting the authority structure of the floriculture industry, but as using the instruments the industry itself has provided women to resist household male domination.

As the following life story will demonstrate, women's conscious resistance of household male domination is the result of combining the feelings of affirmation they experience at the flower farms with the alienation, the lack of male support, and the domestic abuse they experience in the households. Mercedes Vega has four children, two with her first *marido* (husband by habitation not by marriage) and two with her second *marido*.[7] In describing her life story she says with a big grin, "Yes, I had two husbands, the first one because I was innocent, the second one because I was experienced." Another worker, approaching us out of curiosity, overhears Vega's comment and, laughing, retorts, "Hmm, the first one because of inexperience, and the second one because of *sinvergüenza* [shamelessness]." Vega tells her, playfully, to go put her scissors to work, meaning to go mind her own business. Vega was married for seven years to her second husband and has been separated for five years. The word Vega uses is *separated*, not divorced, because she and her *marido* were never legally married. Had they been legally married, the term for him would be *esposo*, and the word for divorce would be *divorcio*. Vega has worked for Muisca Flowers for two years, and in floriculture for sixteen years. With her usual straightforwardness and acuity of mind she summed up the change in her life since her separation. It is worthwhile to keep her words in Spanish since they contain so much meaning:

> A mi no me gusta que me pongan el pié encima, y en mi casa. No lo hacen aquí, menos allá! Eso es que lo humillen a uno. Aquí nadie lo humilla a uno.

> "Agradezca que le doy de comer, agradezca esto, agradezca lo otro." No le parece que es mejor tomarse una agua de panela tranquila que un pollo amargado?

Vega's statement insinuates many issues hard to capture with a simple translation:

> I don't like to be under anyone's foot, and less so in my house. They don't mistreat me here [at the flower farm], less are they going to mistreat me there [at my house]. Here, there is no one humiliating me and saying "be thankful that I feed you, be thankful for this, be thankful for that." Don't you think it is better to drink an *agua de panela* [local brown sugar drink] with tranquility than to eat a chicken with bitterness?

Mercedes Vega points out the intentional choices that she, like other women, has made. She decided she wanted to live alone and asked the father of her two younger children to leave the house. Mercedes' comparison between agua de panela, an inexpensive local beverage common among poor people, and chicken, a food that is a luxury in most households in Fagua and Canelón, exhibits the difference in material well-being between the time the *marido* lived with her and after he left. Mercedes points out that the losses in standard of living she experienced by becoming a single mother are outweighed by the emotional benefits of living alone and in peace.

Like many women who work in the flower farms, Mercedes Vega consciously draws a comparison between the farms and the household when she states that she is not in a submissive position on the flower farms and even less would she allow herself to be in a submissive position in her own household. Vega's declaration that she dislikes a man's putting his foot on top of her denotes the physical restrictions, all too literally, of gender inequality she and other women experience inside the household. In Spanish *el pie encima* (to have someone's foot on top) is the colloquial form that José Rodríguez verbalized more elegantly as *sometimiento* or submission. Later in the interview Vega states directly her position that at home women are humiliated by male partners when the husband demands submission simply because the men bring income to the household. The metaphor for income is "bringing the food to the house."

Vega supports her four children without any financial or emotional help from their fathers, who have no interest in having any contact with the children. She is aware that her family has less financial security now than when she lived with her *marido*, but she also articulates the frustration many women in the region express that even when there is a male partner at home there is no assurance that they will bring their earnings home consistently. Most men spend a considerable portion of their salaries on beer, and some have several households or other women to contribute toward financially. Although living in a household with two or more working adults provides for a better standard of living, too often this idea of dual incomes is only just an idea, a potential.

Mercedes Vega's case is specific to women who used to live in a nuclear household with a male partner and children but currently live in households with their children and no partners. Women, however, also talk about the humiliation they have to put up with from grandfathers, fathers, uncles, and brothers. This is the case of Susana Hincapié, thirty-two, single mother of a seven-year-old boy, whose father abandoned them. Hincapié comes from a *raizal* family, and her father yields a lot of power and is well respected in the region. As Hincapié talks about her father, however, she rolls her eyes and her face shows repulsion. She wonders what people would think if they knew the quality of life such a "respectable" man gives the women in his home. He leaves the men of his household, his sons and grandson, alone, but the women receive both physical and verbal abuse from him and from the eldest brother, Alvaro, who is twenty-six years old.

Feelings such as Susana Hincapié's have existed in the community for a long time and contain plenty of hidden transcripts.[8] What is extraordinary in Fagua and Canelón is that such feelings against abuse, coupled with the affirmation women get at work, are now being aired and acted upon so that one can say that a new public transcript is being created with regard to gender relations inside the household. This revision is happening in various ways that I will detail in chapter 6. Here let me say that many women are challenging the authority of their partners and are temporarily or permanently leaving their partners, and sometimes even their children. Women also decide to have children on their own without partners. Having serial mates is becoming more common in the region. A handful of women choose to remain single and celibate.

Of course, one cannot say that women do not wish to have partners and do not need or want relationships, because most single women talk about their desire to find a partner. Many single mothers voice similar desires, and many women living with partners state they want to remain with them. There is no hidden script of hatred toward men.[9] There is a trend toward single motherhood. On the farm where I conducted fieldwork, 23 percent of the women are single mothers living on their own with their child or children (see table 2.8). What is certain is that the older a woman gets, the more radical her choices become in making sure she is autonomous financially and emotionally.

The flower industry is giving women tools to resist the local practices of gender inequality at home and at work. The industry is openly addressing sensitive issues such as spousal abuse and conflict resolution within the family. The industry "talks the talk and walks the walk," giving women classes on self-esteem and the equality they should have at home with male relatives at the same time it provides them with jobs at equal pay.

Notes

1. Antioquia, in northwestern Colombia, also produces flowers, but at a lower scale. The ratio of female to male workers is apparently the reverse: 70 percent of workers are men. A comparison of management practices between the two regions is the perfect subject of future research.

2. It is worthwhile to point out that the experiences do not invalidate men as individuals in the process. Their position in Fagua and Canelón's society has always been important.

3. For example being a potato carrier is at the very bottom because it requires no skill, only force, and the work implies getting dirty from head to toe from carrying sacks on the shoulders.

4. There is an inconsistency between the way women feel about their jobs and the high numbers who quit after a year or two. I will come back to this in the last chapter.

5. See for example Ong (1987). Bettina Aptheker (1989), however, deprives the concept of any meaningful analytical power by arguing that plain survival is an act of resistance.

6. See for example Kevin Yelvington (1995) and Devon Peña (1997).

7. In Spanish a woman does not have children *con* (with) a husband; rather, the children *son del* (are from) the husband.

8. Juanita Barreto Gama and Yolanda Puyana Villamizar write about the socialization process in Colombia where abuse and violence are common. This ethnography uses exclusively female voices to understand the internalization of patterns of abuse in the identity of the individual (1996).

9. The reactions people have when I have talked about my work in Colombia and in the United States have been radically different. Listeners in the United States hear a subtext of male hatred. Listeners in Colombia do not understand the argument as polarized between camps of good and evil, men and women.

CHAPTER FIVE

Land, Housing, Money, and Social Networks

The realm of work is stratified and filled with power differentials between employees, supervisors, managers, and owners. The previous two chapters have shown hierarchical dynamics in the floriculture industry in Colombia. Power stratification also influences social interactions outside of the work setting. Indeed, households are composed of individuals with different needs and wants and different resources. Within the household, power differences between men and women and young and old are exercised daily in various ways. For instance, deciding to buy a radio or who gets to visit relatives are interactions saturated with power struggles whether intense or mild. Such interactions can be teased apart by analyzing the power dynamics embedded in gender relations and generational differences in relation to the allocation of resources and time.

In the next two chapters I examine bargaining and asset-formation within households in Fagua and Canelón. In this chapter I introduce the theoretical framework of household economics and specifically of intrahousehold bargaining. Property ownership, wage income, social capital, domestic abuse, and self-esteem are a few of the key elements in the analysis of intrahousehold bargaining. I will examine in detail the distribution of land and housing ownership for the employees of Muisca Flowers, disaggregating the data by gender and residential status. In addition I will study the cultural parameters of the distribution of income and housework of individuals living in Fagua and Canelón. The following chapter will examine in more detail how property ownership, wages, social capital, and self-esteem are put in motion as negotiating tools among members of households in Fagua and Canelón. In chapter 6, I weave together the quantitative and ethnographic data.

Household Economics

Until relatively recently, the economic processes of households had remained largely unexamined. Although previous anthropological studies of production and consumption in Latin American peasant societies defined the household as the basic unit of production and consumption (Hoyos 1996; Netting 1989; Shanin 1971), they did not look at the actual economic activities and relationships around consumption and production operating *within* the home but rather focused on the definition of household and household boundaries (Bentley 1984; Hammel 1984; Wilk 1984).[1] The assumption that peasant households, rather than the individuals inside the households, are the basic units of consumption and production for a long time foreclosed the study of actual economic processes of decision making and resource allocation within the household. Furthermore, the assumption of the unitary household has precluded the analysis of asset distribution by gender as well as the study of the effects of asset distribution on intrahousehold bargaining. My study provides a link between assets and intrahousehold bargaining.

The paucity of studies on household economics came to a halt with a groundbreaking article titled "A Theory of the Allocation of Time" by Gary Becker (1965). He recognized housework[2] as a topic of interest for economics, at last acknowledging that the house is not only a site of consumption but one of production as well.[3] The new theory came to be known as "New Household Economics," which holds that households behave as units. According to the model (Becker 1965, 1991; Gronau 1973) households have one joint utility[4] function.[5]

Over the past twenty-five years, however, scholars from various disciplines have challenged this view, arguing that the significant power differences between members of a household affect its economic choices and behaviors. Formal economic models initially critiqued the notion of the unitary household (Becker 1991) by developing bargaining models as a way to circumvent the single utility problem in Becker's model (Manser and Brown 1980; McElroy and Horney 1981). These models enable the examination of intrahousehold allocation of resources by assuming that households are not units, that its members may have different and competing preferences, and that resource allocation decisions result from a bargaining process. Bargaining models assume that households may (cooperative) or may not (uncooperative) pool their income. There are cooperative bargaining models (Manser and Brown

1980; McElroy and Horney 1981),[6] non-cooperative models (Wooley 1988), and models that allow individuals to have separate spheres of activities while still cooperating with each other within the household (Lundberg and Pollak 1993).[7]

The current cross-disciplinary scholarly consensus is that in most parts of the world households do not behave as cohesive units. Individuals living in households do not always pool their material, income, and time resources, nor do they make decisions in unison or reach agreements without conflict and negotiation. In fact, the negotiation or bargaining over the allocation of resources, the decision-making processes, and the allocation of resources itself is intensely conditioned by gender-based and age-based power differences (Bruce 1989; Dwyer and Bruce 1988; Deere 1995; Deere and León 1982; Doss 1996a and 1996b; Ronald Duncan 1999; Folbre 1988; Haddad, Hoddinott, and Alderman 1997; Hoodfar 1988; Pfeiffer 2003; Roldán 1988; Schwede and Papanek 1988; Whitehead 1981; Wolf 1992).

In recent years, the economics of households has been examined in relationship to women's labor in a variety of environments including global assembly line labor. These studies' foci span from the effects of formal employment in export-oriented factory work (Friedemann-Sánchez 2006; Korovkin 2003; Newman 2002; Newman et al. 2002; Ong 1987; Tiano 1994), informal employment (Grasmuck and Espinal 2000), and agricultural contract work (Carney and Watts 1991; Raynolds 2002; Watts 1994) of women on intrahousehold dynamics to the specifics of bargaining models from an economic perspective.

Intrahousehold Bargaining

A central concept used for the analysis of intrahousehold bargaining processes is called the *fallback position*. Bargaining models assume that resource allocation within the household results from a bargaining process in which the power that individuals hold is an important factor, a major deviation from the New Home Economic model where power cannot be taken into account in human economic behavior.[8] The concept of fallback position is borrowed from the Nash game theory model, which takes into account conflict and cooperation and is particularly useful in studying the economic life of households in Fagua and Canelón. The fallback position, also referred to as the threat point or breakdown point, is "the level of utility that each party will attain if they do not cooperate" (Hart 1992, 115). It reflects the amount of power that each individual brings to the bargaining process. Indeed, the person with the strongest threat point or fallback position (that is, power) will obtain the best outcome. This manipulation of power is accomplished through the pressure and influence each individual is able to bring to bear according to the individual's threat point, which reflects the material, social, and emotional assets each individual possesses. For instance, a spouse who has relatives nearby is more likely to threaten to leave the house than a spouse who does not have access to such a support system. In this case, the proximity of relatives becomes a social and logistical asset for the individual.

Scholars studying intrahousehold bargaining are focusing in understanding the ways in which bargaining elements, such as income, property ownership, social capital, and self-esteem, determine the fallback positions of household members. This is precisely the area of inquiry that bridges studies focused on export-oriented industries and those that examine household economics. For the most part, with a few exceptions (Korovkin 2003; Newman 2002; Ong 1987), the two have been kept apart. Are women exploited or empowered by global assembly line work? Such a question can only be answered when we also ask the following: Are women exploited or empowered by their relatives and intrahousehold conditions? How do wages from export-oriented industries, relative to property ownership, and social capital affect the intrahousehold power individuals hold? How do these affect their fallback positions?

Resolving these questions in particular and the main theoretical question of what determines fallback positions in intrahousehold bargaining requires finding quantitative and qualitative measures of bargaining power. Bina Agarwal's (1994) pioneering elaboration on the importance of land rights and its effective control in improving women's fallback position has been pivotal in advancing the analysis of quantitative measures, by segmenting the topic into coherent portions. Agarwal states that land ownership and control strengthen women's fallback position and improve the returns from other forms of income (1994, 65). On the other hand, Safa (1995a) has examined the role of wage income on women's intrahousehold bargaining power finding, among other scholars (Rahman 1986; Roldán 1988), that women's wage income enhances women's decision making and improves the treatment they receive from husbands but does not necessarily improve women's bargaining position inside their households. Other studies have included looking at shares of income (Hoddinott and Haddad 1991; Kennedy 1991), asset inheritance (Quisumbing 1994), value of assets (Doss 1997; Quisumbing and de la Brière 2000), and control of assets (Quisumbing and Maluccio 2000).

Qualitative measures based on ethnographic data can capture context-specific ways in which additional measures of power are used in bargaining. In fact, they reveal how material assets are leveraged in bargaining processes. The need to find culturally appropriate measures of power based on qualitative data is recognized by economists (Frankenberg and Thomas 2001; Quisumbing and de la Brière 2000). Agarwal (1997) and Hart (1997) have pointed out that the field needs to move toward a less restrictive formulation by incorporating qualitative data, as endogenous variables, such as the roles that social capital, ideology, and self-esteem play in intrahousehold bargaining. The difficulty of incorporating local gender ideologies and cultural and social constructions into the analysis was pointed out early on by Whitehead (1981) and Benería and Roldán (1987), and the challenge was subsequently taken up by several scholars (Wolf 1992; Tiano 1994; Carter and Katz 1997; Guyer 1997; Hart 1997; Grasmuck and Espinal 2000; and Raynolds 2002). However, a critical lack of data presents an ongoing obstacle to the effective incorporation of quantitative measures of physical assets, such as property ownership, into studies of intrahousehold bargaining.

The field of intrahousehold bargaining raises the following questions in this research: How does wage work in the cut-flower industry compare to property ownership in determining relative power within a household? Is wage income enough to provide women a strong fallback position in Fagua and Canelón? In what ways does social capital, in relation to property ownership and wage income or independent from them, affect fallback positions? How do the rules that govern social structure and thus social capital affect bargaining? How do self-esteem and emotional stamina moderate women's fallback positions? How is domestic abuse incorporated in the power dynamics of bargaining processes? In Agarwal's words, "what is the role of social norms in determining bargaining power and in setting the limits to what is bargained over?" (1997, 6). In the next two chapters I will explore the role of property ownership, labor, kin and solidarity networks, ideologies, domestic abuse, self-esteem, and emotional stamina in intrahousehold bargaining. In the remainder of this chapter I will explore the types of and links between physical and social assets.

Property Ownership, Property Rental, and Residential Location

Agarwal's argument for the study of property rights is well recognized. However, there is a dearth of knowledge regarding the distribution by gender of physical assets such as land and housing for Latin American countries, including Colombia (Deere and León 2000 and 2003). Traditional tools for assessing resources, such as census data or even floriculture corporate data, do not segregate asset ownership by gender, revealing an underlying assumption that households are headed by males and that household members pool their resources and income (Deere and León 2000 and 2003).[9] The lack of data on the distribution of physical assets by gender limits the analysis of the effects of asset distribution on intrahousehold bargaining.[10] In addition, it limits the possible comparison between the role of wage income, property, and social and human capital on intrahousehold bargaining.

Twenty years ago the region was dedicated to subsistence agriculture in *minifundios* and extensive cattle farming in *haciendas*, both described in chapter 1. Since then, however, high fertility rates and bilateral inheritance patterns that divide property of parents into equal portions among all siblings regardless of sex have contributed to intense subdivision of the land. The *minifundios* have become so small they no longer function as subsistence plots but are rather urban-type lots used only for housing. When one walks the streets of Canelón and Fagua, it is hard to tell how many houses there are behind each frontage house, which usually has a wall in front to mark the property line (see figure 5.1). The lots continue to be divided through inheritance law, even when neither parent has died. What used to be agricultural land is now urbanized and so densely populated that there is no space even for trees.

Subdivision of property is more intense in land owned by *raizal* individuals because they have held the land longer. For example, on July 25, 2000, I went to visit Maria Mercedes Teusabá, twenty-two, and her husband, Alfredo Cabra, twenty-three, both *raizal* individuals. I rang the doorbell of what I thought was their house. The wall that ran from one end of the property to the next was

Figure 5.1. Housing in floriculture region

made of brick and cement, though not covered with plaster and paint; it is common in Colombia for people to build the basic structure and never finish the surfaces since it is so expensive. Maria Mercedes's sister, Maria Clemencia, twenty-seven, opened the door. She did not know if her sister was in her house. So we walked to the edge of the wall, where there was a metal door, and we went though a tight corridor between Maria Clemencia's house and the neighbor's property, which was partially demarcated by barbed wire, wall, and a wooden fence. Behind Maria Clemencia's house stood another house, and after that an empty lot with a mound of sand on it, and after that a prefabricated house, and then finally Maria Mercedes and Alfredo's house. Such an arrangement is common among *raizal* families in the region (see figure 5.2). All of these houses plus the one empty lot occupy space that used to be one property; the original owner had acquired it by working at Hacienda Fagua during the first half of the twentieth century. Teusabá's mother, owner of the land, has given portions of that land to each offspring as they have married and have needed a place to live. The entire family compound has one plant: a fig tree.

The Teusabá family property, subdivided into small lots, exemplifies the housing pattern common among *raizal* families who tend to have bigger land holdings and also more extended families than *antiguos* and migrants. As a consequence, one can trace the genealogy of families through the ownership

Figure 5.2. Behind the frontage wall and original houses, one can see three additional houses built after the land was subdivided

of land, even if this means ownership of only a few square meters. One can also see this division of property in *antiguo* families, although their extended families and the amount of land that they own are both smaller. They are also more likely to rent out rooms to the new migrants than are *raizal* people.

In much of Latin America, rural women are less likely to own land or housing than men (Deere and León 2003). However, as stated above, gender-segregated data of property ownership is not available (Deere and León 2003). In fact, censuses for rural areas in Latin America do not ask who holds the title of the property (Deere and León 2003), making research on property ownership by gender a challenge. In the towns of Chía and Cajicá and in Veredas Fagua and Canelón it is possible to live in one's own house built on a kin-owned lot, usually foreseeing that one will eventually inherit the lot on which the house stands. Thus, property ownership data is here reported separately for lot and house and is disagregated by residential category.[11] A detailed analysis of gendered patterns of ownership and acquisition are reported in Friedemann-Sánchez (2006). My main focus here is on ownership by residential categories as it sheds light on social networks and qualitative measures of power used in intrahousehold bargaining.

I asked floriculture workers whether their housing was rented or owned. Those who indicated they lived in owned property were then asked, in separate questions, who owned the lot and who owned the house. Individuals' answers fell into the following categories: respondent was sole owner, spouse was sole owner, respondent and spouse owned jointly, or the property was owned by other kin. In effect, the survey question provides two kinds of information: property ownership and living arrangements. The latter, living arrangements, provides further information on the importance of the kin network as a social asset and its role in acquiring property as well as in household bargaining.

Since I will focus on property ownership for a bit, I would like to stress that the majority of cut-flower workers do not own property. In fact, the more precarious situation of migrants, compared to their *antiguo* and *raizal* counterparts, is apparent in their rates of renting housing. As shown in table 5.1, migrants in the cut-flower industry are more likely than *antiguos*, who in turn are more likely than *raizales*, to be renters. Note that the percentage of individuals renting decreases as their longevity in the region increases, a pattern true for both men and women. Seventy-five percent of migrants, 57 percent of *antiguas*, and 18 percent of *raizal* women rent; 86 percent of migrant men, 39 percent of *antiguos*, and 26 percent of *raizal* men rent.

The data reports not only on property ownership but on residential patterns as well. Thus one can observe that the longer an individual, whether male or female, has lived in the region, the more likely they are to be living with kin. For instance, only 6 percent of migrant women live with kin in kin-owned property, while 13 percent and 30 percent of *antigua* and *raizal* women, respectively, do so.

As table 5.1 shows, residential longevity in the region is much more important than gender to individual property ownership (that is, sole rather than joint ownership). Among both men and women, *raizal* individuals are more likely than *antiguos* to be sole owners; *antiguos*, in turn, are more likely than migrants to be sole owners. Furthermore, living in kin-owned property allows some individuals to avoid the onus of paying rent. This social asset is differentially available to *raizales*, *antiguos*, and migrants because the extensiveness of an individual's local kin network is directly related to residential longevity. In other words, how many potentially property-owning kin live in the area is related to how long an individual (and his or her family) has lived there. Not surprisingly, *raizales* are more likely than *antiguos*, and *antiguos* more likely than migrants, to live with kin in kin-owned property or otherwise.

Rates of property ownership among male and female *raizales* who responded to the survey and who work in the flower industry are roughly equivalent (Friedemann-Sánchez 2006). Gender is a determining factor in property ownership, but only among *antiguo* residents. *Antiguo* men are twice as likely as *antigua* women to own their lot (39 percent and 17 percent, respectively), and three times more likely to own their house (50 percent and 17 percent, respectively). This is a particularly important finding in that, compared to *raizales*, *antiguos* have fewer kin in the region with whom they can potentially reside; thus they are highly motivated to purchase property in order to avoid the monthly expense of renting. Current ownership for women contrasts dramatically to that recorded by Diana Medrano in 1980 in Chía, Cajicá, and Zipaquirá. She found that 70 percent of female floriculture workers who were interviewed owned between 1/7 of a hectare and 4 hectares of land (1982, 47).

The difference in how men and women acquire their property illustrates how much harder it is for women to accumulate enough capital to purchase property. Inheritance is important for men and women, but men are more able to accumulate savings and purchase property than are women. Women rely more on the Employee Fund loan. Ironically though, men receive a disproportionate share of loan fund money, as we shall see later. In addition, *raizal* female property owners have worked in the flower industry longer than have *raizal* male property owners. *Raizal* women who own their own lot have, on average, worked in flowers for fourteen years. In comparison, *raizal* men who own their own lot average eleven years in the flower business. All women who

Table 5.1. Property Ownership and Residential Location as Reported by Cut-Flower Workers

	Women			
	Migrant	*Antiguo*	*Raizal*	All
N =	108	46	77	231
Lot ownership:				
Respondent only	7%	17%	31%	17%
Spouse only	6%	11%	10%	9%
Joint (couple)	4%	2%	1%	3%
Other kin	6%	13%	30%	15%
Owned, no info	1%	0%	6%	3%
House ownership:				
Respondent only	7%	17%	34%	18%
Spouse only	5%	4%	6%	5%
Joint (couple)	5%	7%	4%	5%
Other kin	6%	13%	30%	15%
Owned, no info	1%	0%	6%	3%
Renter	75%	57%	18%	52%
No response	1%	0%	1%	1%
	Men			
	Migrant	*Antiguo*	*Raizal*	All
n =	76	18	35	129
Lot ownership:				
Respondent only	5%	39%	34%	18%
Spouse only	7%	17%	11%	9%
Joint (couple)	0%	0%	0%	0%
Other kin	1%	6%	23%	9%
Owned, no info	0%	0%	6%	2%
House ownership:				
Respondent only	8%	50%	43%	23%
Spouse only	3%	0%	3%	2%
Joint (couple)	0%	0%	3%	1%
Other kin	3%	11%	17%	8%
Owned, no info	0%	0%	6%	2%
Renter	86%	39%	26%	63%
No response	0%	0%	0%	0%

Notes: Migrants have been in the region for fifteen years or less, *antiguos* have been in the region between fifteen and thirty years, and *raizales* have been in the region for two generations or more and have *hacienda* labor relations. Percentages add up to more than 100 percent because lot ownership and house ownership are separate considerations. "Other kin" includes own family members and spouse's family members. "Owned, no info" indicates that respondent reported living in an "owned" house (as opposed to renting) but did not report who, in fact, is the owner.

are property owners have worked in floriculture, on average, three more years than men, a significant difference (Friedemann-Sánchez 2006).

Many people combine a variety of modes of property acquisition to achieve property ownership. These modes include those already mentioned: actual or expected inheritance, savings from wage labor, informal loans (usually from kin), and formal loans including from the Employee Fund. Table 5.2 shows that, on average, women require 1.71 different modes to acquire either a lot or house while for men it takes just 1.17 different modes to acquire a lot and 1.28 to acquire a house, shedding additional light on why women take longer to acquire property. Thus, not only does it take men less time working in the flower industry to become property owners than women, they also require fewer modes of acquisition (Friedemann-Sánchez 2006). In other words, a typical woman may require a loan in addition to her savings from wages, while a typical man may be able to save enough to purchase property without a loan or borrow enough to purchase property without saving in advance. Even so, it is important to keep in mind that modes of acquisition are a reflection of gender ideology and social networks as well as of financial wealth or lack therof. Thus, the quantitative data measuring how many modes of acquisition women and men must combine in order to acquire property cannot answer the qualitative question of *why* people use the strategies they do.

Table 5.2. Number of Means Used to Acquire Property among Cut-Flower Workers

	Women			
	Migrant	*Antiguo*	*Raizal*	All
n =	8	7	23	38
Means of acquiring lot	1.4	1.3	1.8	1.6
n =	6	5	23	34
Means of acquiring house	1.5	1.6	1.7	1.6
	Men			
	Migrant	*Antiguo*	*Raizal*	All
n =	4	7	12	23
Means of acquiring lot	1.5	1.1	1.0	1.1
n =	6	9	14	29
Means of acquiring house	1.0	1.6	1.1	1.2

Women must combine more modes of acquisition in order to purchase property in part because an individual's financial responsibilities to parents differ by sex. While young single women are expected to contribute a share of their wage income and unpaid household labor to their parents, there is no such expectation of men. Single men living with their parents do not share their income and do not perform household chores. This practice of privileging men is supported by the ideology, as studied by Safa (1995a and 1999), that men are the breadwinners and women's income is complementary. Thus the needs of men and women are perceived to be different. My ethnographic data reveal the cultural perception that young men need to save to buy land and housing in order to establish an independent household. Despite evidence to the contrary, women are not similarly perceived as needing to save because they are not believed to be the main financial contributors to their households.

This gender-based allocation of responsibility remains practically the same over the life course of individuals, whether they are men or women. For instance, older women are more responsible for their older aging parents than are their brothers. That is, daughters of aging parents are the primary physical, emotional, and financial caretakers of their parents.

Because an analysis of the various modes of property acquisition used by individuals shed light on fallback positions and hence on the amount of power individuals hold, I asked flower workers how they had acquired their land and house. By exploring what facilitates property acquisition, I can analyze the gender and residential effects of wage income and patron-clientship and kin networks on property ownership. My research finds that social networks, financial wealth, and property ownership are interrelated forms of capital, which makes the analysis of intrahousehold bargaining complex, as the same elements (in addition to self-esteem, emotional stamina, and presence of domestic abuse) provide an individual with a fallback position. In short, what determines property ownership also influences intrahousehold bargaining.

As we have seen, with regard to land and housing acquisition in Fagua and Canelón, wage workers are able to acquire property through two processes: inheritance or purchase. First, those who are local to the region may inherit property. *Raizal* men and women are far more likely than their migrant and *antiguo* counterparts to inherit (Friedemann-Sánchez, 2006). Land ownership patterns among *raizales* suggest that for the most part bilateral inheritance patterns in Colombia are not only the law but are in fact taking place in Chía and Cajicá as neither men nor women are disadvantaged in this route to property acquisition.

There are two issues with respect to inheritance that may be addressed in future research and would help explain the context of property ownership further. First, recent laws from the 1990s require couples living together, regardless of their type of union (de facto union or marriage), to have joint titles of their property (Deere and León 2000, 408).[12] In my research no individual reported inheriting from both parents. This might be because the law has not been enforced or because, in the short time from the passage of the legislation to when this survey was conducted, no one had yet inherited property held jointly by father and mother. Second, in 1982 the family code gave equal inheritance rights to children born out of wedlock. Since most of these children grow up with their mothers, they clearly inherit from their mothers. However, neither respondents to the survey nor individuals I interviewed addressed the possibility of inheritance from an absent father. I would argue that, in spite of the law, the social norm has not changed and neither has the inheritance pattern among children called *hijos naturales*, a pejorative term meaning born out of wedlock and with an absentee father. The norms that in actuality guide inheritance from parents to offspring might be social instead of legal, as is the case with rules that govern property ownership among spouses.

Second, social networks facilitate the accumulation of savings toward the purchase in two ways. Workers may combine loans from kin, from the floriculture farm's Employee Fund, state subsidized loans, and regular mortgages as well as using savings and severance payments. As described in chapter 1, many *raizal* workers have patron-clientship ties to the flower industry owners who previously were owners of former *haciendas* or large landholdings. These people use their *hacienda* labor networks to move up the employment hierarchy and access the well paying jobs that enable them to buy property. *Antiguo* residents and some *raizales* without comparable social capital use kin resources (housing and childcare) in order to save enough money to buy property.

Labor, Kin, and Female Solidarity Networks

The property ownership differential by residential longevity (*raizal*, *antiguo*, and migrant) can be further explored by looking at each group's social capital. People in Fagua and Canelón employ their social assets through living arrangements; living with family implies sharing living expenses and rent, the single most expensive living cost, as well as having family available to provide childcare. In this section I will explore property and residential arrangements by marital status, parenthood, and gender. Residence patterns of single women and men illustrate how all individuals, but women in particular, rely on their kin network and how they are disadvantaged when few kin are available.

In table 2.8, I showed that 15 percent of all women in the sample are single (unpartnered) and childless compared to 26 percent of all men and that 23 percent of women are single mothers while only 2 percent of men are single fathers. In this section I will examine the property ownership and residential patterns of this group of single people, both childless and with children, as laid out in table 5.3. Recall that for this discussion, having children is defined as having children in the household, not as having produced biological offspring. Thus, the migrant woman who left her daughter with her mother and came to the Sabana to work in the flower industry is, for this discussion, considered childless because she is not actively raising the girl. Similarly, men who have fathered children but do not live with them are considered childless. In other words, I am exploring *household composition* not procreation.

Those engaged in parenting tend to be older than childless individuals. Recall that my sample includes only people working in the floriculture industry (excluding by necessity older individuals who are no longer engaged in wage labor). In my sample, the average age of childless single women is twenty-four years (ranging from eighteen to thirty-nine years) compared to thirty-five years among single women raising children (ranging from seventeen to fifty-nine years). Among single men, fathers average thirty-four years (ranging from twenty-seven to forty-six years), and childless men average twenty-five years (ranging from seventeen to forty-six years). These averages do not vary significantly by residential category (migrant, *antiguo*, and *raizal*).

The most revealing aspect of this subsample is that the majority of single women are raising children (n=53, 61 percent), while the majority of single men are not (n=3, 8 percent). The analysis of property ownership and reliance on kin network is relatively simple for the men. Seventy-one percent of single childless men, corresponding to 65 percent of all single men, live with relatives. All three single fathers live independent of kin. Similarly, 62 percent of all single women live with relatives; childless single women (96 percent) are more likely than single mothers (42 percent) to live with kin.

The importance of social assets in the form of kin networks is most clearly revealed when the household composition of single women is compared across residential categories. The worst off are migrant single mothers, the majority of whom (65 percent) rent and live independently, indicating that they do not share living costs or household chores with kin. In contrast, 42 percent of *antigua* and only 19 percent of *raizal* single mothers are in similar financial and logistical straits. Including those who share this monetary and time expense with kin, fully 90 percent of migrant single mothers rent, compared to 67 percent of *antiguas* and 33 percent of *raizales*.

Table 5.3. **Living Arrangements of Single Cut-Flower Workers**

	Single Women							
	Migrant		*Antiguo*		*Raizal*		All single women	
	with children	no children	with children	no children	with children	no children	with children	no children
n =	20	17	12	4	21	13	53	34
Independent household								
own property	0%	0%	0%	0%	19%	0%	8%	0%
kin-owned property	5%	6%	0%	0%	5%	0%	4%	3%
rent	65%	0%	42%	0%	19%	0%	42%	0%
no information	0%	6%	0%	0%	5%	0%	2%	3%
Live with extended family								
own property	5%	0%	8%	0%	0%	8%	4%	3%
kin-owned property	0%	18%	25%	50%	29%	69%	17%	41%
rent	25%	71%	25%	50%	14%	0%	17%	41%
no information	0%	0%	0%	0%	10%	23%	4%	9%

(continued)

Table 5.3. *(continued)*

	Single Men							
	Migrant		*Antiguo*		*Raizal*		All single men	
	with children	no children	with children	no children	with children	no children	with children	no children
n =	2	23	1	1	0	10	3	34
Independent household								
own property	50%	0%	100%	0%	-	10%	67%	3%
kin-owned property	0%	0%	0%	0%	-	0%	0%	0%
rent	50%	35%	0%	0%	-	10%	33%	26%
no information	0%	0%	0%	0%	-	0%	0%	0%
Live with extended family								
own property	0%	0%	0%	0%	-	50%	0%	15%
kin-owned property	0%	4%	0%	0%	-	0%	0%	3%
rent	0%	61%	0%	100%	-	30%	0%	53%
no information	0%	0%	0%	0%	-	0%	0%	0%

Among single women, *antiguas* and *raizales* are more likely than migrants to be living with their parents. *Raizales* have been in the region for generations and are most likely to have a large kin network. *Antiguas* have been in the region at least fifteen years and often migrated with their families of origin. Half of *antigua* single mothers (50 percent) live in their parents' household and one additional *antigua* single mother (8 percent) shares housing with her siblings. Among *raizal* single mothers (53 percent) live in their parents' household, while 30 percent of migrant single mothers live with kin (half with parents and half with siblings or cousins). Conversely, 70 percent of migrant single mothers have established independent households, compared to only 42 percent of *antigua* single mothers and 48 percent of *raizal* single mothers. As we have seen, the average age of single parents does not vary significantly among residential categories. However, among single mothers, those living independently are an average of eight years older than those living with kin (thirty-eight years and thirty years, respectively).

Among childless single women we see an even greater reliance on kin and a lower incidence of renting. Almost three quarters (71 percent) of single childless migrant women rent, all of whom live with family. Two of the four childless *antigua* women rent and, again, both live with family. None of the childless *raizal* women rent, either independently or shared with extended family.

Among *single* mothers, *raizal* women are more able to purchase property than migrant or *antigua* women. Among twenty-two *raizal* single mothers, four (18 percent) own their lot and house. Of these four, one inherited her property from her mother, one inherited her lot and purchased her house with earnings, and two purchased both lot and house with earnings. One *antigua* woman inherited property from her mother, thereby needing to invest no personal earnings. Only one migrant single woman owns property; having been widowed one month before I interviewed her, she in fact reinforces my finding that migrant women are unable to acquire property unless partnered.

All other migrant women property owners in the sample are married and have acquired their property through a combination of inheritance (rare for migrants), loans, and savings. Thus, single migrant women do not have enough economic resources to accumulate and buy property. For migrant women, acquiring property requires being married in order to save money for individual or joint ownership (13 migrant women, or 12 percent). These thirteen include the 8 out of 108 migrant women who report sole ownership plus the 5 out of 108 migrant women who report joint ownership with their spouse.

Raizal mothers are able to accumulate earnings thanks to a social network that provides the economic resources to buy property. A social network can provide support such as childcare and a place to live, allowing them to accumulate their wages. Fewer migrant women have an extensive kin group in the region and thus have to pay for childcare and get loans to purchase property. In addition, local women are more likely to inherit property. Fifteen (65 percent) *raizal* women who own a lot acquired it through inheritance compared to one migrant (13 percent) and no *antiguo* women.

The availability of childcare provided by relatives also lessens the economic burden of *antiguo* and *raizal* women relative to that of migrant women and denotes the amount of social capital individuals have by residential longevity in the region (see table 5.4). Only 14 percent of *raizal* mothers pay for childcare while 63 percent percent rely for childcare on relatives, including the other parent or extended family. By comparison, 38 percent of migrant mothers pay for care and only 36 percent have relatives providing care.[13]

Floriculture Employees' Fund Credit

Floriculture farm credits constitute a portion of the Florverde Program instituted by Asocolflores and implemented by individual farms. Table 5.5 shows the type and amount of credit made available to men and to women from

Table 5.4. Sources of Childcare among Cut-Flower Workers with Children

	Women			
	Migrants	*Antiguo*	*Raizal*	All
N =	75	38	57	171
The other parent	4%	5%	9%	6%
Another family member	33%	32%	61%	42%
In-home childcare	29%	16%	5%	18%
Childcare center	13%	8%	9%	11%
School	48%	76%	42%	52%
	Men			
	Migrants	*Antiguo*	*Raizal*	All
n =	48	18	29	95
The other parent	25%	17%	45%	29%
Another family member	29%	28%	48%	35%
In-home childcare	21%	17%	3%	15%
Childcare center	8%	11%	14%	11%
School	31%	61%	21%	34%

Note: Percentages total more than 100 percent because respondents may name more than one source of childcare. "In-home childcare" and "childcare center" are both paid sources of childcare.

1993 to 1998 at Muisca Flowers flower farm. Some flower companies, such as Muisca Flowers, have established a system called *Fondo de Empleados* or Employees' Fund to loan money to workers for health, education, and housing needs. The fund is supported with monthly savings from every worker and managed by the farm's administration. Every worker contributes 5 percent of his or her monthly salary to the fund, and every worker has the right to request a loan. The money deposited is relinquished to the worker upon request. While a few workers did voice opposition to the retention of 5 percent of their wages, most workers I talked with preferred to provide money to the fund foreseeing that they themselves might use the loan program eventually. In addition to individual company efforts, in the southern section of the Sabana the industry has also collaborated with financial institutions to develop housing, and with the government to set up childcare and recreational facilities (Friedemann-Sánchez 1999). In my study I can only speak about individual farm efforts, as such collaborations with the government of lending institutions, to my knowledge, have not occurred where this research took place.

The flower farms do not keep records on the number of loans requested or the number that are turned down. This limits our understanding of how this employee resource functions within the sociocultural context. Most importantly, it is impossible to know whether women request loans as frequently as men or whether requests by either women or men are disproportionately rejected. However, some observations can be made based on data about loans actually extended.

In Muisca Flowers specifically, from 1993 to 1998, 19 percent of the number of loans and 47 percent of the monetary loan value received from the fund were for housing. By gender, 24 percent of all loans received by men were for housing, amounting to 53 percent of loan money extended. Among women, 16 percent of all loans were for housing, amounting to 42 percent of loan money extended to them. Women are more likely to get loans for their children's education than men: 31 percent of the loans to women compared to 18 percent of those to men. Male and female investments in health are approximately the same (see table 5.5).

In general, though, and consistent with the literature (Agarwal 1994; Deere and León 2000 and 2003) and my qualitative findings, women do not have parity in access to loans from the employee fund. Over the course of the six years in question, 1,230 loans (63 percent of all loans) were made to women and 721 (37 percent) to men. When comparing the amount of the average loan made to women (US$99) to the average loan to men (US$149), we see that loans to individual men tended to be 50 percent larger than loans made to individual women (Friedemann-Sánchez 2006).

Table 5.5. Muisca Flowers Employee Loan Fund Activity, 1993–1998

Year	Purpose of loan	Women: number of loans	Women: average loan*	Men: number of loans	Men: average loan*	Difference in average loan size by gender
1993	Education	20	$ 35	8	$ 38	9.6%
	Housing	17	$ 78	16	$ 127	62.8%
	Health	20	$ 34	16	$ 53	58.4%
	All loans	87	$ 47	57	$ 72	51.0%
1994	Education	40	$ 53	14	$ 50	-5.7%
	Housing	23	$ 166	23	$ 260	56.8%
	Health	27	$ 45	18	$ 78	76.2%
	All loans	137	$ 69	80	$ 121	75.5%
1995	Education	87	$ 39	29	$ 55	39.6%
	Housing	42	$ 244	39	$ 317	30.0%
	Health	33	$ 44	15	$ 80	81.1%
	All loans	242	$ 77	131	$ 140	81.1%
1996	Education	57	$ 51	32	$ 73	40.8%
	Housing	38	$ 333	41	$ 377	13.3%
	Health	26	$ 54	20	$ 54	0.0%
	All loans	226	$ 104	165	$ 147	41.9%
1997	Education	58	$ 66	15	$ 82	24.3%
	Housing	34	$ 261	30	$ 423	61.8%
	Health	40	$ 65	18	$ 75	15.2%
	All loans	218	$ 111	125	$ 175	57.8%
1998	Education	121	$ 97	32	$ 110	13.7%
	Housing	48	$ 301	24	$ 375	24.5%
	Health	39	$ 83	32	$ 104	24.7%
	All loans	320	$ 132	163	$ 179	35.2%
All loans, all six years	Education	383	$ 64	130	$ 74	15.3%
	Housing	202	$ 254	173	$ 332	30.7%
	Health	185	$ 57	119	$ 77	35.3%
	All loans	1,230	$ 99	721	$ 149	49.9%

Source: Data provided by Muisca Flowers.

Note: Loan amounts are provided in dollars and are not adjusted to a standard year. A conversion of US$1=2,000 Colombian pesos was used, the approximate exchange rate for the years 1999 and 2000 when fieldwork was conducted. Not all loan categories are itemized (loans were also made for vehicles, household appliances, household emergencies, etc.). *Difference in average loan size by gender* calculates the difference between the average loan to men and the average loan to women in percentage terms. Thus, last line in the table shows that for all loans over all six years, the average loan to men was 49.9 percent larger than the average loan to women: ($149–$99) / $99 = 49.9%.

Multiplying the total number of loans by the average loan amount, we arrive at the total value of all loans payed out. Thus, women received US$122,114 (that is, 1,230 x US$99.28) from the employee loan fund over the course of six years; at the same time, men received US$107,321 (that is, 721 x US$148.85). All together, the total amount loaned from the fund was US$229,435. In other words, men received 47 percent and women 53 percent of all money loaned out of the employees fund over that six-year period. When considering these numbers, it is important to recall that women are disproportionately represented in the flower industry, comprising 64 percent of workers. It is obvious then that, on average, individual women have had less access than men to money available through the employee fund. They consistently receive smaller individual loans and less money overall than their male counterparts proportional to their representation in the industry.

When asked, the executives of Muisca Flowers attributed this difference to women's situation rather than to discriminatory lending, stating that women employees are reluctant to take loans as large as men because their family financial responsibilities limit the flexibility in their budgets for repaying larger amounts of credit (Friedemann-Sanchéz 2006). The human resource manager of Muisca Flowers states that women most often ask for loans from the employee fund to cover the educational and health expenses of their children while men ask for loans to cover housing expenses, motorcycles, and stereos. This portrayal is not accurate as women do in fact ask for loans to purchase property. Future research could shed a great deal of light on this subject by inquiring how much of the gender gap in access to credit is due to women's financial limitations, which are quite real, and how much is due to discrimination. To be most useful, research should examine applications for loans from the employee funds (both number of requests and amounts requested) as well as information on loan denials and loan approvals, and the data should be analyzed by both gender and residential category (*raizal*, *antiguo*, and migrant).

Non-Kin Social Networks

As we have seen, social networks affect and are affected by property acquisition (or the lack of acquisition). Furthermore, they play a role in intrahousehold bargaining. Before going into the dynamics of bargaining, I would like to describe a bit more the social characteristics of the region with regard to household economics.

Of course, individuals who are not affiliated with the floriculture industry constitute a large and influential sociocultural group in the region, and they too, like cut-flower workers, have social networks that provide them with support. Female relatives living nearby, female friends, and female neighbors, for instance, provide day care for young children and supervision for older children. These female networks ensure childcare, mobility, and freedom for mothers. Women who do not work at the flower farms also have strong networks with people working in the farms. These networks are not exclusively female, but since the majority of workers are women, by default the networks end up being predominantly female. An individual who works at a flower farm and has good labor relations can influence managers, supervisors, or business owners, which is called having *palanca*. This influence can be exercised to get friends and family outside of the industry jobs at the farm or to ascend within the farm, for example. For cut-flower workers, it is common to use *palanca* to change positions laterally within the flower farm, as some jobs are more desirable than others. Working in fillers, for example, provides more contact and conversation, while work in the rose section is lonely.

Loan guarantor networks are primarily male. There are stores in town that sell such goods as refrigerators, stereos, and televisions on credit. In order to buy an item on credit, the buyer needs to have a *fiador* or loan guarantor. Men more than women tend to trade favors that involve some object going back and forth: lending the boss's *guadaña* (circular weed cutter) to a neighbor, fixing a broken television, and lending a bicycle or motorcycle. Trading favors constitutes and reinforces a network when the lender requests from the borrower to reciprocate the favor and to be a loan guarantor, for example.

The residents of Fagua and Canelón also form networks exclusively created and maintained for an accumulation of money called *cadena* (chain). A *cadena* is formed by a group of individuals who give a certain amount of money to one person in the group for redistribution among group members. Each individual in the *cadena* contributes the money once every two weeks, on payday. Every two weeks a different individual in the *cadena* receives the total amount of money collected by the person in charge of disbursing it. People in Fagua and Canelón often say "I'm in a *cadena* of ten with eight," which means being in a chain of 10,000 pesos (US$5) per person in a group of eight people. The person responsible for collecting and disbursing the money has to be trusted by all that she or he will not leave with the money from two weeks' work. There have been instances, however, where the person collecting the money disappeared, which is why flower farms discourage people from entering *cadenas*. Usually *cadenas* formed by men are of larger amounts of money and include more people than those formed by women. Talking about it with a group of women one afternoon, they all agreed that such groups involved too much risk. Usually female *cadenas* are of 10,000 pesos and only include ten people. For individuals who do not have loan securers and who have difficulty setting money aside, *cadenas* provide an alternative way to be able to buy big items such as refrigerators, stereos, and young cattle, because they force an individual to set aside a small amount of money from every pay period.

Women, like Rosa Moreno, also develop networks of friends who can provide support. Almost every afternoon during the rainy season, there is conversation and *agua de panela*, a hot drink made with raw sugar and lemon, at Moreno's house. Even though Moreno and her husband are tenant workers and thus do not own the house, it is an asset to them because of its relatively large size when compared to other houses in the region and because it has gardens around it. The house is one of the best in the region, one of only two with two floors. The first floor contains Moreno's bedroom, a bathroom, and a kitchen and living room that share one space. Most of the space in the large room is used to store scraps of electric appliances, tools, old stereos, blenders, radios, speakers, and boxes of old magazines and newspapers. But the room has two small sofas, the only sofas I saw while doing fieldwork, made of *cañabrava* (native bamboo) and even a small coffee table—a welcoming setting for social reunions. The wood stove heats up the room, and in the cold rainy season Moreno's friends arrive even before 4:00 P.M., the usual time for *onces* (*agua de panela* or coffee time). The network supplies Moreno with information on available informal ironing and cleaning jobs at local houses and occasional childcare. For Moreno's son, Joaquín Piragua Moreno, the network provides the exchange of reciprocal favors such as helping a friend fix up a bike in exchange for borrowing a motorcycle one morning. For the house visitors, there is also an investment: a potential daycare provider or a loan securer, for example. The versatility of assets, whether they be material or social, show, as Jane Guyer (1997) points out, that they can change from being investments to being consumption items and yet again to being prestige items.

Elements of the Household Economy in Fagua and Canelón

In Fagua and Canelón household members negotiate their control over decision making in three main areas: the allocation of income, the performance of chores, and the exercise of human rights. These, then, are the issues that constitute the foundation of household economics in the region.

First, with regard to income allocation, family members agree, disagree, and bargain about how money is spent, what goods to purchase, and who benefits from the items bought. People bargain about the amount of money that each income-earning person will contribute toward rent, market, clothes, diapers and milk, bikes, motorcycles, makeup, beer, and other goods. Second, people negotiate about non-income earning chores, which nevertheless are included in the economics of a household. For example, who takes care of children? Who feeds, plays, supervise, disciplines, and bathes the children? Who takes them to the doctor? Even whose children are cared for can be a contentious issue. Household members might disagree whether the youngest adult woman should care only for children who are relatives, or if she will care for the neighbor's children too. Who washes clothing, and whose clothing gets washed? Who shops at the market and with whose money? Who takes the children to and from school or day care? Who cooks, serves, and packs meals? Who picks up the dishes from the tables? Who washes them? Who runs the errand for the grandmother? Third, people negotiate control over their own lives; in a sense, they bargain over their human rights. Within the household, members negotiate who works for pay and who, if anyone, stays at home doing unpaid chores. People bargain about getting and using leisure time. Individuals, women in particular, negotiate their freedom to move beyond their socially sanctioned space and the amount of control and knowledge their relatives have with regard to their whereabouts. More intimately, family members may bargain over how much physical abuse or infidelity they will accept and negotiate family planning and birth control, including what type of birth control they use and who is responsible for it.[14]

The amount of power that individuals have within the household is embedded in all the processes enumerated above and shifts according to circumstances as member try to shift the balance of power to their advantage. In Fagua and Canelón, assets, whether they be material and/or social, tilt the threat point one way or another and give their holder more or less power to take a stance.

Resource Distribution: Time and Money

The pattern of money and time allocation in Fagua and Canelón is gendered. Although there is not one identifiable pattern of behavior for the whole region, there are clusters of patterns that vary depending on the social structure of the household, housing ownership, the wages individuals earn, and the type of jobs, if any, that individuals hold. In general, women in *raizal* households that do not have family members working in non-traditional occupations, such as floriculture, have less power in making decisions than men do, are more often and brutally subject to domestic abuse than women working in floriculture, are expected to perform all household chores, and often struggle with their husbands to be allowed to work for pay. In these households, men typically are the sole decision makers, bear almost all financial responsibility as long as they live in the home, and have control of the physical movements of the other members of the household including their wives. In addition, men most often decide if the family will use family planning and what method *he* will use, as some women are not allowed by husbands to use any birth control themselves. The pattern of birth control is different for some couples with women working in floriculture. Women may challenge male decision making by choosing a method and hiding its use from their husbands or by deciding with their husbands on a method. In households where the adult women are employed, women have more decision-making power, more financial responsibility, and more physical mobility, although they too may be subject to domestic abuse and perform virtually all household chores. In these households, men almost always bear less financial responsibility but may occasionally still control family planning methods. In the few households with financial and gender equity, financial responsibility is shared equally, men contribute to one or two household chores, there is no domestic abuse, and women decide what method to use for family planning. Consistent with findings in the Caribbean (Safa 1995a), these are typically the households of childless young couples where both work in floriculture. Of course, there are the households that have no male partner present, in which women bear all decision-making power and responsibility.

Perception and Observations on Money Management

The patterns outlined above are framed by a cultural distinction made in Fagua and Canelón between individuals who consider that their household is managed with a joint budget and those who are, in the local idiom, managing their budget as *plata aparte*, meaning monies are kept separate. Most of the households that do openly state they have *plata aparte* are households that have no members of the family working in the flower industry or more traditional households, including migrant families and single male migrants who come from more traditional rural areas, from *el campo*. Although my observation while doing fieldwork was that in most households in Fagua and Canelón, regardless of their emic distinctions, in fact manage their money as *plata aparte*, though individuals might not *perceive* their households as functioning with *plata aparte*.

The majority of single male cut-flower workers who live with extended family perceive their money to be theirs solely while some single women living with kin do. Single males are not expected to contribute to their parents' household and in fact do not do so. Meanwhile, single women are expected to contribute, and in fact they do. I observed that single women who live with only their mothers contribute the largest portions of their income to the household while single males living with their mothers only contribute minimally if at all.

People consider the income they earn to be their individual money and talk about *mi plata* (my money), *mi casa* (my house), *mi vaca* (my cow). Husbands and wives will ask each other for loans, which are literally meant as loans, money to be returned. In households with less gender asymmetry, the opposite gendered perception exists of joint budgets. More women than men talk about resources being pooled. Households that consist of an adult woman, her children, and sometimes the grandchildren in perception and in effect pool their resources.

In Fagua and Canelón financial responsibilities are broken into areas that are gender determined, areas in which an expenditure is paid by gathering resources from various members of a household, and expenses that belong to individuals according to ownership. Examining the latter of these categories powerfully reveals how people in Fagua and Canelón think about ownership of material property, financial responsibility, and money management. In general, physical assets like land, houses, and vehicles are considered individual property, even if used by several members of the family. This is very clear with land and house ownership and it is common in the region, as stated before, for older people to give their children land or houses as inheritances while they live. For instance, in one case I observed, the wife had inherited one *fanegada* of land from her mother. To transfer the property title from her mother's name to her own, she needed, at the time, 500,000 pesos (US$250), or the equivalent of two and a half month's salary calculated at minimum wage working full-time. Since she only worked part-time, she asked her husband of seventeen years to provide the money. He refused, however, stating it was her lot and it was up to her to figure out how to make the legal transfer. When I later asked him why he had not just given her the money and asked her to put his name on the deed, he stated it was her lot, just like the house they now live in is his. This pattern is common in the region, and even old couples refer to their property as "hers" or "his."

If a house is located on a lot that the man or woman of the household has inherited, whether or not this house was acquired or built within the marriage, the person who inherited is responsible for *la cuota*, a term for the monthly loan payment on the property (whether the loan is formal or informal and regardless of whether the loan was for the the house itself, building materials only, or another major house purchasing or building expense), if there is one. The financial responsibility for a house or lot goes along with the ownership title, no matter who lives in the house or for how long the house has been inhabited by a family.

Over half of female (54 percent) and male (64 percent) respondents reported living in rented rooms or houses. For these individuals, rent is their largest expenditure, as stated above, usually amounting to at least half their monthly wages. This is why buying lots or houses, even prefabricated ones, is usually a priority for those who do not own one. As a result of this desire to own lots and housing, the land is being subdivided even further into small sections and turning some areas into slums. What is interesting is that even in cases where the lot or house is purchased rather than inherited, one person assumes the loan, the payments, and the ownership of the property. The ownership of a house or lot conferred by responsibility for payments is an asset that an individual may use as leverage at one moment or another. I will examine this in more detail in chapter 6.

Because money is managed individually, most households have clear definitions of who pays for what. When a couple lives in a house that is owned by a member, then the person who does not own the property is responsible for paying the utilities: water, gas, and electricity. At the time when fieldwork was conducted, no one in the region had a telephone, and gas is bought in *cilindros* (metal bottles) from trucks that drive through the region every two weeks.

Gendered Financial Responsibility

Women bear individual financial responsibility for their children from previous unions. In general, the expenses related to children whose father is absent fall solely on their mothers, even if those children were born into a two-parent family. In the few cases where absent fathers financially help the children they have fathered, they do so minimally and sporadically, usually spending more money monthly on beer than on child support. In fact, while child support is legislated it is still, in effect, non-existent because it is not enforced. In another pattern I found in the region, the maternal grandmother of the child takes care of the child physically all of the time because the mother has migrated to work in floriculture leaving behind the child. Women whose children live with their mothers send money and buy food for that household when they visit.

In most of the households I visited and interviewed that considered themselves as having *plata aparte* or separate pockets, the marketing is done and paid for by the husband (see figure 5.3). *Hacer el mercado* (going to the market) is divided into two chores: *hacer mercado de plaza* or *ir a la plaza* and *hacer mercado de grano*. The first refers to buying fresh produce: fruits, vegetables, and potatoes. The second means buying dry goods such as beans, rice, candles, sugar, meat when possible, and hygiene items for the wife and young women of the house. The fact that men do the marketing is an extension of the tradition of women remaining close to the home, and it is the one household chore that men regularly perform. One way of finding out the position of women and the level of equity in a household is to ask *quién hace el mercado* (who does the marketing) and who pays for it. In households where there is less gender asymmetry, both women and men purchase the groceries. However, disposable diapers, milk and powdered milk, and formula for babies are not included in the *mercado de plaza* nor in the *mercado de grano* but are always the woman's responsibility. These are seen as extensions of the milk produced by the mother and diapers washed by the mother. In general, women also pay for school uniforms, tuition, and supplies and clothes for the children.[15]

Women who have little control over what is bought in the *mercado de plaza* and *mercado de grano* often resist their lack of control by hiding groceries and overstating what is needed in the household, constituting an indirect arena of bargaining and fighting for equity. For several couples I talked with, the men addressed this issue as an example of not being able to trust their wives, while the women feel they are in a double bind: they do not control what groceries are bought, yet they are held accountable for not having sufficient groceries to carry the household over the required period of time or, worse yet, for not having the right food on the plate. Obviously, women without male partners do their own shopping. Women living on their own expressed satisfaction at being able to decide what to buy and what to eat.

Figure 5.3. The market

Extraordinary medical expenses are generally paid by whoever has the resources. In 1991 Colombia's new constitution decreed that health care is a right for all Colombians. The implementation of the constitutional law in 1993 establishes a system of compulsory insurance with a combination of contributory and subsidized regimes. Every employer, including floriculture farms, contributes at least half of the premiums, the other half being the responsibility of the worker (Panapoulou 2002). Since the system is new its implementation has its problems and it has taken time for all services to be covered, forcing flower workers to resort to loans to cover medical expenses (see table 5.5). Individuals who are not formally employed usually resort to kin loans to cover medical expenses.

The disbursal of money and gifts of goods from offspring to parents is also gendered. Usually only daughters give gifts to mothers, generally in the form of bank deposits or clothing, food items, and little sums of cash. I heard of only two men who bought groceries for their mothers. As in other parts of Latin America and despite evidence to the contrary (Safa 1995a and 1999; Tiano 1994), men's salaries are assumed to be essential to their own household and thus cannot be dispersed to extended family while women's salaries are conceived of as disposable. I also heard of only one case where a father was a recipient of gifts or money.

Money and Control

Control of family members, of money, and of the decision-making process are all connected. In households where women have no wage income, men have total or near total control of expenses and of decisions regarding those expenses. These men also try to control their wives physically. Men whose wives start to work, either in the formal or informal labor market, once the children entered school often find it difficult to give up control of decision making and of the physical mobility of their wives. The case of Armando Olaya, a day laborer in the region, is typical. His wife, Luz Bernal, began work as a domestic worker when their youngest child started school, a year before our interview. When I asked him if he liked the money she brought in, Olaya did not answer the question directly but said that she never consulted him about the use of that money and that he strongly disagreed with her working outside the house. "What is the use of her bringing money home if I cannot decide how to spend it?" he replied. He stated that even though she spent the money on sheets, clothes for the kids, and blankets, he did not agree with the purchases because she had bought on credit. If she had consulted with him, he said, he would have agreed on buying the same items he now opposed. He stated he had never failed in providing for the home, so he did not understand why his wife should go out and work. Bernal stated she likes the independence that the little money she is making gives her, adding that before she began working for pay she could not wait to have some of her own money, to be able to decide on purchases, and to be able to get out of the house. Armando, like many men in the region who have seen the routine of their household change, objects to the *process* and his loss of control as the sole decision maker.

In younger couples where both work in the flower industry, gender-based financial obligations still exist, but not as dramatically. While women are still financially more responsible than men for expenditures that have to do with children, men and women share the expenses for rent, food, furniture, and housing; similarly, they share the decision making. Many women state they like it when their spouses work in the floriculture industry because then they know how much money their husbands are actually making. Four flower farm managers I interviewed stated that salaries are deposited directly into people's bank accounts in part as an effort to deter the men from spending it on alcohol. A few years ago, before that policy was put in effect, there would be crowds of men drinking beer at the cantinas on payday; but now there are no crowds, just a few men here and there. Direct deposits have made spending money on alcohol one step harder; however, when both men and women in the same couple work in the flower industry, women still spend a larger percentage of their salary in household goods than men.

Such is the case of Carolina Suárez and José Vaca. At the time of the interview Suárez was nineteen and married for a year to Vaca, twenty-two; they have a boy who was eighteen months old. Both work in the flower industry, though in different companies, and both earned minimum wage, which at the time was 240,000 pesos a month (US$120). Vaca spends 100,000 pesos (US$50) a month, a little less than half his monthly salary, on household goods, part of the groceries, and part of the payment for the prefabricated house they both built on a lot she expects to inherit from her mother. The remainder he spends mostly on his hobby, cycling. Although Suárez is not certain, she thinks he occasionally sends money to a child he fathered two years ago. In contrast, Suárez spends her entire salary on house payments, utilities, groceries, milk, diapers, minimal daycare payments to a sister who lives next door with their parents, and small sums of money she gives to her mother. Suárez has asked Vaca to leave the house on several occasions because she is not satisfied with his contribution to the house and claims she should have never married. She wants to pay off a debt she acquired buying clothes, finish a *cadena* she is in, save a little money, and then she will ask him to leave again, an option she has since they live on a lot her mother gave her.

Los Señores a la Tienda, las Señoras a la Casa

Regardless of their level of financial participation in the household, women perform the majority of household chores. The two exceptions are men shopping for groceries and transporting their preschool children to the house where they are cared for. When asked what they do after working at the flower farm, women invariably respond *recoger a los niños y hacer el oficio* (pick up the children and do housework), which includes washing clothes by hand, ironing, cooking, cleaning the house, and overseeing the children. Men have a variety of responses, which include *ir a hacer diligencias* (run errands), *ir a la tienda* (go to the store) with the subtext of having a beer, and *descansar* (rest). Of all the interviews I conducted, only a couple of men responded they do housework to help their wives. The patterns of mobility reflect the public-private distinctions common in Latin America and "fostered by Catholicism, wherby women were relegated to the home and men to the street as a way of maintaining family honor and female virginity" (Safa 1995b, 45). An old saying in the region, which reflects the pervasive public-private distinction, is that *las señoras son de la casa, los señores de la tienda* (women *are of* the house, men *are of* the canteen), which has been revised to reflect cultural changes: *las señoras van a la casa y los señores van a la tienda* (women *go to* the house and men *go to* the canteen).

Alfonso León, twenty-seven, a migrant from Bogotá, is one of two single fathers working at Muisca Flowers. He has clear visions of gender and of what housework requires in terms of time and money. León, like most men, was brought up with no expectation of being the primary caretaker of a child and of the household. León is very conscious of all his responsibilities involving childcare and house chores, describing, for instance, how many minutes it takes him to ride his bike from work to pick up his child and then to the room he rents, the time it takes to clean up after dinner and to wash clothes. He even lists the minutia of his boy's needs. Most women do not recite the activities of childcare, child rearing, and housework in detail because it is a given they are the ones who have to do it. For León, the double workday is still a shock and was the first thing he talked about when interviewed. He is well aware that both child rearing and housework are unpaid labor and are not remunerated socially.

There is a paradox at work in the way resources are distributed and managed in Fagua and Canelón which leave women in a double bind, especially in traditional households where monies and assets are separate and mostly male controlled. How are women supposed to pay, for example, for the legal transfer of papers if at the same time they are not supposed to work for money? The paradox contributes to a culture where disagreement is pervasive and conflict and bargaining are used to resolve household economic issues. The following chapter examines the exercise of fallback positions within the household bargaining process.

Foreshadowing

In this last section I summarize the research results in this chapter and foreshadow a bit its theoretical implications, which are tied to the theoretical overview that opens up this chapter. My study finds that social capital, financial wealth, and property ownership are interrelated. Women with the most labor-related social capital can access high paying positions, accumulate wealth, and buy property. These are the women, as we shall see in the next chapter, with the strongest fallback position to bargain their living conditions. Women without labor networks but with kin networks use family as a logistical and financial resource, which facilitates property purchase. I found that women who have a combination of wage income and property ownership are more likely to bargain inside their household before choosing to exit the household and live on their own or with their children.

On the other hand, landless women who rely solely on their minimum wage income, migrants for the most part, use their wage income and the social and self-esteem benefits of wage employment to opt out of the traditional family structure: they do not bargain about their living conditions. I found, as will be described, that among the 23 percent of women who are single mothers (27 percent when widows are included), 15 percent are migrants, 26 percent are *antiguas*, and 26 percent are *raizales*. Among the partnered women (60 percent), most of those in *unión libre* (de facto union) are migrants, while most of the married women are *raizales*. And finally, 15 percent are single. While women are abandoned, a significant portion of single mothers are single because they use their income to exit abusive relationships and choose not to reenter into a relationship. I estimate that half of landless migrant women who remain married are physically abused by their partners. Some local single women, aware of the incidence of domestic violence, are able to emulate other single mothers by using their kin social capital to avoid potentially abusive relationships; they can still have a family by choosing to be single mothers.

In accordance with findings in Ecuador's floriculture industry (Korovkin 2003) my research shows that women's income increases their household bargaining possibilities, especially when such income is combined with housing ownership and strong social capital. However, income alone, while necessary, is insufficient to bargain *inside* the household, but it is sufficient to *exit* the household. What this research shows, differing from findings in the

Caribbean (Raynolds 2002), is that the income women earn is a sufficient means of support outside of marriage. Culturally, women who choose to exit or to never enter into a permanent partnership (by electing to be single mothers) are the individuals who have most visibly redefined the family contract by lowering the cultural threshold of male control and violence that they will tolerate. In this way, as will be described in the coming chapter, migrant landless women workers improve not only their own situation, but also that of more financially and socially privileged women.

Notes

1. Formalist economic anthropologists apply the neoclassical economic framework to the analysis of culture. They look at production, consumption, and distribution of resources among diverse human groups.

2. Cleaning, organizing, cooking, shopping, sewing, bearing children, rearing children, and creating and maintaining a social network are all part of housework.

3. Nancy Folbre (1991) traces the history of the construction of the concept of housework as unproductive, beginning in the nineteenth century, noting the importance of gender bias in the definition of productive work and its implications for analyzing female labor force participation.

4. Utility indicates the level of enjoyment or preference an individual has for anything: a chocolate, a song, a painting, and so on. The utility a person derives from drinking a glass of water on a hot day might be higher than on a cool day. A utility function will be the relationship between utility and several goods given a constraint. So for example if the individual has ten dollars, there are several ways to spend the money. Each combination, let us say, two chocolates, one apple, one juice; or four apples and two juices will provide the individual with x amount of utility. Either way, according to microeconomic theory, the individual will try to maximize the utility of a given amount of resources. Because individuals are so different, *it is impossible to compare utility among individuals*. Thus, to be able to apply the basic assumptions of neoclassical economics to households, the New Household Economics model assumes households to have a *joint utility* function. The assumptions in the neoclassical model are:

a. Individuals are rational.
b. Individuals make decisions on a rational basis to maximize utility.
c. Interpersonal utility comparisons are impossible.
d. Tastes are determined outside of economic models
e. Tastes are consistent through time; they do not change.
f. Actors are selfish in markets and thus have independent utilities.

5. The assumption of joint utility function has been heavily critiqued by economists and other social scientists because it assumes the commensurability of value (Gudeman 2001; Blau and Ferber 1992; Ferber and Birnbaum 1977; England and Farkas 1986; England 1993; Pollak 1985; Ben-Porath 1982). Becker's (1991) rotten

kid theorem has also been critiqued. For a detailed feminist critique of the theorem see England (1993).

6. Cooperative bargaining models assume that resource allocation within the household is a bargaining process in which power is a major factor. This assumption is a major deviation from the New Home Economic model where power cannot be taken into account in human economic behavior (Becker 1991).

7. See Hart (1992) and Doss (1996a and 1996c) for reviews of household economic modeling and Agarwal (1997) for a framework on household bargaining including qualitative categories of analysis.

8. As some scholars have noted, the neoclassical model does not take into account that the household has a decision-making structure and that there are frictions and power struggles within it (England and Farkas 1986; Blau and Ferber 1992). Power means that one of the spouses, possibly the husband, "gets more of what he wants" (England and Farkas 1986, 49). The difficulty here is that this realization about power transgresses the assumption within neoclassical economics that it is not possible to compare the utility of two individuals (England and Farkas 1986).

9. The shortcomings of census data have also been documented by Deere and León (1982), Folbre (1991), and Grasmuck and Espinal (2000).

10. Deere (1995) presents an analysis of the implications of considering gender as an analytical category in Latin American peasant studies.

11. Trying to triangulate qualitative information, I asked in the survey "In whose name does the electric bill arrive?" as it is standard practice when setting up an electric account to put it in the name of the person who holds legal title to the property. However, in doing kinship charts, I found that many of those names present in electric bills were deceased. Since there is no connection between *Catastro*, the office where property titles are held, and the power companies, it is up to the current owner of the property to update the name; thus the question proved unreliable.

12. Under Colombian law two years of cohabitation mark the time when a couple is considered a permanent union. Permanent unions that are longer than two years are subject to the same property regime as any marriage by the church or the state. However, in Fagua and Canelón the social norm predominates over the legal norm. A couple in *unión libre* or cohabitating will not regard property as joint. If the partnership dissolves, the division of land and housing ownership follows the individual trail of inheritance or purchase. More on this subject can be found in Deere and León (2000).

13. These percentages eliminate double counting of respondents who indicated utilizing both types of for-pay childcare (in-home childcare and childcare center) or both types of family childcare (the other parent and another family member). As a result, they are not produced simply by adding together percentages found in table 5.4.

14. Birth control and male domination has been analyzed among microentrepreneurs in the Dominican Republic by Sherri Grasmuck and Rosario Espinal (2000).

15. Even public schools in Colombia require tuition.

CHAPTER SIX

Cultivating Homes

The overall purpose throughout this book has been to examine the effects of formal employment in the fresh-cut flower industry on intrahousehold dynamics of rural women and on that basis assess whether the floriculture export-oriented industry is at all beneficial to women. The beginning chapters provided the historical and sociocultural context of the region where this research took place. They also analyzed the cut-flower industry from a global assembly line industry perspective. The middle chapters provided an ethnography of the flower farms at work and its effects on women workers' self-esteem. In chapter 4 I have presented the changes in the consciousness of workers in the floriculture industry including women's realization of their own value and of the value of their knowledge. In chapter 5 I discussed the minutiae of the distribution of physical assets, and social assets by gender and by the local emic categories of residence. This chapter gathers together all the elements presented in previous chapters to examine how individuals put in motion fall back positions within the household. I will examine the effects of the industry's policies on the gendered ideology of household equality in combination with people's command of physical assets, wage income, and social assets, in intrahousehold bargaining. My evidence regarding intrahousehold bargaining processes and outcomes of households with women workers and non-workers in the floriculture industry speak to the overarching question of this research: What are the gendered effects of wage employment in a global assembly line industry in Colombia?

Specifically, in this chapter I examine the alternatives to traditional households that can be found in Fagua and Canelón. The chapter examines the challenges women are posing to the inequitable distribution of financial responsibilities and of household work. Most important, it examines the challenges that women are posing to being abused emotionally and physically by their partners and husbands. By contesting male domination of households, women are claiming their human rights.

I conducted in-depth interviews of women who work in floriculture, and also had passing conversations with other women of the region, regardless of their employment status. Most have devised diverse bargaining strategies within and exit options from their households. This is evidence of both the socioeconomic constraints within which they live and their resourcefulness in creating threat points and fallback positions within those constraints. Despite sharing those constraints, local and migrant women, cut-flower workers and non-workers, have differing physical, financial, and social assets with which to bargain, as was described for workers in the previous chapter. Table 6.1 provides an idea of the variety and number of household arrangements and strategies.

The ethnographic record that follows will demonstrate a sample of the variety of new household arrangements forged by women in their search for gender symmetry in Fagua and Canelón. Given the number of variables in consideration, it is not possible to provide a case study for each strategy. The case studies provided are illustrations of how wage income, land and/or housing ownership, social networks, emotional stamina, and human capital are used as leverage in intrahousehold bargaining. In general *raizal* women and women from *antiguo* families who live in households with husbands and children and work outside the home may use the threat or act of leaving as a way to gain more equality within their families. In this way they leverage their wage income, lot and/or house ownership if they have it, knowledge of housework and childcare, and emotional stamina in the bargaining process.

In varying degrees, some younger women in Fagua and Canelón, including those from all three emic distinctions, *raizal*, *antiguo*, and migrant, may opt out of the bargaining process by refusing to form households with male partners. They instead may choose to focus their lives around work and children, and establish households without permanent male partners. Women approximately eighteen to thirty-five years old may chose not to marry or pair up with men at all. They may either remain single and childless or have children on their own. This is a trend that is taking force, and in future years it will undoubtedly include even more young women as long as they have stable wage employment and the cultural parameters of the marriage contract remain in-

Table 6.1. Matrix of In-Depth Life Histories of Cut-Flower Workers

	Migrants		Non-migrants		
	no land	landowner	no land	landowner: lives with kin	landowner: does not live with kin
Women					
Single, no children	OO		OO		
Single with children: by choice	OO			O	
Single with children: abandoned by male	P		POOO		
Single, with children: left, took children with	PPP		P		
Left home and children: haven't returned	P				P
Left home and children: returned	P		P		P
Married	VVOO	POO	PV		O
Men					
Single, no children	Δ			Δ	
Single with children, abandoned by female	Δ				Δ
Left home and children: no child support	ΔΔ				Δ
Left home and children: contribute child support	ΔΔ				
Married		ΔΔΔ	ΔΔΔΔ		Δ
n=	20	6	14	2	6

O = female interviewee who has not experienced domestic violence
V = female interviewee who is currently subjected to domestic violence
P = female interviewee who has experienced domestic violence in the past, but no longer does
Δ= male interviewee

equitable by gender. Some of those in their early twenties who are living with male partners also working in floriculture have more equity in the distribution of time and household chores than other households. For their part, more women within marriages are claiming their right to work, to control resources, to be decision makers, and to refuse to be victims of domestic abuse.

The Importance of Domestic Abuse

I would like to stress that intrahousehold bargaining in the Sabana de Bogotá not only includes the allocation of income, labor, material goods, and time resources that are considered by most economic research, but also women's human rights in households in which men use the threat of physical force as a means of exercising power. In other words, intrahousehold bargaining analysis may be biased when domestic abuse is omitted as an anaylitical variable. To fully understand why women choose to opt out or to leave the home it is necessary to recognize that family violence in rural Colombia is pervasive, understudied, and underreported.[1] Domestic abuse in Colombia's provinces of Cundinamarca and Boyacá is especially pervasive due to the Hispanic patriarchal system that replaced the more equitable indigenous system (Wartenberg 1992). Domestic abuse against wives and daughters and exercised by fathers or older household males is in effect part of the marriage contract in Cundinamarca, where Chía and Cajicá are located. Furthermore, since serial and parallel sexual relations with other women is a cultural norm for men, men use physical control and domestic abuse to avoid any questioning regarding their behavior from their permanent partners (Wartenberg 1992, 415). In addition, in spite of the existence of laws, the judicial system does not provide an effective mechanism for enforcing laws against domestic violence or for punishing those who commit the crime.[2] My data in Colombia show women negotiating their freedom of movement, their right to work for pay, and their right to live free of domestic violence as a central component of their intrahousehold dynamics and bargaining processes. Studies that further explore the links between property ownership, income, and intrahousehold bargaining should benefit from incorporating social assets, domestic abuse, and cultural change as elements of analysis. Research on domestic abuse and its relationship to intrahousehold bargaining processes is necessary to understand whether Colombia's rate of domestic abuse has increased very recently, whether existing research has not highlighted the issue, or whether the absence of this analytical category in other studies simply reflects a different local reality.[3] Based on my findings, I argue that domestic abuse is the decisive contextual feature in understanding intrahousehold bargaining in the northern section of the Sabana de Bogotá.

Given the prevalence of domestic abuse, women's increased self-esteem empowers them and provides them with bargaining power.[4] That a portion of the women, even if it is not a majority, are willing and able to drive such hard bargains denotes the level of domestic violence against women in Colombia. Previous studies have highlighted women's formal employment in the industry and the breakdown of traditional patriarchal families as the culprit of "family disintegration" (Velez 1995). Furthermore, the industry, instead of being perceived as providing a means of subsistence to women who are abandoned and abused, is seen as "imposing [harsh] economic conditions" (Díaz and Sierra 1995, 28). In my sample, only 1 percent of women reported having children elsewhere, while 15 percent of men reported having children elsewhere (see table 6.2). This dramatic difference may be even larger if one considers that men who appear in this statistic are only those who actually *acknowledge* their fatherhood. It is unknown how many do not even recognize the children they fathered and abandoned. The shallow analysis on the detrimental effects of floriculture on families, that is, assuming that the "problem" in family disintegration is women's wages rather than men's violence and abandonment, echoes the local chauvinistic view of the effects of female employment expressed to me as well as to other researchers (Hoyos, 1996; Meier 1999). My research found that, in contrast, women workers use their employment in the industry to challenge male domination of households and drive forward a more gender equitable notion of what a family can be. Domestic abuse is not emerging because of women's employment in floriculture; rather it is diminishing because of it. This finding concurs with research results in Ecuador's floriculture region (Newman et al. 2002). The women who challenge the status quo are culturally redefining the terms of the marriage contract to exclude domestic violence.

Men are culturally allowed to contribute very little financially (if at all) to the household. This reality motivates women further to bargain actively in the household or to opt out of bargaining entirely. However, I also found that the prevalence and severity of domestic abuse raises the stakes for women and prompts them to bargain or exit in dramatic ways. The women who took the drastic decision to live on their own risked ostracism and isolation, as living alone as an adult woman is not regarded positively in Colombia's central region (Wartenberg 1992, 417). However, in Fagua and Canelón, so many women live alone that in doing so they have challenged and changed the cultural parameters of acceptable behavior for women overall, and they are no longer ostracized.

Of importance for the literature on global assembly line and structural adjustment and the questions that underlie this study on the exploitation or empowerment of women is the comparison of Colombia's marital and decision-making outcomes with the experience in the Caribbean and the experience elsewhere in South America. According to Safa (1999), women in the Dominican Republic are choosing to be alone because the "marriage market" of men able and willing to be breadwinners has diminished due to adjustment. As Safa summarizes, "female-headed households need to be seen as the outcome of poverty rather than producing poverty" (1999, 303). In Colombia a similar pattern emerges but for dramatically different reasons: female headed households are the outcomes of male abandonment or of female choice in order to avoid domestic abuse or its risk as it is culturally sanctioned in the marriage contract. Women in Colombia sometimes leave their partners in spite of the fact that men are perceived as the main breadwinners and in fact have more and higher paying employment possibilities. With regard to household decision making, Sherri Grasmuck and Rosario Espinal find that in the Dominican Republic the amount of income partners earn relative to each other impacts intrahousehold decision making, but they also find that gender ideology can bypass the income effect and take women's income-based leverage away (2000). Raynolds finds, in the same country, that the amount of income women earn is not enough to allow for an increase of female power inside the household, much less for the woman to exit the household (1998). Barrientos and colleagues, studying seasonal employment of women in Chile's fruit industry, find that women are seasonally and partially empowered as their wage labor is on a temporary basis (1999). In contrast, Colombia's floriculture women are empowered on a permanent basis and earn enough income to exit the household.

Household Strategies

The income from floriculture wages and the stability of those jobs is an indispensable component of bargaining or of living alone while the social network facilitates acquisition of property, high wages, and provides logistical and financial support to individuals. To answer the claims of those who argue that floriculture employment breaks down the traditional family unit, this research demonstrates the opposite. Families are already "broken down" or do not function in equitable ways for all members due to cultural ideologies of male domination. It is the wage income from floriculture, in fact, what allows women to envision new family arrangements and cultivate such visions into reality.

The households described below reflect the thoughts, lives, and patterns of behavior of many of the families I interviewed regardless of whether they are *raizal*, *antiguo*, or migrant. I chose these examples because two of the women, Olga Sutáuta and Celia Quindío, are very clear and eloquent regarding their choices, while the case of Omaira Perilla and Yesid Gachalá represents well the traditional household.

The strategies of partnered women vary according to whether they work for pay at all, and, if they do, by whether their employment is in the formal or informal sector. For those employed, the amount of income is determined by the sector, physical assets they own, whether they are in joint ownership, and the type of social networks they possess. In turn, as described for single women who are cut-flower workers, the amount of income earned hinges in some measure on the type of social assets an individual has.

Sixty percent of women workers are partnered (see table 6.2). The majority of the women I interviewed chose to remain in the home and only began to challenge the household order when their smallest child reached school age, as will be seen in the case of Omaira Perilla. However, I did find a number of women who challenged male domination of households by threatening to leave or in fact leaving temporarily (see table 6.1). The fact that the challenge is accomplished in such a drastic way is of great significance, qualitatively and culturally, because it demonstrates an entirely new mode of behavior that some individuals, whether they work in floriculture or not, are emulating.Leaving the home temporarily is a strategy put into motion mostly by well-paid workers who belong to the upper-class peasantry due to their ancestors' connection to current or old *hacienda* owners or owners of large landholdings (*latifundio*). Those who have long-standing personal or family labor connections to former *hacienda* or large landholding owners (*terratenientes*) are more likely to own land and/or housing or to be supervisors with high-paying jobs in flower farms located within these large estates. In addition, due to their labor relations with ex-*hacienda* owners, those individuals have virtually guaranteed jobs. Their high salaries, especially when they earn as much or more than their husbands do, provide them a strong fallback position to press for better living conditions. Whether they own property or foresee inheriting property is secondary to high wages since the property essentially represents what they will not have to pay in rent. High wages, on the other hand, provide forceful leverage as their withdrawal has immediate effects on the welfare of the family.

Strikingly, among cut-flower workers, women are more likely to live with their children than to live with a partner, while men are more likely to live with a partner than with their children. Three quarters (76 percent) of all women surveyed live with their children, while only 58 percent live with a partner. Among men, 71 percent live with a partner, but only 59 percent live with their children. One-fourth (23 percent) of all women in the cut-flower industry are single mothers; among *antiguo* and *raizal* women single motherhood approaches 30 percent, while only 2 percent of men are single fathers.

Table 6.2. Family Composition of Cut-Flower Workers

		Women			
		Migrants	*Antiguo*	*Raizal*	All
n =		108	46	77	231
Single:	with children	15%	24%	26%	23%
	children elsewhere	1%	2%	0%	1%
	no children	18%	9%	16%	15%
Live with partner:	with children	57%	63%	51%	56%
	children elsewhere	1%	0%	0%	0%
	no children	8%	2%	6%	6%
Unknown	no children	0%	0%	1%	0%
		Men			
		Migrants	*Antiguo*	*Raizal*	All
n =		76	18	35	129
Single:	with children	3%	6%	0%	2%
	children elsewhere	5%	6%	17%	9%
	no children	24%	0%	11%	17%
Live with partner:	with children	50%	78%	63%	57%
	children elsewhere	7%	6%	3%	5%
	no children	9%	6%	6%	8%
Unknown	with children	1%	0%	0%	1%
	no children	1%	0%	0%	1%

Note: "Single" includes both never married and separated individuals. "Live with partner" includes respondents who are in civil, church, or de facto marriages as well as the few widows in the survey pool. Percentages add up to more than 100 percent because of rounding.

Bargaining inside the Marriage

Temporarily abandoning the home is a strategy used by those women who have strong fallback positions because of their financial or physical wealth and social capital, like Olga Sutáuta. The family of Olga Sutáuta is well respected in the region, where they have lived as long as they can remember. Sutáuta is thirty-eight years old. She studied in elementary school until the second grade and started working in the fresh-cut flower farms when she was twelve years old. Sutáuta is a supervisor in the flower business and earns four times the base salary most flower workers earn. Her husband of seventeen years, Eleuterio Rozo, earns a third of what she does. They have four children from the ages of four to sixteen years. Sutáuta reported that she began to have significant marital problems about ten years earlier because of her long work hours at the flower farm as she begun to ascend the corporate ladder. At that point, Sutáuta argued, her husband began to exert physical control over her:

> He could not stand that I spent so much time here [at the farm]. He was always saying that I had another man, that he was the reason why I was spending so much time in the farm. He used to drink [alcohol] a lot, and hit me every time he was drunk. He would never hit me when he was sober, only drunk. But he was drunk every weekend. The girls were also getting very afraid of him. When he would arrive home they could not find fast enough a place where to hide. So I saw that this was happening and I left him. *But* I left him with the children. Carlos was small. He was still wearing diapers, so he had to change him, and wash the diapers. *And all the work children are . . .* [laugh].

Sutáuta related that, when they were fighting, he would threaten to leave and take the children with him. While Colombian penal and civil laws do recognize cohabiting couples who have been together for at least two years and accord them every protection of civil or religious marriage, Rozo was leveraging with the social norm that women do not seek legal council in case of being abandoned by a cohabitating partner. Women do not seek counsel nor have the law enforced either because they do not know about it, as I found in the interview process, or because enforcement of the law, as in many instances in Colombia, is perceived as being near impossible.

Laughing hard and showing her perfect teeth, Sutáuta said she gave him what he threatened: she left him with the three children they had at the time. In her description she emphasized the "but" (*pero*), which highlighted her leverage. Leaving him was dramatic, especially in a culture where women do not leave men. It is assumed and sometimes even expected that men will leave women and children, but not the other way around. Sutáuta admits that emotionally it was difficult to leave her children behind, although her purpose was not to leave her children, *but* to leave him *with* the children. Her goal was clear. She wanted to have a home with her husband but under different conditions. She went to a town called Líbano and stayed there for five months working in a restaurant and renting a room nearby. She avoided all contact with her family, his family, her children, and her husband for the entire time she was gone.

Sutáuta's additional assets at this point were her knowledge of childcare and household administration and her emotional strength. By leaving, Sutáuta leveraged her skills in childcare and housework and her partner's lack of skills in these areas of work. The laughter denotes another asset: the time that childcare and housework require, but that is unaccounted for monetarily and unrecognized socially. Sutáuta had a strong fallback position: either her husband stopped hitting her and threatening to leave her childless or she would leave him with all the work, which in addition he did not know how to do. In effect she left him without her housework, childcare, financial contribution, and emotional support. Leaving him with all the responsibilities was a way for Sutáuta to make her work and her person visible.

The statements of men like Martín Serrano, also a cut-flower worker who migrated to the region five years ago, married with two children, demonstrate that the knowledge and time housework require do constitute additional leverage in bargaining, as the threat of female abandonment is deterring him from practicing domestic abuse and high alcohol consumption. It also acknowledges that female abandonment of the household is not an isolated strategy. "If she were to leave me with the children, my life would become very complicated. I have seen it happen to other men; people have told me that that is what women are doing now. Plus, I would not be able to care for the children as well."

By leaving the children behind, Olga Sutáuta took away her husband's leverage: the threat to leave her childless. By leaving, Sutáuta made evident one more asset: her emotional tenacity, which she has continued to exercise.

Sutáuta's income was also an asset. Before leaving him, she would give all her salary to her husband as soon as she received it, and he would decide on the purchases and manage the money. What is important to note is that Sutáuta exercised the power and leverage of all of her assets, including income, when she deprived her husband of them. However, income was not an asset that she had put into use before. While income is thought to be a "hard" asset and one effective as a threat point tool, it can only be so if the individual who earns the income controls it. Sutáuta decided to use her income as leverage only when she left. But in effect, withdrawing her income, since she would not earn it either, was not a fallback position or even a threat point. It was the absence of the income that she used as leverage.

If either Sutáuta or Rozo were to leave the house, however, it had to be her because they lived next to her in-laws, in a rented house owned by her husband's father. Thus the place of residence was her husband's leverage. Rozo also had as an asset the physical control that his mother, who stayed home, could exert on Sutáuta. His mother knew when Sutáuta would come home and when she went out. Even though Rozo's mother did not say anything directly to Sutáuta, Sutáuta knew she was being watched. This surveillance was part of the physical control Rozo exerted over Sutáuta. In addition, he abused her physically, which was culturally sanctioned and even encouraged. Thus violence, threats, and physical monitoring were among Rozo's assets. In traditional households the threat of abuse and the abuse itself give leverage and power to men. This was true for the first years of Sutáuta and Rozo's marriage, when, Sutáuta stated, she would do everything Rozo demanded. After a few years, however, this asset had become a liability for Rozo.

After five months away, Sutáuta came back. Sutáuta was eager to tell the rest of her story:

> He convinced me to come and live with him again. I did, maybe because of pride or because I knew I could make it alone financially. Today, I do not ask him for anything. I tell him, if we cannot get along, let's separate, but you remain with the children. I will not take them. That is the *weapon* I have used so that he would not hit me, insult me, or threaten me with taking the children. Since the youngest daughter was born we made a shared agreement that we would not fight. And he has changed. Things are now nice for me. In the beginning he would not even pick up his socks; I would have to do all the housework. Now, it is different. It is nicer for me. Women before had not only to ask their husbands for permission to spend money, but had to give their salaries to their husbands. And the husbands decided how the money was spent. My parents were that way. We were that way before.

Since Sutáuta, a rose supervisor, now earns four times more than her husband, her position is even stronger than when she left him several years ago. In addition, Sutáuta and a male sibling who is also a supervisor at Muisca Flowers have guaranteed jobs, largely as a result of their father's social assets. *Señor* and *Señora* Sutáuta, Sutáuta's parents, worked all their lives for a relative of Muisca Flowers' owner when the land was still used for dairy cows. They lived in a house inside the farmland, under the same conditions as *concertados* or tenant laborers in *haciendas*, as is described in chapter 1. The social and labor relationship that the Sutáuta parents had with their employer extended to their children, and there is an implicit guarantee that the Sutáuta family will provide the owner's family with labor and will use its social network to recommend individuals as workers at the flower farm. In turn, the owner's family guarantees the Sutáuta family employment. This arrangement has been kept through two generations and through the dramatic shift from using the land for cattle and agriculture to an agro-industry. The guarantee of a job for Sutáuta at the flower farm provides her with one more asset to use for leverage inside her household. This particular asset carries weight in Sutáuta's household given that Sutáuta's husband has no such guarantee. His family never worked for the *hacienda* or any other large landowner in the region.

As mentioned, before Sutáuta left the household she would give Rozo her salary, and he would decide how to spend it, going to Chía on Sundays, market day. Sometimes he would buy the groceries, and sometimes he would use the entire salary for individual entertainment. Now Sutáuta decides on the groceries, and Rozo accompanies her to carry them home. In spite of the increased gender equality and possibly because of her fallback position, Sutáuta continues to use her assets as a threat point. Sutáuta keeps reminding her husband, and brings it up in the conversation repeatedly, that she has an *arma* (a weapon) she can use: leaving, but leaving him with small children who require a lot of work. She states that when they fight she will remind him of what she is capable of doing. Here, her emotional tenacity is also an asset, and thus a source of power and leverage.

The house they live in now was built with construction materials paid for by Sutáuta and with Rozo's labor. It is one of six houses in one *fanegada* (6,400 square meters) of land. The other five were built by Rozo's siblings, although Sutáuta also bought the lot where the house now stands. Sutáuta does not perceive her work at home to be overwhelming because she has her husband doing his share, as do the children.

Rozo is a construction worker, and with his salary he pays for the utilities and the market. Sutáuta pays for school and childcare tuition, clothing, and medical services. She also pays for her father's and Rozo's father's needs. In addition she paid for the car they own, one of the few owned by families of the region. She considers the car and the house as owned by them both; according to Sutáuta it is one home and one purse.

Sutáuta is conscious that her situation is different now because she earns more than her husband. "What he does not make in income," she stated, "he makes up in housework." This highlights a gender difference regarding earned income and the way it is perceived. In the first part of the marriage, even though Sutáuta earned the same income and worked the same number of hours as Rozo, she was expected to do all the housework. With her income four times larger than his, in addition to the leverage she has used, he has felt obligated to compensate in kind doing housework. There is, then, a difference in perception regarding the importance of income: men's income is perceived to be more important, and to have more value. Women will perform the majority or all of the housework and childcare even if their income is the same as their partner's. In the face of cultural expectations, income is less of an asset for women than for men, when the amount of income each individual earns is equivalent in currency. This cultural perception is prevalent in the region not only between spouses, but also between siblings. Daughters are expected to do a large portion of childcare and housework even if they earn minimum salary just like their brothers. In addition, daughters are expected, when they leave the household, to send in-kind or cash remittances to their mothers. Sons have no monetary, in-kind, or chore obligation in the household. This gender and generational dynamic is in effect among Sutáuta's extended family. Sutáuta's brother Miguel Sutáuta is also a supervisor at Muisca Flowers flower farm and earns the same amount of money; nevertheless, it is Olga Sutáuta who cares physically, emotionally, and financially for their ill, widowed father.

Exiting the Marriage

But not everyone has wages as high as Olga Sutáuta. Minimum wage workers who own property use it less as a threat, a fallback position: if conditions inside their household do not improve, women ask their partners to leave if the couple is living in her house, or they themselves leave if the couple is not living in her property. As stated earlier only a small percentage of couples own property jointly (see table 5.1). In either case, the stability of jobs and the income makes it possible for women to live on their own if need be.

Recall Mercedes Vega in chapter 4, an *antigua* single mother in her mid-forties, who has worked in floriculture for sixteen years and who has four children, fathered by two men. The first abandoned her, and the second she intentionally left because she was tired of the emotional and physical abuse she received from her *marido*, as she put it. In our conversation she weighed the choice she had made of living alone and with less financial security but with improved emotional freedom. She made the analogy of eating chicken with a bitter attitude or drinking the inexpensive local drink in happiness.

Her analysis clearly had not only occurred while we talked. She had planned how she could live on her own. With four children to support, her goal was to control the lot and own the house where she currently lives with her children. Having permanent employment in the flower industry guaranteed she would be able to support herself and her children. While she does not have *hacienda*-like social capital with the flower owners, she has achieved seniority and was able to build her house with a combination of family and farm loans. The lot which she expects to inherit from her mother and the permission her mother gave her to build a house on it provided her with a fallback position: she would eventually have a place to live if she and the children left the house and her husband, their father and step-father. While the house was being built she accessed one more asset: she could live with her mother while she saved money and found a loan to build the house.

Not Marrying

The most dramatic interviews I conducted, in terms of cultural change and the conscious use of assets as leverage, were with female migrants. Celia Quindío is a thirty-two-year-old woman from Chaguaní, a lower-altitude village five hours away by bus from Bogotá. She has been working in the flower business for twelve years, ten of those in Fagua and Canelón, and I talked with her on several occasions and different settings. This particular day was hot, especially under the plastics inside the greenhouse. The gypsophila section, called by everyone the gypso section, is like a waist-high sea of small white flowers. The white sea is sprinkled with the red of workers' uniforms. I could see Quindío from a distance. She was cutting gypsophila at incredible speed. In fact, she is the fastest in the whole group, always winning first place. She had on a wide straw hat but was not wearing the gloves the company provides workers, as she finds them uncomfortable. Quindío was stripping away excess foliage from the cut branches of the flower plant with the tip of her thumbnail, which was stained green.

Quindío has three children, all by different fathers. Their ages are sixteen, fourteen, and two years. The last child she had with a man she has been seeing for ten years. I asked her where this man lives, and she said with his family. He has a wife and children. Naively, I asked if she had not been able to convince him to live with her. She looked at me with anger and as if I was out of my mind: "And why would I want to do that for?" She paused for a long time working vigorously cutting and stripping the gypso, perhaps trying to simmer down from my incendiary question. After a while she continued:

> Live with a man? That is too much work. Then I have to cook, iron, I can't go out, and I will be controlled. Just like this is better. Over there with his family he has someone else who cooks, cleans, washes, and irons for him. He pays for half of the rent, the utilities, and the expenses for the girl [daughter]. He sometimes wants to have lunch at my house. I tell him to go have lunch at the place he did the market for. I don't like him helping with the groceries; then I have to cook for him. Just like this we have a life of husband and wife [smile], except he does not control me or order me around.

Quindío's case, like that of many other women I interviewed, is the most extreme in cultural change, as Quindío openly challenges the traditional patriarchal organization of households. A common theme among women, here expressed by Quindío, is the unequal distribution of housework. The women who openly challenge patriarchal household culture perceive living with a male partner as a job that requires a lot of labor that is not recognized as productive by their husband or their society. Quindío and women like her are aware of their emotional, sexual, and financial needs. Living in partnership with a man, whether husband, father, or brother, is regarded as a burden. In particular, they talk about marriage as "too expensive a trade" in exchange for those needs. The trade is perhaps having a financial contribution from a husband, who will possibly abuse them emotionally and physically, disrespect them, and add to their burden of household chores. Many women, Quindío among them, are opting out of that bargaining process because the patriarchal culture makes it difficult to have parity. They opt out mainly in two ways. One of their options is to remain single and childless, and the other is to choose to have families alone by being single mothers. This way, they are the sole earners, the sole decision makers, and the sole person controlling their lives. In a sense, single mothers channel their lives in two avenues: children and work.

Celia Quindío was clear also about her emotional needs. She stated she did want a relationship, but just one that is not too close. When her fourteen-year-old was nine, Quindío and her boyfriend had a closer relationship, and he started to hit her. At that point she told him to go hit his wife and to respect her (Quindío). Since then, she has kept her emotional distance and described the relationship as one of *novios* (boyfriend-girlfriend) rather than as *compañeros* (partners) or *esposos* (husband and wife), highlighting how domestic abuse is culturally sanctioned within households whether the relationship between man and women is one of marriage or of *unión libre*. Domestic abuse from fathers toward young children of both sexes and older daughters also occurs. But domestic abuse is not approved when there is no cohabitation. As Bergmann states, "A woman who considers entering a housewife job, usually from a paid job, knows that cohabitation is a condition in keeping it, and considers the attractiveness of her suitor (or her husband if she is already married) in deciding whether to accept the 'job offer'" (1981, 82). While this position might seem unsettling to Western cultures whose ideal relationship is based on love, among the group of women in Fagua and Canelón that openly challenge the male dominated status quo, Bergmann's assertions are a close representation of their reality. By keeping her boyfriend out of the house, Quindío is keeping control of her life inside the house. Quindío even decided she wanted another child, seeing that her older two were growing and would soon be on their own, without consulting with her boyfriend because in the end, the responsibility would be hers anyhow, and that is how she wants it. He has asked to move in with her, which she refuses. Since the daughter was born, he has given her money for rent. In our conversations Quindío never mentioned his name, calling him only by the personal pronoun "he," even as my interviews and visits with her became more familiar. Perhaps this is also a way to keep him out of the house mentally as well. Likewise, she refers to the child as *her* daughter, not *theirs*.

The Importance of Wage Income

Safa (1995a and 1999) concludes that women employed in assembly-type export in the Spanish-speaking Caribbean gain little from employment if their wages only substitute for men's income, although her research (1995b) demonstrates that women gain more decision-making authority in the household because structural adjustment has diminished men's wages and created jobs for women. She argues, with regard to female-headed households, that the result may be that women's breadwinning role leads to higher levels of marital instability. Safa finds that most of the women in her study fall between two extremes: being female heads of households and being in egalitarian partnerships. I found that 23 percent of women are single mothers, 58 percent are partnered, and 17 percent are single. However, contrary to Safa's findings, in my research the causality, on one hand, and reason, on the other, behind a portion of female-headed households appear to be different (see table 2.8). In the Caribbean, declining real wages and growing inflation have negatively affected the formal labor sectors dominated by men (Safa 1999, 291). As a response to having lower wages than their female partners, men abandon them (Safa 1999, 291). In Colombia, in contrast, men abandon women despite being able to support the household. In contrast to the Caribbean experience where women avoide marriage because they perceive that men cannot support a household due to declining wages or lack of employment, in Colombia a significant portion of women exit the marriage despite the fact their partners can support the household. They use their income to exit abusive relationships and choose not to re-enter a new relationship. In Fagua and Canelón, though, despite the fact that men, in general, earn more than women and can support a family, in practice they often do not use their money to support their household. In Colombia, though and in contrast to other parts of Latin America (Raynolds 2002), one can state that women choose to exit because they *can* support themselves with their wage income and it is domestic abuse that they seek to avoid.

Aware of the incidence of domestic violence, some women, mostly *raizal* or *antiguas*, choose not enter into potentially abusive relationships but still have a family by opting to be single mothers. The socioeconomic constraints that each group lives with and the patterns of property ownership denote the level of social capital each is able to tap in order to exercise their choice.

Local women find it easier to be a single mother and opt out of the bargaining process before having any children because they have greater social resources to draw on, such as living with kin and inheriting property. With regard to the local single mothers, it remains to be seen if they will eventually choose to partner. In my interviews I did not encounter any who had. The desire of women to raise their children on their own was so evident while doing fieldwork that I included the question in the survey. In general 43 percent of women who answered the question stated they would prefer to raise their children on their own while 57 percent stated they would prefer to raise them with a partner (see table 6.3). Interesting is the fact that 35 percent of married women stated they would prefer to raise their children alone. In terms of current single mothers, it is not surprising that more migrants (64 percent) and *antiguos* (70 percent) report the same desire than *raizal* women (47 percent) as *raizal* women have more at stake socially than women in the other two groups.

While income from wages is indispensable to women's increased intrahousehold bargaining power and their bargaining or exit options, social capital facilitates the accumulation of wealth as well as women's bargaining power. Non-kin social assets facilitate the accumulation of wealth by providing high-earning employment and through it the acquisition of property

Table 6.3. Childrearing Preferences of Female Cut-Flower Workers by Marital Status

	Childrearing preference	Migrant	*Antiguo*	*Raizal*	All
Single women, no children	n =	12	3	10	25
	Raise children alone	50%	33%	80%	60%
	Raise children with partner	50%	67%	20%	40%
Single mothers	n =	11	10	17	38
	Raise children alone	64%	70%	47%	58%
	Raise children with partner	36%	30%	53%	42%
Partnered women	n =	65	24	38	127
	Raise children alone	32%	33%	39%	35%
	Raise children with partner	68%	67%	61%	65%
All women	n =	88	37	65	190
	Raise children alone	39%	43%	48%	43%
	Raise children with partner	61%	57%	52%	57%

Note: "Single" includes never married, separated, or abandoned. "Partnered" includes women in civil, religious, and de facto marriages as well as the seven widows in the survey who responded to this question. This table includes only those women who answered the question.

ownership, while the social capital of kin support facilitates the accumulation of wealth by providing younger people with living quarters and saving them from rent expenditures.

In Colombia women's cut-flower work income increases their household bargaining possibilities, especially when such income is combined with housing ownership, strong social capital, and high self-esteem. My findings appear to be somewhat in line with those in Ecuador's floriculture working communities. A time allocation of paid and unpaid work by gender conducted by Constance Newman in highland Ecuador shows that women's employment in floriculture "led to increases in men's housework through a bargaining effect" (2002, 394). Tanya Korovkin's research, also in Ecuador, finds that households with members working in floriculture are less inequitable, although she argues that is it unlikely that such a trend leads to women's empowerment (2003, 36).

Future research might focus on trying to understand, aside from income, what is necessary to acquire more gender equitable households. Landless migrant women in Colombia, for instance, with limited social assets choose to opt out rather than bargain inside the household. Their opting out of intra-household bargaining is exercised precisely because they lack strong enough leverage but also because their earnings are enough to support them. Remarkably, their exit option is reshaping local cultural constructs of marriage. Women with slightly stronger fallback positions (a combination of salaries, higher salaries, stable jobs, property ownership, and/or strong social capital) use women who opt out as examples that life is possible outside of marriage, and they thereby boost gender equity within the household.

Of course, migrant women are not devoid of social capital. They are diligent at cultivating solidarity networks, aware that failing to cultivate such social networks is akin to social bankruptcy, if not social suicide (Guyer 1997). Without them, the choice of living alone would be harder. In effect, flower companies provide all women an arena in which to resist the domination of men over women and to cultivate the social net in the form of the workplace. As stated in chapter 4, while men have always had the *tienda*, where beer is consumed, as a male socializing arena, women traditionally have not had an equivalent public place to socialize. The flower farms currently constitute this new female public place that is sanctioned socially. That migrant women opt out is a sign that they do not have many social or material assets they can pull in as leverage *inside* the household, and, thus, they opt out. Migrant single mothers are more likely to choose not to re-enter into a partnership once they have had children and base their decision on past experiences with domestic abuse. The assets that they identify to exit relationships, at least cohabitating ones, are the stability of their jobs in floriculture, which implies having a stable source of income, the amount of their wage income, their physical stamina, and the support that their solidarity networks may provide.

Cultivating Homes and Self-Esteem

It needs to be noted that a shortcoming of looking at assets, whether they be social or material, as predictable measures of women's power and leverage, is that their actual value is linked to self-perception (Sen 1990). Women with a low perception of their value are likely to settle for less, either perceiving their interests as less important than those of other family members or not bargaining assuming that their chances to succeed are low. In other words, a woman's fallback position might be diminished not because she lacks actual assets or other measures of power but because of her own low self-esteem. For that reason, I argue that high perceptions of self-worth and emotional stamina are assets in their own right as can be seen in the cases described above. I found that bargaining, challenging, and resisting male-dominated household arrangements is due in large part to the affirmation and high self-perception that women experience at the flower farms, in contrast to the alienation, the lack of male support, and the domestic abuse they experience in their households. Women not only expressed their improved self-esteem but in fact credit it directly to their employment and to the education on domestic abuse that they receive at the farms. Thus the flower farms are not only promoting gender equality by hiring women, retaining them, and providing a salary and benefits equal to those of men, but by actively discouraging domestic abuse.

As the ethnographic record shows in this chapter as well as in chapter 4, the awareness women have that their housework is valuable is a sign of their self-perception and level of self-esteem. A woman with low self-esteem will more likely follow the gender ideology and undervalue her own housework. However, for women with high self-esteem, housework and childcare activities themselves become leverage. In line with Raynolds's (2002) analysis of household dynamics in the Dominican Republic, I found that in Colombia's cut-flower industry "traditional gender norms about wives as 'helpmates' of husbands" and as the individuals responsible for the domestic activities provides women with leverage, as their knowledge is their human capital for men but not vice versa. However, that capital is only realized once a woman is aware of the value of her work and can use the threat of withdrawing it, which is ostensibly possible only if she can support herself through her wage income.

Women in Chía and Cajicá who work in floriculture consider their bodies an asset, not in terms of sexual barter within the household, but by envisioning their physical stamina and capacity to work as a tool to gain their livelihood. To be strong and in good health is what allows them to make the choice of living alone or with their children. Whether that notion will hold with time remains to be seen.

I described in chapter 4 the perceptions of men who are from *el campo* regarding the changes from an economy based in subsistence agriculture to one that uses the land as an export industry. The core of the base, or, as they state, *fundamento*, is the land. How has thinking about the base changed now that almost no one lives off subsistence agriculture and few own their houses? Women have reconceptualized the term and think about their capacity to work as the base, but have men done so too? In particular, have men begun to acknowledge that female work is, along with their work, the new core component of the base? In the interviews I conducted, women were aware that in exiting or opting out they are withdrawing their income, unpaid labor, human capital, and social assets. In short they are debasing men, using Gudeman's concept (2001); however, I would argue that men have yet to realize, acknowledge, or acquire the language to express the changes.

The effectiveness of the floriculture employment is evident when one examines the bargaining options of traditional households where women do not work in floriculture. Such is the case of Omaira Perilla's household.

Staying In and "Putting Up With"

The changes occurring among individuals and families that have people working in the flower business have transferred over to the region as a whole. Even more traditional *raizal* families, rooted in the land and in their customs, perceive the changes and act accordingly. But the changes are harder to act on and institute. Such is the case in the household of Omaira Perilla and Yesid Gachalá. However, some of the assets and the way they are exercised as leverage to have more power in the household differ from the previous case.

Yesid Gachalá, thirty-four, is *raizal* as he was born and raised in Canelón, just as his parents and grandparents were. Gachalá is short, slim, and muscular. He has a small moustache, big brown eyes, and an ever-present smile. He clearly is of Indian ancestry, reflected in his last name of Chibcha origin as well as in his looks. He works as the caretaker of one of the country houses in the region. His responsibilities are to take care of the gardens surrounding the house and any maintenance that the property requires. He receives an above-minimum salary plus gets housing, utilities, and some use of the land for crops to consume with his family. The labor arrangement is a blend between current labor contracts that guarantee the employee minimum salary and health insurance, among other benefits, and the labor agreement that corresponds to *hacienda* labor contracts between *hacendado* and *concertado* (tenant laborer) described in chapter 2.

Omaira Perilla, thirty-three, is Gachalá's wife. Unlike him, she has fair skin, green eyes, and freckles. She comes from Tabio, a neighboring town that is known for its fair skinned inhabitants. They have four children who range from seven to thirteen years of age. Until a year ago, Perilla did what was traditional for the region in terms of gender roles: she took care of the children, made the meals, washed the clothes, and tended the animals—one or two cows that pastured on the side of the road by the house, ten hens, and a few doves. But a year ago, she started to work as a part-time maid cleaning and cooking for a middle-class family that lives nearby. The following section is translated into English from my field notes in 1999:

Perilla, Gachalá's wife, is arriving by bike. As I see her, I ask Gachalá: "Who is the person washing clothes? She has been there for two hours." I had assumed it was Perilla, Gachalá's wife, since I could only see the back of the woman and we were at a distance. He replied disapprovingly: "You see what I was telling you, she had to hire someone because she does not have time." Gachalá has been telling me for a week now that he does not agree with Perilla's working outside the house. She has been doing so for the last four months. He says he did not tell her anything, he let her work to find out what would happen and that things inside the house would not work out. He had assumed that after a while Perilla would quit her job. However, this has not happened. So according to Gachalá, the housework is behind. Lunch is never ready for him, the clothes are behind, and no one is taking care of the children now that they are on vacation.

By June of 2000 Perilla was working every day outside of the house. She has a network of friends who tell her where her cooking and cleaning services are needed, and now has more work offers than she can accept. At that time there were intense disagreements between Perilla and Gachalá. She told him that he should help her make lunch and dinner while she is outside working, while he states, as he did the previous year, that she should not work outside because her place is in the house.

By emulating other women in the region, Perilla is rocking the household order, and breaking several cultural rules and assumptions. The first one is that the woman is "of the house" and should stay the majority of the time within the physical limits of the house. Like Olga Sutáuta, Omaira Perilla does not want to be controlled and has been slowly opening her possibilities.

First she worked nearby, just a few hours a week. Then she worked a few hours every day. In a brief visit to the region in January 2001 I talked with Gachalá, though I was not able to talk with Perilla because she was in Bogotá, 40 kilometers away![5] At that time she would ride her bike to Gachalá's parents house by the main road, take a bus to the highway, and there transfer to the new urban transportation system called *Transmilenio*. She was gone from 7:00 A.M. to 5:30 P.M. working as a day maid. In contrast, traditional families perceive the city as a foreign space that does not need to be explored. While the capital of Colombia is only one hour away, traditional individuals see themselves as separate from the city or its reality. They do not perceive the city as a potential place to get jobs and live, nor do they consider visits as a way to spend leisure time. This perception of the city is what makes Perilla's decision to work in Bogotá a radical challenge to the patriarchal organization of her household. Some of the women friends who visit the Perilla and Gachalá household provide child care for Perilla when she is working away from the house, reciprocating for years of child care she herself provided for them. In turn, this is one reason she could work outside of the house: her social network has proven to be an asset.

By bringing money home and deciding on purchases, she is usurping Gachalá's monopoly on decision making and is breaking additional cultural rules. She challenged his authority and his source of self-esteem. According to him, the man of the house should be the sole provider for the family. Only when Perilla stopped doing housework did her work become visible and did Gachalá acknowledge that her housework was also a contribution to the household. Furthermore, before working outside the home, Perilla used to do chores that are part of Gachalá's paid job. Perilla, as well as the older children, performed unpaid jobs just like in the *haciendas*, a part of the *hacienda* culture that remains present in the region. But through the years Perilla slowly began to pressure Gachalá for more liberty and less physical abuse by not performing some of those jobs. Having no income, no family nearby, her leverage became resistance (Scott 1990), the job not done as Gachalá's employers would admonish him for the tasks not performed. Perilla stopped watering the flower gardens and the herb garden and no one took notice until nearly all the plants had died. When asked if she knew she was getting her husband in trouble, Perilla has only a naughty and affirmative smile. Gachalá was unaware that she had broken the tacit agreement between them (reinforced by the *hacienda* culture) of performing some of his jobs. Perilla, who takes care of the property and opens up the gates for the owners when Gachalá leaves in the evenings or weekends, has stopped being unconditionally available. She now goes to her friends' houses before Gachalá can leave. She states: "If he wants to go *parrandiando* (go partying), he has to ask me the favor of staying here." Perilla is challenging the culture of *hacienda* labor relations.

But the challenge in 2001 to Gachalá's authority proved to be too much. In yet another visit to the region in 2003, Gachalá reported the events of the past two years. Early in 2002 he had abandoned the household, while managing to maintain his employment. He stopped providing the household, including his children, of any financial support as leverage to force Perilla to stop working for pay and acquiesce to his authority. In turn a few months later, Perilla abandoned the household for four months, leaving her children in the care of the oldest one. Her abandoning the household, in effect, forced Gachalá to return home and take care of the children. After four months, Perilla returned home and is not working for pay at all.

Perilla knows that Gachalá is unlikely to leave his job and thus possibly never leave the household. Gachalá is privileged to live in a big and nice house. He has land to cultivate and employers that respect and trust him. Since the estate he takes care of is the second home of the owners, Gachalá on a daily basis is in effect his own boss. No one controls him, and he decides how to pace his work. On many days he even works fixing electrical appliances, and is known in the region as a man who fixes radios, stereos, irons, and so on. Gachalá's appreciation for his job has intensified in recent years as Colombia has fallen into economic recession, and he sees people all around the region struggling with unemployment and a shortage of housing. However, unlike previous tenant laborers would have, he does not regard the house as belonging to him. He, like female flower workers, knows that he can support himself and find a place to rent.

The dynamics in this household are different than in the previous cases in part because Yesid Gachalá and Omaira Perilla are more traditional. In her view, also shared by Gachalá, fresh-cut flower work is demeaning to a woman's reputation. Perilla, in some respects, has no immediate fallback position. Her only recourse, until the children are bigger, is to *aguantar* (to put up with). It is commonplace that physical abuse is most intense when the children in the household are small; as the children grow, the woman has more freedom of movement, and feels less at risk if abandoned. When Perilla's children were babies, Gachalá used to hit Perilla on the back with the flat end of a *machete*, which he does no longer.[6] He still argues that in those times, she was guilty of "looking around" and almost being unfaithful. Gachalá's reluctance about Perilla's work outside the house, then and now, is not because she really might be unfaithful; rather, he is painfully aware that he was losing ground in the home in terms of the decision-making process. However, like Perilla and Olga Sutáuta, many women wait until the smallest child is seven years old and is attending school to challenge the status quo in the house. By the time women become grandmothers, they yield a lot more power within the house and are seldom victims of domestic abuse.

For now, though, Perilla has to keep a careful balance between how much and how far she challenges Gachalá. An issue at play and used as leverage by Gachalá is one of labor specialization: until Perilla started to work outside of the home she had not acquired skills in labor relations with anyone or exercised her network to further her employment. Meanwhile, Gachalá has had many years of practice in several trades and has developed excellent labor relations with his employers. As Bergmann (1981) puts it, Perilla is living the risks of being a housewife. Time spent outside of the labor market has a negative effect on women's potential earnings. A woman who specializes in housework when children are present invests in their human capital, but not in her own. When the children are grown, as pointed out by Bergmann, the women's labor value decreases, whereas her husband's reaches its peak years. Indeed, Gachalá has invested diligently in his own human capital and his labor-related assets. Perilla has no comparable investment. What is worse, if Perilla and Gachalá were to live apart again, he would be able to buy some of the services performed by his wife, but Perilla, who specialized in housework, would be left with insufficient earnings and labor skills to replace her lifestyle or even set up another household. This is why Perilla and other women living in traditional households and not earning formal sector wage incomes, while challenging patriarchal household rules, unlike Olga Sutáuta, do so slowly and tentatively. Yet Perilla's decision to work outside of the home once the smallest child has reached school age is based in part on a realization that her labor value within the home decreases as the children's needs lessen.

Gachalá did not want to drive Perilla out of the house through brutal domestic abuse either, since this would give him the dubious distinction in the region as being *un animal* (an animal). Even though physical abuse is sanctioned in the region, there are limits to it and rules about how much is acceptable. What he does try to do is to drive her away by increasing the number of parallel relationships he has and by becoming more overt about them.

From the ethnographic descriptions of household bargaining processes and dynamics we can see how gender ideologies of inequality are more likely to be challenged in households with female members working in floriculture. While the changes are due, and in fact possible, due to women's wage income, income alone, while necessary, is not sufficient. Social assets, physical assets, and the ideological changes brought forward and implemented by the floriculture industry are critical. Echoing Grasmuck and Espinal, ideology matters. Intrahousehold bargaining research might benefit from including variables that account for ideology, ideological change, and the ways that it is culturally transmitted to produce outcomes such as the reshaping of the marriage contract in the whole of the region via individuals who work in floriculture.

Social Control: Gossip and Employment

As mentioned in chapter 4, flower companies struggling with the high rate of worker rotation experience "worker insecurity," as opposed to the common finding in global assembly line research that it is workers who have no job security. The industry faces the challenge of providing worker training knowing that many workers will leave within the first two years of employment, a problem compounded by the fact that companies are taking on the task of providing literacy classes and further technical training for the many workers who have low literacy skills. From the companies' view, by providing seminars on health, literacy, and human relations, among others, they are improving the quality of their workers. Thus when losing workers, companies not only lose those who have been trained in horticulture, but also the basic education provided for them.

I argue that the reasons behind the high level of worker rotation lie in the local gender asymmetry and culture of violence in the marriage contract. Not only individual men but traditional individuals, government representatives, and the Catholic Church oppose the cultural changes taking place inside households and in the social structure of the region that challenge patriarchal control over women. The opposition occurs in the form of social control, first, by defining female flower workers as loose sexually (*floristeras*), which incidentally is also the case for Ecuadorean workers (Korovkin 2003), and second through deploying gossip and domestic abuse. The result, as we shall see, is that many women move from one company to another to protect themselves and escape being harassed and abused.

Female fresh-flower workers in the Sabana are known as *floristeras*, and although the literal translation of the term is florist, within local culture, the word has a public transcript that refers to female flower workers as being promiscuous. In the local culture, men have greater sexual freedom than women; married or single men are expected to have serial or simultaneous partners. Local culture does not sanction this behavior for women, however. This particular transcript is supported in particular by individuals who do not work in the flower industry, regardless of gender, and by the local Catholic clergy.

Women who work in the fresh-cut flower companies face the label of *floristeras* coupled with gossip and domestic abuse. Gossip is the mechanism that enforces the meaning of the *floristera* concept. As one flower company manager stated, "*En las flores se maneja mucho el chisme*" (Gossip is handled a lot in the flowers). Seeing, hearing, or imagining some woman talking to some man becomes a thread of gossip that can smother women, usually a young one, until she cannot resist the social pressure. If the woman has a partner, she may face beatings at home. At this point, such women usually talk with their supervisors to look for alternative areas in the same flower farm in which to work. The most common option, however, is to resign and find work in another flower company to keep beatings and household troubles at bay. By doing so, they effectively acquiesce to the social pressure. On occasion, when the company wants to keep a valued worker, it will intercede by talking to the partner of the woman. By intervening, the company attempts to educate the male partner, explaining the role of the female worker in the company, the schedule, and the fact that she is indeed at work where she is needed. In effect, the company tries to change the way female behavior is perceived. The company also talks to the partner about domestic abuse and alternatives for solving conflict. Of course, it is impossible for companies to address each case individually, which is one reason why flower farms have set up the seminars on family violence, domestic abuse, and conflict resolution. Their hope is to educate the population and reduce the incidence of domestic abuse.

However, for many women, such social control is still difficult to resist. For a few, like Perilla, flower work is out of the question. For her as for other women, the deterrent is domestic abuse as well as gossip and her social standing in the community as she would acquire the label of being a *floristera*. For others, including those who come from families that have had flower workers, the alternative is to remain single and celibate. Women who acquiesce to the pressure are most often first-generation flower workers. Second-generation flower workers have, in their own words, *cancha* (experience), in part acquired through relatives, in dealing with this type of social control. All the women I interviewed who held positions of power in the company—supervisors, monitors, and laboratory technicians—have unconventional household arrangements. All of them have made decisions that challenge the cultural pattern. Half are single and expressed no desire to set up households with partners.

Unfortunately, the plight of women is not easily understood in Colombian society, and women's decisions can create a backlash among different segments of society. Take, for example, Velez's study, mentioned above, of female floriculture workers in a village called Suesca, who were pressured by men to have more children as a condition of living together and were later abandoned by those same men. Velez focuses exclusively in the paid labor of women workers, disregarding altogether her own information on male pressure to have more children and their subsequent abandonment of the household. Velez states that "women's access to this new income [from floriculture work] translates into a process of family dissolution, [complete] families where household chores represent the perpetuity of the domestic unit" (1995, 50, my translation). Not only does Velez fail to see men's behavior as causal in the breakup of what she considers the ideal family unit, but she holds women and their paid labor responsible for its dissolution, accusing women of not doing their gendered assigned household chores, and disregarding male abandonment!

Views like those expressed in Velez's work are reinforced by the Catholic Church, which bans the use of contraceptive methods. This ideology is useful to males who do not want their partners to avoid having children. Pablo Puentes's feelings echoed those of most men interviewed:

> I do not allow her to take any pills or do anything. I'd rather have her have many children than have her be out of control and going [to have sex] with anyone. It is enough having to deal with her being out of house and in the flowers all day. There are too many opportunities in the flowers. This way, at least I know she will not go around looking for what she shouldn't.

The views of men and the church reinforce each other by linking women's supposed lack of sexual control, the patriarchal natural order of society, and the work in floriculture.

The transcript of women's sexual deviance is also supported by the church by publicly excoriating female flower workers and flower companies for their supposed lack of morality. In particular, the clergy supports the image of female workers as *floristeras*. According to the church, flower companies are promoting promiscuity in their farms and in so doing are responsible for the demise of morality in the region.[7] However, neither the church or the majority of men similarly condemn male abandonment (physical and/or financial) of the home, the lack of paternal acknowledgment of the children men produce, physical abuse, and men's supposed right to have serial sexual partners even when married. In contrast, the flower companies do challenge this double standard.

In spite of this, the notion that female fresh-cut flower workers are loose sexually is a powerful sign of women's newly acquired freedom and successful strategies for forging different personal and family lives for themselves. The *floristera* public transcript is a cultural tool created to prevent such cultural changes from occurring. It is also often effective; as one supervisor states: "Women who consider working in flowers are more worried about their social reputation than about occupational health." Although this is the main reason why worker turnover is so high, many women nonetheless continue to challenge the social order. Women's "bad reputation" is a sign of attempted social control and a measure of the autonomy they are acquiring.

The role the industry has taken in educating workers and setting up the social component of the Florverde program is one that benefits both workers and the industry. It can be claimed that such work is being done by the companies because they benefit one way or another by it. Seen from another perspective, however, the flower companies are doing the social work the state (if not the church itself) should be doing, but is not.

Conclusion

The women in Olga Sutáuta and Celia Quindío's category who have taken floriculture as their lifelong employment see their position in the flower industry as their careers. They talk about their job satisfaction and their respect for the owner, the supervisors they work for, and their fellow workers. While the loyalty of some is attached to one flower farm in particular, for the majority it is attached rather to the industry. In this sense, the results presented here are generalizable to the floriculture industry in the northern section of the Sabana. This includes the cut-flower industry located in Chía, Cajicá, Cota, La Calera, Suesca, Tabio, Tenjo, and Zipaquirá. Given the large number of farms, the large extension of the Sabana de Bogotá, and the wide variability among farms, this research cannot state that all of its findings are generalizable to all of Colombia's flower industry. What it does present are topic areas, methodologies, and above all the use of gender as an analytical category, all of which may be helpful for policy and implementation oriented work. This research shows in stark ways how categories of analysis make a difference for research results. By looking at gender and at households, not as units, but as composed of individuals with different preferences and leverage, one finds that the flower industry facilitates the breakdown of the male dominated structure of decision making, providing women with the tools to build more equitable homes.

Women like Omaira Perilla, who are more traditional and do not seek employment in the industry, demonstrate how challenges that other women pose to male domination of households permeate social expectations more generally. But her case also illustrates the enormous trial that women who belong to traditional households face ahead.

A way to understand the radical decisions of women like Celia Quindío is that they do not have access to physical assets like land. What they have as a base is themselves and the social networks they build in the area. Once migrant women who migrate without family decide to leave their town they, in effect, decide to leave everything they know, including the traditional family arrangement. They opt out of life as they know it and forge a new reality.

To study household economics in Fagua and Canelón is to examine the conflicts people are caught in between emotions, material and financial scarcity, and distribution of time. It would be misguided to state that most women are not interested in having partners. In the Muisca Flowers flower company, 60 percent of the women live with partners. But they do so with the realization that being partnered means living under unequal conditions with regard to men.

The four life stories above show the diversity in household dynamics as well as household composition. In all four the patriarchal social structure is being challenged. The pattern of change is spearheaded by women. Flower work is a desirable job for women, but not for men who only work at the flowers if they find no other employment, preferably in construction. Women seek and guard their employment at the flower companies, as working at the flower farms has meant that they ascend socially in the steep class structure of Colombian society. Being a proletarian is better than being a peasant or a maid, or an agricultural laborer in lower altitude regions. But the biggest change occurring in the region is the decision of many women to revise their definition of family and their attitude about life. Many women are deciding to focus their lives entirely in terms of work at the flower farms and in terms of their children.

Notes

1. Some geographic-specific studies on family violence in Colombia include Espinosa and Useche (1992), Wartenberg (1992), Uribe (1995), Jimeno and Roldán (1998), Moser and McIlwaine (2000).

2. Law 248 of 1995 and Law 294 of 1996 and procedural codes for applying the law: Resolution 1812 of 2002.

3. In a study of potters in La Chamba, Tolima, Ronald J. Duncan explores the relationship between gender and age and the distribution through time of household tasks (2000). In accordance with my findings, Duncan finds that as women get older,

the amount of domestic abuse they receive at the hand of husbands decreases along with the control that men have over the women's labor.

4. "In Colombia, 30 percent of women have been victims of domestic abuse, while 19 percent are victims of habitual violence at the hands of their partners" (Women in Action 1993 as cited in Lama 2000). Official statistics on rates of domestic violence, including home abandonment by the husband, are unavailable.

5. Perilla and Gachalá's third child, ten-year-old Edison, had never been to Bogotá until I took him. As we walked through the city, he compared everything to what he had seen in television. When we got back to Canelón, he complained about dizziness (looking at the buildings) and bad smells.

6. Laws against domestic abuse have been legislated in Colombia, but in practice they are punitive and do not have the victim in mind. When women report abuse to police, it is, women state, to make men pay literally and metaphorically—*para que le duela* (so that it hurts him)—as men are imposed a fine.

7. Attendance at formal religious services, including mass, is almost non-existent in Fagua and Canelón. When I asked people about their religiosity and the local church, people laughed and asked "What should we go to church for?" The evangelical church's following has increased, however. According to Manuel Castells (1998), evangelicalism actually reinforces patriarchy.

EPILOGUE

Gendered Development

The neoliberal policies that have been instituted in Latin America since the 1980s and in Colombia in full force since the 1990s have had a significant effect on the labor markets. Structural adjustment programs have been shown to significantly increase women's participation in the formal and informal labor force. The consensus remains that women have not benefited from it. Arguments point to women's marginalization in the economy, their unshifted double burden of formal and house work, and the unsubstantiated benefits women gain at the household level from their formal wage employment (Radcliffe 1999). In summary, the usual image of third world women industrial workers, viewed from a global perspective and structural analysis, is still one of exploitation.

Can the picture of the effects of structural adjustment be complete without considering the economic and household roles of both men and women prior to the neoliberal policies? What looks like exploitation from a global perspective may be seen quite differently, as a welcome individual opportunity, when viewed in the context of available alternatives. To disregard this local perspective is to ignore the reality that women are active agents, making calculated choices to promote their own wellbeing and that of their families.

Sarah Radcliffe asks, "What makes gender relations 'flexible' under processes of adjustment, crisis, and restructuring?" (1999, 196). I counter by asking, Can gender relations ever become flexible without radically changing cultural ideologies of male domination or without holding men accountable for their inflexibility at the household level? My research presented here has found that, as those traditionally having less leverage within the household, women have always been the ones doing the adjusting. That is, it is *women* who are flexible, not the "relationship." The cultural changes described here now taking place at the household level are being forged by women precisely because of their flexibility and in spite of the inflexibility of men, who have enjoyed overwhelming social, financial, political, and physical power in and outside of the household and have, therefore, never needed to be flexible in their relations with women. To fully examine the effects of structural adjustment on women, men, and gender relations, research must incorporate the cultural models at play beyond the global assembly line factory floor.

This research challenges the consensus that global assembly line industries always and systematically reinforce patriarchal relations of reproduction. My study argues that the floriculture industry in Colombia facilitates the breakdown of patriarchal marriage contracts and the male domination of households. In fact, the fresh-cut flower industry in Colombia has been instrumental in cultural changes that forge household gender equity and, outside of household partnerships, allow women to live free of domestic violence and in control of their lives. Women remain as workers for flower companies not because they are exploited. They benefit both financially and in their quality of life. While women and men alike enter the flower industry compelled by financial need, for women floriculture work in Colombia presents the best employment alternative. As in all other formal sector employment, floriculture workers receive employment-related social benefits, and within the industry their pay is no different than that of men. In addition, cut-flower work has a much higher social and salary remuneration that other work available to women in the informal sector.

Women's employment in floriculture has forced the acknowledgement of women's labor capability and their contribution as members of society. Colombia's floriculture industry consistently has hired a majority of women of a variety of ages and marital statuses. Floriculture's employment of women has generated intense social and political criticism directed against both workers and employers. Even so, the industry continues to hire women and to collaborate with its workers in the challenges they face in their daily lives.

Despite the conventional representation of global assembly line industries as extracting rather than adding value to the societies in which they operate, the floriculture industry in the region studied here is performing some of the public duties the government should perform but does not. In so doing the industry functions as a para-governmental institution serving its largely female workforce by providing education, mediating private conflicts, and lending money. Despite its global market, the management in the fresh-cut flower industry has an intimate knowledge of the people in the region gained from dealing on a daily basis with the needs of its workforce, which are the basis for the loan programs, the education seminars, and workshops provided to the workforce. An important goal of the industry has been to make people aware of the violence in the country at large and its effects upon the individual and the family. The industry has met this challenge with seminars on self-esteem, domestic violence, child abuse, and positive parenting skills. Indeed, the industry has done so, in part as described in the previous chapter, out of its own self-interest as women who are not restricted physically and abused are more able to stay on the job and be productive.

The main quality of life issues for workers are housing and education. Local government has no housing program of any kind, including low-income housing, so cut-flower companies fill the gap by administering workers' loans to buy land and materials for house construction. Because long-term loans through financial institutions or public rural credit institutions are almost non-existent, the region operates as a cash economy in which cars, land, cattle, and houses are bought with cash or informal short-term credit. The female fresh-cut flower workforce is deterred from seeking loans from formal financial institutions because two-thirds of them do not own land or housing locally that they can present as collateral. Women have an additional cultural barrier to securing credits, as rural credit institutions, accustomed to extending credit to men, are reluctant to extend it to women regardless of income, and women have no experience in dealing with banks or governmental offices to apply for credit. Instead, women workers perceive their own labor as an asset or base, a perception reinforced by being able to use that labor as collateral for credit from the companies or the employee loan funds where they work. By offering loan programs based on good faith, the social relations of production, and social networking, the floriculture industry fills in the governmental void.

The large economic and social role taken on by the flower industry as well as their silence regarding occupational health and environmental issues has subjected it to intense local criticism and backlash from government representatives of municipalities in the Sabana. Through lobbying and pressure, some towns have been successful in limiting and even decreasing the number of hectares dedicated to flower production. Paradoxically the official opposition to flower farms has, in some towns, actually accelerated the loss of land by small landowners. Inability to pay the dramatically higher property taxes resulting from their proximity to Bogotá or to support themselves through agriculture and milk and cattle production, rural inhabitants have been left with the options of selling their land or seeking employment in floriculture. Thus, in some areas like Sopó and La Calera, many small landholders (*minufundistas*) have been able to retain their land, directly or through their daughters, by earning income in the flower farms. Rather than being displaced by the industry, people use cut-flower work to maintain their socioeconomic status. This trend is also taking place between peasants and floriculture in Ecuador (Korovkin 2003).

The negative perceptions of many government officials about the industry are due in part to the industry's lack of direct aid to municipalities in the form of tax revenues and to secrecy about its use of water and chemicals. Yet while their complaints are well founded, unfortunately official resentment frequently gets couched as a gender discourse about appropriate roles for women and men, further fueling the national and international image of women being exploited by the industry. Paradoxically, the industry, by avoiding other public duties such as discussions about water and chemical use, also aids the public rethoric to be directed against women.

The complaints of several government officials from two different towns, for example, are based on an assumption of women's lower status and men's natural right to be employed. The following representative statement frames the official negative discourse about the floriculture industry and its female workforce: "*Son asentamientos de personas subnormales*" (they are shanty towns of *subnormal* people). Other phrases that fit into such discourse are: "They only hire women"; "99 percent of the workforce is female"; "To earn a salary, those women give up their quality of life"; and, "Only low class people come here to work. They are pulling us down socially." Most telling is the rhetorical question, "Why do they hire only women? Why not regular people?" The reasoning behind all of these complaints appears to be that women are abnormal which accounts for the willingness of the companies to hire them. As the logic goes, if women were normal, they would have as much status as men and either would not be hired or would not accept floriculture jobs. In short, the lower status of women reinforces the bad reputation of the industry and vice versa.

I argue that if the floriculture workforce were predominantly male, the industry would face less direct and indirect opposition from municipalities, the church, the press, and the larger culture. In fact, it would probably be heralded and promoted by the government as a source of much-needed employment, as is a beer factory located forty miles north of Bogotá that hires mostly men. In spite of the fact that this beer company also presents environmental problems and makes excessive use of water resources, it faces no opposition.

The employment it provides is culturally sanctioned because men hold those jobs, doing what they are naturally meant to do: be employed. This implies that women's employment is somehow unnatural, presumably because they do not face the same financial obligations as men, making women's employment solely a choice. The claim by government officials that women give up their quality of life for a meager salary assumes a stereotypical image of patriarchal nuclear households where men are the "breadwinners," an unrealistic perception of Colombia's political context and the quality of life faced by people, women in particular, in the countryside. In this context, the flower industry in the Sabana deserves credit for raising the perceptions of women in a culture that devalues them on a consistent basis. One might even propose that the backlash against the industry is due precisely to floriculture's positive effect on the lives of women in the region.

My results support the thesis that, from a feminist perspective, the floriculture industry in Colombia has been a catalyst for positive cultural change for women. The growth of Colombia's export business, including its connection to global processes, has provided women with new opportunities to oppose gendered patterns of domination. Whether women working in the global assembly line industries are better off in terms of human rights, labor laws, and gender discrimination must be examined within the specific cultural and historical context at both a local and a national level. Comparing labor conditions in the third world to labor conditions in Europe is unrealistic. Because the cultural and historical context is different, the meaning of work is not comparable. Work brings qualitative benefits as well as quantitative financial benefits, although the former are more difficult to measure. My research has addressed the relative and absolute benefits of global assembly line work by examining it in the context of employment alternatives, the local historical moment, and the local social structure. Furthermore, I question the claim that structural adjustment global assembly line employment imposes a double work day for women. These findings support the need to reexamine the distribution of work by gender in rural communities in Latin America. For instance, Deere and León (1987) point out that women's participation in farming is extensive at the same time that their household chore responsibilities are a major source of inequity within the household. Thus, women's double burden is not new, nor is it caused by floriculture or any other export industry in Latin America. In fact, Newman concludes that women employed in floriculture do not work more hours in both paid and unpaid work (2002, 394). This body of research must become a part in analyzing the gendered effects of structural adjustment labor employment patterns. In addition, national and international pressure on behalf of women and children could focus on gender equitable divorce, paternal responsibility laws, and effective enforcement. Such policies, if enacted, may begin to address household and family inequities that shift the reproductive role almost solely onto women's shoulders.

This investigation points to an alternative route for examining global assembly line industries. Future research would benefit from focusing on the relationship between global assembly line industries and household economic processes. Otherwise, we run the risk of merely replicating the dominant model that perceives women merely as victims to be "saved." That model denies women their agency and individuality. Furthermore, my study speaks of the importance of social context to the analysis of structural adjustment and the enactment of development programs.

At present, research on global assembly line industries and on household economics represent two separate areas of scholarly activity that, while beginning to communicate theoretically, have few practical studies focused on the links between industrial employment and intrahousehold dynamics. The two approaches, for the most part, have not been examined together in a systematic way. My research attempts to bridge those two areas by looking at the effects of employment in the household. To conduct such an examination is not possible if all the analytical categories are not differentiated by gender. To my knowledge, I am the first researcher of Latin America to ask gender-specific questions in relation to property ownership and property acquisition. The importance of who owns property and how they acquire it is already known to be a key component of development. This knowledge must inform the concrete practices of any entity involved in development work. In fact, it should be taken on by Colombia's floriculture industry itself in order to make its social development efforts more effective and visible.

I have often been asked with suspicion, Why is the industry doing all of this? What is in it for them? Clearly, floriculture industrialists are in their business, like all business people, to make a profit. Their business would not be sustainable long term if they were to ignore the social context of their workforce. Unlike industries that employ much smaller numbers of workers, the floriculture guild cannot ignore the worker's social conditions and the effects on them, both positive and negative, that floriculture work may have. The social work they do would, perhaps, be more effective if they were to incorporate gender as an analytical category in they data systems: Are women getting a fair share of loan funds in number of loans as well as total value? Are female workers as able to buy property as male workers? In addition, while the floriculture industry is open to discussing its social program, it is not as open to discussing water and chemical use as well as occupational and environmental health issues. An open forum would benefit the workers and the environment and would dispel outside suspicion.

By adopting the concepts of threat point, social assets, and base I address issues of power and gender within the household and within the global assembly line. By using complementary quantitative and qualitative methodologies I have been able to answer the larger question of what happens when workers leave the assembly line and arrive home. I have examined the relationship between work, self-esteem, wage income, property ownership, social networks, and empowerment. I have established that because women assemble flowers at work, when they go to their families they are enabled to cultivate their homes.

Bibliography

Abraham-Van der Mark, Eva. "The Impact of Industrialization on Women: A Caribbean Case." In *Women, Men, and the International Division of Labor*, ed. June Nash and María Patricia Fernández-Kelly, 374–86. Albany: State University of New York Press, 1983.

Acevedo, Luz del Alba. "Feminist Inroads in the Study of Women's Work and Development." In *Women in the Latin American Development Process*, ed. Christine Bose and Edna Acosta-Belén, 65–98. Philadelphia: Temple University Press, 1995.

Achío, Mayra, and Patricia Mora. "La Obrera Florista y la Subordinación de la Mujer." *Ciencias Sociales* 39 (1988): 47–56.

Agarwal, Bina. "'Bargaining' and Gender Relations: Within and Beyond the Household." *Feminist Economics* 3, no. 1 (1997): 1–51.

———. *A Field of One's Own: Gender and Land Rights in South Asia*. Cambridge: Cambridge University Press, 1994.

Amin, Sajeda, and Nagah H. Al-Bassusi. *Wage Work and Marriage: Perspectives of Egyptian Working Women*. Policy Research Division Working Paper 171. New York: Population Council, 2003.

Amin, Sajeda, Ian Diamond, Ruchira T. Naved, and Margaret Newby. "Transition to Adulthood of Female Garment-Factory Workers in Bangladesh." *Studies in Family Planning* 29 (1998): 185–200.

Anderson, Bridget. *Doing the Dirty Work? The Global Politics of Domestic Labour*. London: Zed Books, 2000.

Aptheker, Bettina. *Tapestries of Life: Women's Work, Women's Consciousness, and the Meaning of Daily Experience*. Amherst: University of Massachusetts Press, 1989.

Arango, Luz Gabriela. "Mujeres Obreras, Paternalismo e Endustrialización." In *El Trabajo Femenino en América Latina: Los Debates en la Década de los Noventa*, ed.

B. Bustis and G. Palacio, 271–94. Guadalajara: Universidad de Guadalajara, Instituto Latinoamericano de Servicios Legales Alternativos, 1994.

Arango, Luz Gabriela, Magdalena León, and M. Viveros. *Género e Identidad: Ensayos Sobre lo Masculino y lo Femenino*. Bogotá: TM Editores, Ediciones Uniandes, 1995.

Ardila Galvis, Constanza. *The Heart of the War in Colombia*. London: Latin American Bureau, 2000.

Arocha, Jaime. *Utopía para los Excluidos: El Multiculturalismo en Africa y América Latina*. Bogotá: Universidad Nacional de Colombia, Centro de Estudios Sociales (CES), 2004.

Asocolflores. *Cifras 2002*. Available at: <www.colombianflowers.com/info/info_cifras2002.php>. Accessed September 9, 2004a.

———. *Datos de Interes*. Available at: <www.colombianflowers.com/info/info_datosin.php>. Accessed September 9, 2004b.

———. *2001 Statistics Exports*. Available at: <www.colombianflowers.com/4000/4041.htm>. Accessed May 26, 2001.

Babb, Florence E. *Between Field and Cooking Pot: The Political Economy of Market-Women in Peru*. Austin: University of Texas Press, 1989.

Barham, Bradford, Mary Clark, Elizabeth Katz, and Rachel Schurman. "Nontraditional Agricultural Exports in Latin America: Toward an Appraisal." *Latin American Research Review* 27, no. 2 (1992): 43–82.

Barreto Gama, Juanita, and Yolanda Puyana Villamizar. *Sentí que Se Me Despredía el Alma: Análisis de Procesos y Prácticas de Socialización*. Bogotá: Indepaz, 1996.

Barrientos, Stephanie, Anna Bee, Ann Matear, and Isabel Vogel. *Women and Agribusiness: Working Miracles in the Chilean Fruit Export Sector*. New York: St. Martin's Press, 1999.

Bauer, Arnold. *The Hacienda El Huique in the Agrarian Structure of Nineteenth-Century Chile*. Berkeley: University of California, Center for Latin American Studies, 1972.

———. "The Church and Spanish American Agrarian Structures, 1765–1865." *The Americas* 28, no. 1 (1971): 78–98.

Bauer, Arnold, and Ann Hagerman Johnson. "Land and Labour in Rural Chile, 1850–1935." In *Land and Labour in Latin America*, ed. Kenneth Duncan and Ian Rutledge with the collaboration of Colin Harding, 83–102. Cambridge: Cambridge University Press, 1977.

Becker, Gary. *A Treatise on the Family*. Cambridge: Harvard University Press, 1991.

———. "A Theory of the Allocation of Time." *The Economic Journal* 75, no. 299 (1965): 493–517.

Benería, Lourdes. *Gender, Development, and Globalization: Economics as If All People Mattered*. New York: Routledge, 2003.

Benería, Lourdes, Maria Floo, Caren Grown, and Martha MacDonald. "Introduction: Globalization and Gender." *Feminist Economics* 6, no. 3 (2000): vii–xvii.

Benería, Lourdes, and Marta Roldán. *The Crossroads of Class and Gender: Industrial Homework, Subcontracting, and Household Dynamics*. Chicago: University of Chicago Press, 1987.

Ben-Porath, Yoram. "The Economic Analysis of Fertility in Israel: Point and Counterpoint." *Journal of Political Economy* 81 (1982): 202–33.

Bentley, Jeffrey. "Eating the Dead Chicken: Intrahousehold Decision Making and Emigration in Rural Portugal." In *Households: Comparative and Historical Studies of the Domestic Group*, ed. Robert Netting, Richard Wilk, and Erik Arnould, 73–90. Berkeley: University of California Press, 1984.

Berger, Peter, Brigitte Berger, and Hansfried Kellner. *The Homeless Mind: Modernization and Consciousness*. New York: Random House, 1973.

Bergmann, Barbara R. "The Economic Risks of Being a Housewife." *American Economic Review* 71, no. 2 (1981): 81–86.

Bergquist, Charles W., and Ricardo Peñaranda. *Violence in Colombia: The Contemporary Crisis in Historical Perspective*. Wilmington, DE: SR Books, 1992.

Berik, Günseli. "Mature Export-Led Growth and Gender Wage Inequality in Taiwan." *Feminist Economics* 6, no. 3 (2000): 1–26.

Blau, Francine, and Marianne Ferber, eds. *The Economics of Women, Men and Work*. Upper Saddle River, NJ: Prentice-Hall, 1992.

Blumberg, Rae Lesser. "Fairy Tales and Facts: Economy, Family, Fertility, and the Female." In *Women and World Development*, ed. Irene Tinker and Michèle Bo Bramsen, 12–21. Washington, DC: Overseas Development Council, 1976.

Bolaños, Bernando, and Hannia Rodríguez. "La Incorporación de la Mujer en el Proceso Productivo de las Flores en Costa Rica." *Ciencias Sociales* 39 (1988): 57–68.

Borah, Woodrow Wilson. *New Spain's Century of Depression*. Berkeley: University of California Press, 1951.

Bosé, Christine E., and Edna Acosta-Belén. *Women in the Latin American Development Process*. Philadelphia: Temple University Press, 1995.

Bosnak, K. "Pride of the Andes." *Supermarket Floral* (1993): 12–16.

Bourdieu, Pierre. *Distinction: A Social Critique of the Judgment of Taste*. Cambridge, MA: Harvard University Press, 1984.

Bracamonte y Sosa, Pedro. "Haciendas y Ganado en el Noroeste de Yucatán, 1800–1850." *Historia Mexicana* 37 (1988): 613–39.

Branding, David. "The Hacienda as an Investment." In *Haciendas and Plantations in Latin American History*, ed. Robert Keith, 135–40. New York: Holmes & Meier, 1977a.

———. "Hacienda Profits and Tenant Farming in the Mexican Bajio, 1700–1860." In *Land and Labour in Latin America*, ed. Kenneth Duncan and Ian Rutledge with the collaboration of Colin Harding, 23–58. Cambridge: Cambridge University Press, 1977b.

Bruce, Judith. "Homes Divided." *World Development* 17, no. 7 (1989): 979–91.

Cambio 582 (August 23–30, 2004): 36–38.

Carney, Judith, and Michael Watts. "Disciplining Women? Rice, Mechanization, and the Evolution of Mandinka Gender Relations in Senegambia." *Signs* 16, no. 4 (1991): 650–81.

Carr, Marilyn, Martha Alter Chen, and Jane Tate. "Globalization and Home-Based Workers." *Feminist Economics* 6, no. 3 (2000): 123–42.

Carrillo, Jorge, and Alberto Hernández. *Mujeres Fronterizas en la Industria Maquiladora.* Mexico City: Secretaría de Educación Pública, Centro de Estudios Fronterizos del Norte de México, 1985.

Carter, Michael, and Elizabeth Katz. "Separate Spheres and the Conjugal Contract." In *Intrahousehold Resource Allocation in Developing Countries: Models, Methods, and Policy*, ed. Lawrence Haddad, John Hoddinott, and Harold Alderman, 95–111. Baltimore: Johns Hopkins University Press, 1997.

Castells, Manuel. *La Era de la Información: Economía, Sociedad y Cultura. Vol. 2, El Poder de la Identidad.* Translated by Carmen Martínez Gimeno. Madrid: Alianza Editorial, 1998.

Chang, Grace. *Disposable Domestics: Immigrant Women Workers in the Global Economy.* Cambridge: South End Press, 2000.

Chevalier, François. *Land and Society in Colonial Mexico: The Great Hacienda.* Berkeley: University of California Press, 1966.

———. *La Formation des Grands Domains au Mexique: Terre et Société aux XVIe–XVIIe Siècles.* Paris: Institut d'Ethnologie, 1952.

Chía, Alcaldía Municipal de. *Plan de Ordenamiento Territorial, Municipio de Chía.* Technical Report. Bogotá: Universidad Nacional de Colombia, 2000.

Clark, Gracia. *Onions Are My Husband: Survival and Accumulation by West African Market Women.* Chicago: University of Chicago Press, 1994.

Colen, Shellee. "'Like a Mother to Them': Stratified Reproduction and West Indian Childcare Workers and Employers in New York." In *Conceiving the New World Order: The Global Politics of Reproduction*, ed. Faye D. Ginsburg and Rayna Rapp, 78–102. Durham, NC: Duke University Press, 1995.

Constable, Nicole. *Maid to Order in Hong Kong: Stories of Filipina Workers.* Ithaca, NY: Cornell University Press, 1997.

Cravey, Altha J. *Women and Work in Mexico's Maquiladoras.* Lanham, Md.: Rowman and Littlefield, 1998.

Cubides, Fernando. "Los Paramilitares y Su Estrategia." In *Reconocer la Guerra para Construir la Paz*, ed. María Victoria Llorente and Malcolm D. Deas, 151–200. Bogotá: Cerec, Ediciones Uniandes, Grupo Editorial Norma, 1999.

Cushner, Nicholas P. *Lords of the Land: Sugar, Wine and Jesuit Estates of Coastal Peru, 1600–1767.* Albany: State University of New York Press, 1980.

Deas, Malcolm. "A Colombian Coffee Estate: Santa Barbara, Cundinamarca, 1870–1912." In *Land and Labor in Latin America*, ed. Kenneth Duncan and Ian Rutledge with the collaboration of Colin Harding. Cambridge: Cambridge University Press, 1977.

Deere, Carmen Diana. "What Differences Does Gender Make? Rethinking Peasant Studies." *Feminist Economics* 1, no. 1 (1995): 53–72.

Deere, Carmen Diana, and Magdalena León. "The Gender Asset Gap: Land in Latin America." *World Development* 31, no. 6 (2003): 925–47.

———. *Género, Propiedad y Empoderamiento: Tierra, Estado y Mercado en América Latina*. Bogotá: Tercer Mundo, 2000.

———, eds. *Rural Women and State Policy: Feminist Perspectives on Latin American Agricultural Development*. Boulder and London: Westview Press, 1987.

———. *Women in Andean Agriculture: Peasant Production and Rural Wage Employment in Colombia and Peru*. Geneva: International Labour Office, 1982.

Departamento Administrativo Nacional de Estadística (DANE). *Encuesta Nacional de Hogares Diciembre de 2000*. Bogotá: Departamento Nacional de Estadística, 2004. Available at: <www.dane.gov.co/inf_est/empleo.htm>. Accessed September 28, 2004.

———. *Evidencia Reciente del Comportamiento de la Migración Interna en Colombia a partir de la Encuesta Continua de Hogares*. Bogotá: Departamento Nacional de Estadística, 2003.

———. *Censo: República de Colombia*. Bogotá: Departamento Nacional de Estadística, 1993.

Díaz, Maritza, Humberto Rojas, María Cristina Salazar, and Gabriel Rueda. *Trabajo de Niños y Jóvenes en la Floricultura en el Municipio de Madrid, Cundinamarca*. La Floricultura en la Sabana de Bogotá. Proyecto Piloto en el Municipio de Madrid, Cundinamarca, Technical Report 5. Bogotá: Universidad Nacional de Colombia, Centro de Estudios Sociales, 1995.

Díaz, Maritza, and Patricia Sierra. *Dinámica Sociocultural Comunidad, Género y Familia*. La Floricultura en la Sabana de Bogotá. Proyecto Piloto en el Municipio de Madrid, Cundinamarca, Technical Report 2.2. Bogotá: Universidad Nacional de Colombia, Centro de Estudios Sociales, 1995.

Dombois, Rainer, and Carmen Marina López P., eds. *Cambio Técnico, Empleo y Trabajo en Colombia: Aportes a los Estudios Laborales en el VIII Congreso de Sociología*. Bogotá: Fescol, 1993.

Doss, Cheryl. "The Effects of Women's Bargaining Power in Household Health and Education Outcomes: Evidence from Ghana." Williamstown, MA: Williams College, 1997.

———. *Do Households Fully Share Risk? Evidence From Ghana*. St. Paul: University of Minnesota, Department of Applied Economics, Staff Paper Series, 1996a.

———. *Women's Bargaining Power in Household Decisions: Evidence from Ghana*. St. Paul: University of Minnesota, Department of Applied Economics, Staff Paper Series, 1996b.

———. "Testing among Models of Intrahousehold Resource Allocation." *World Development* 24, no. 10 (1996c): 1597–609.

Douglas, A. Irwin. "Antidumping: How It Works and Who Gets Hurt." *Journal of Economic Literature* 32, no. 3 (1994): 1,243–44.

Drori, Israel. *The Seam Line: Arab Workers and Jewish Managers in the Israeli Textile Industry*. Stanford, CA: Stanford University Press, 2000.

Duncan, Kenneth, and Ian Rutledge, eds. *Land and Labour in Latin America: Essays on the Development of Agrarian Capitalism in the Nineteenth and Twentieth Centuries*. Cambridge: Cambridge University Press, 1977.

Duncan, Ronald J. *Crafts, Capitalism, and Women: The Potters of La Chamba, Colombia*. Gainesville: University Press of Florida, 2000.

———. "The Economics of Crafts among Home-Based Workers: The Women Potters of La Chamba, Colombia." *Research in Economic Anthropology* 20 (1999): 197–219.

———. *The Ceramics of Ráquira, Colombia: Gender, Work, and Economic Change*. Gainesville: University Press of Florida, 1998.

Dwyer, Daisy Hilse, and Judith Bruce, eds. *A Home Divided: Women and Income in the Third World*. Stanford, CA: Stanford University Press, 1988.

Ehlers, Tracy Bachrach. *Silent Looms: Women and Production in a Guatemalan Town*. Boulder, CO: Westview Press, 1990.

Ehrenreich, Barbara, and Annette Fuentes. "Life on the Global Assembly Line." *Ms. Magazine* (1981): 53–71.

Ehrenreich, Barbara, and Arlie Russell Hochschild. *Global Woman: Nannies, Maids, and Sex Workers in the New Economy*. New York: Metropolitan Books, 2003.

Elson, Diane, ed. *Male Bias in the Development Process*. Manchester: Manchester University Press, 1995.

England, Paula. "The Separative Self: Androcentric Bias in Neoclassical Assumptions." In *Beyond Economic Man*, ed. Julie Nelson and Marianne Ferber, 37–53. Chicago: University of Chicago Press, 1993.

England, Paula, and George Farkas. *Households, Employment, and Gender: A Social, Economic, and Demographic View*. New York: Aldine, 1986.

Enloe, Cynthia. *Bananas, Beaches and Bases: Making Feminist Sense of International Politics*. Berkeley: University of California Press, 1989.

———. "Women Textile Workers in the Militarization of South-East Asia." In *Women, Men and the International Division of Labor*, ed. June Nash and María Patricia Fernández-Kelly, 407–25. Albany: State University of New York Press, 1983.

Escobar, Arturo. *Encountering Development: The Making and Unmaking of the Third World*. Princeton, NJ: Princeton University Press, 1995.

Espinosa, Mario, and Helena Useche. *Abriendo Camino: Historias de Mujeres*. Bogotá: Ecoe, 1992.

Fairbanks, Michael, and Stace Lindsay. *Plowing the Sea: Nurturing the Hidden Sources of Growth in the Developing World*. Boston: Harvard Business School Press, 1997.

Falchetti, Ana María, and Clemencia Plazas. *El Territorio de los Muiscas a la Llegada de los Españoles*. Bogotá: Universidad de los Andes, 1973.

Fals Borda, Orlando. *People's Participation: Challenges Ahead*. New York: Apex Press, 1998.

———. *El Hombre y la Tierra en Boyacá: Desarrollo Histórico de una Sociedad Minifundista*. Bogotá: Tercer Mundo, 1979.

———. *Campesinos de los Andes*. Bogotá: Universidad Nacional, 1961.

Feldman, Shelley. "Exploring Theories of Patriarchy: a Perspective from Contemporary Bangladesh." *Signs* 26, no. 4 (2001): 1,097–127.

Ferber, Marianne A., and Bonnie G. Birnbaum. "The New Home Economics": Retrospects and Prospects. *Journal of Consumer Research* 4, no. 1 (1977): 19–28.

Fernández-Kelly, María Patricia. *For We Are Sold, I and My People: Women and Industry in Mexico's Frontier*. Albany: State University of New York Press, 1983.

Finger, J. Michael, and Nellie T. Artis, eds. *Antidumping: How It Works and Who Gets Hurt*. Ann Arbor: University of Michigan Press, 1993.

Florescano, Enrique. "The Problem of Hacienda Markets." In *Haciendas and Plantations in Latin American History*, ed. Robert Keith, 129–34. New York: Holmes & Meier, 1977.

Folbre, Nancy. *Who Pays for the Kids? Gender and the Structures of Constraint*. London: Routledge, 1994.

———. "The Unproductive Housewife: Her Evolution in Nineteenth-Century Economic Thought." *Signs* 16, no. 3 (1991): 463–84.

———. "The Black of Four Hearts: Towards a New Paradigm of Household Economics." In *A Home Divided: Women and Income in the Third World*, ed. Daisy Dwyer and Judith Bruce, 248–62. Stanford, CA: Stanford University Press, 1988.

Fossum, M. T. *Marketing Facts for Floriculture*. Washington, DC: Society of American Florists, 1973. Quoted in Catherine Ziegler. "Favored Flowers: Culture and Markets in a Global Commodity Chain." Ph.D. diss., New School University, 2004.

Foucault, Michel. *Discipline and Punish: The Birth of the Prison*. Translated by Alan Sheridan. New York: Pantheon Books, 1977.

Frankenberg, Elizabeth, and Duncan Thomas. *Measuring Power*. Food Consumption and Nutrition Division Discussion Paper 113. Washington, DC: International Food Policy Research Institute, 2001.

Freeman, Carla. *High Tech and High Heels in the Global Economy: Women, Work and Pink-Collar Identities in the Caribbean*. Durham, NC: Duke University Press, 2000.

———. "Femininity and Flexible Labor: Fashioning Class through Gender on the Global Assembly Line." *Critique of Anthropology* 18 (1998): 245–62.

———. "Designing Women: Corporate Discipline and Barbados's Off-Shore Pink-Collar Sector." *Cultural Anthropology* 8, no. 2 (1993): 169–86.

Friedemann-Sánchez, Greta. "Assets in Intrahousehold Bargaining among Women Workers in Colombia's Cut-Flower Industry." *Feminist Economics* 12, nos. 1–2 (2006): 247–69.

———. *Challenging Patriarchy in the Transnational Floriculture Industry: Household Economics, Identity and Gender in Colombia*. Ph.D. diss., University of Minnesota, 2002.

———. *The Self-Regulation of the Fresh-Cut Flower Industry in Colombia*. Master's thesis, University of Minnesota, 1999.

———. *Modernización en Saucío*. Tesis de Licenciatura, Universidad de los Andes, 1990.

Fuentes, Annette, and Barbara Ehrenreich. *Women in the Global Factory*. New York: South End Press, 1983.

Fussell, Elizabeth. "Making Labor Flexible: The Recomposition of Tijuana's Maquiladora Female Labor Force." *Feminist Economics* 6, no. 3 (2000): 59–79.

Gamburd, Michele Ruth. *The Kitchen Spoon's Handle: Transnationalism and Sri Lanka's Migrant Housemaids*. Ithaca, NY: Cornell University Press, 2000.

———. *The Aztecs Under Spanish Rule: A History of the Indians of the Valley of Mexico, 1519–1810*. Stanford, CA: Stanford University Press, 1964.

Geertz, Clifford. *Local Knowledge: Further Essays in Interpretive Anthropology*. New York: Basic Books, 1983.

Gladden, Kathleen. "La Reestructuración Industrial, el Subcontrato y la Incorporación de la Fuerza de Trabajo Femenina en Colombia." In *Cambio Técnico, Empleo y Trabajo en Colombia*, ed. Rainer Dombois and Carmen Marina López, 321–40. Bogotá: Fescol, 1993.

Grasmuck, Sherri, and Rosario Espinal. "Market Success or Female Autonomy? Income, Ideology, and Empowerment among Microentrepreneurs in the Dominican Republic." *Gender and Society* 14, no. 2 (2000): 231–55.

Grimes, Kimberly M., and B. Lynne Milgram. *Artisans and Cooperatives: Developing Alternative Trade for the Global Economy*. Tucson: University of Arizona Press, 2000.

Gringeri, Christina E. *Getting By: Women Homeworkers and Rural Economic Development*. Lawrence: University Press of Kansas, 1994.

Gronau, Reuben. "The Effect of Children on the Housewives' Value of Time." *Journal of Political Economy* 81, no. 2, part 2 (March–April 1973): S168–99.

Grossman, Rachael. "Women's Place in the Integrated Circuit." In *Southeast Asia Chronicle and Pacific Research* 9 (1979): 2–17.

Gudeman, Stephen. *The Anthropology of Economics*. Oxford: Blackwell, 2001.

———. *Economics as Culture: Models and Metaphors of Livelihood*. London: Routledge, 1986.

Gudeman, Stephen, and Alberto Rivera. *Conversations in Colombia: The Domestic Economy in Life and Text*. Cambridge: Cambridge University Press, 1990.

Guyer, Jane. "Endowments and Assets: The Anthropology of Wealth and the Economics of Intrahousehold Allocation." In *Intrahousehold Resource Allocation in Developing Countries: Models, Methods, and Policy*, ed. Lawrence Haddad, John Hoddinott, and Harold Alderman, 112–26. Baltimore: Johns Hopkins University Press, 1997.

Gwynne, Robert, and Cristobal Kay. "Views from the Periphery: Futures of Neoliberalism in Latin America." *Third World Quarterly* 21, no. 1 (2000): 141–56.

Haddad, Lawrence, John Hoddinott, and Harold Alderman, eds. *Intrahousehold Resource Allocation in Developing Countries: Models, Methods, and Policy*. Baltimore: Johns Hopkins University Press, 1997.

Hammel, Eugene A. "On the *** of Studying Household Form and Function." In *Households: Comparative and Historical Studies of the Domestic Group*, ed. Robert Netting, Richard Wilk, and Erik Arnould, 29–43. Berkeley: University of California Press, 1984.

Hart, Gillian. "From 'Rotten Wives' to 'Good Mothers': Household Models and the Limits of Economism." *IDS Bulletin* 28, no. 3 (1997): 14–25.

———. "Imagined Unities: Constructions of the 'Household' in Economic Theory." In *Understanding Economic Process*, ed. Sutti Ortiz and Susan Lees, 111–30. Lanham, MD: University Press of America, 1992.

Hirschman, Albert O. *Exit, Voice, and Loyalty*. Cambridge, MA: Harvard University Press, 1970.

Hoddinott, John, and Lawrence Haddad. *Household Expenditures, Child Anthropometric Status, and the Intrahousehold Division of Income: Evidence from the Côte d'Ivoire*. Research Program in Development Studies Discussion Paper 155. Princeton, NJ: Woodrow Wilson School of Public and International Affairs, Princeton University, 1991.

Hondagneu-Sotelo, Pierrette. *Domestica: Immigrant Workers Cleaning and Caring in the Shadows of Affluence*. Berkeley: University of California Press, 2001.

———. *Gendered Transitions: Mexican Experiences of Immigration*. Berkeley: University of California Press, 1994.

Hoodfar, Homa. "Household Budgeting and Financial Management in a Lower-Income Cairo Neighborhood." In *A Home Divided: Women and Income in the Third World*, ed. Daisy Dwyer and Judith Bruce, 120–42. Stanford, CA: Stanford University Press, 1988.

Hoyos, Maria Cristina. *La Movilidad de las Poblaciones y su Impacto Sobre la Dinámica del Area Metropolitana de Bogotá. Documento de Trabajo 5: Metodología y Resultados de la Encuesta Cualitativa.* Bogotá: Centro de Estudios de Desarrollo Económico (CEDE), 1996.

Human Rights Watch. *2002 World Report*. Available at: <www.hrw.org/wr2k2/americas4.html>. Accessed October 4, 2004.

———. *2001 Beyond Negotiation: International Humanitarian Law and Its Application to the Conduct of FARC-EP*. Report 13, no. 3B. Available at: <www.hrw.org/reports/2001/farc/>. Accessed October 4, 2004.

———. *2000 World Report, Colombia*. Available at: <www.hrw.org/wr2k1/americas/colombia.html>. Accessed October 4, 2004.

———. *1998 World Report, Colombia*. Available at: <www.hrw.org/wr2k/americas-03.html>. Accessed November 2, 2003.

Jaramillo Agudelo, Darío. *La Nueva Historia de Colombia*. Bogotá: Instituto Colombiano de Cultura, Subdirección de Comunicaciones Culturales, 1976.

Jimeno, Myriam, and Ismael Roldán. *Violencia Cotidiana en la Sociedad Rural: En una Mano el Pan y en la Otra el Rejo*. Bogotá: Universidad Sergio Arboleda, Universidad Nacional de Colombia, 1998.

Kabeer, Naila. "Globalization, Labor Standards, and Women's Rights: Dilemmas of Collective (In)Action in an Interdependent World." *Feminist Economics* 10, no. 1 (2004): 3–35.

———. *The Power to Choose: Bangladeshi Women and Labour Market Decisions in London and Dhaka*. London and New York: Verso, 2000.

———. "Tactics and Trade-Offs: Revisiting the Links between Gender and Poverty." *IDS Bulletin* 28, no. 3 (1997): 1–13.

Kaufman, Leslie, and David Gonzalez. "Labor Progress Clashes with Global Reality." *New York Times*, April 24, 2001: A1, A10.

Kay, Cristobal. *Latin American Theories of Development and Underdevelopment*. London: Routledge, 1989.

———. "The Development of the Chile Hacienda System, 1850–1973." In *Land and Labour in Latin America*, ed. Kenneth Duncan and Ian Rutledge with the collaboration of Colin Harding, 103–40. Cambridge: Cambridge University Press, 1977.

Keith, Robert G, ed. *Conquest and Agrarian Change: The Emergence of the Hacienda System on the Peruvian Coast*. Cambridge: Harvard University Press, 1976.

Kennedy, Eileen. "Income Sources of the Rural Poor in Southwestern Kenya." In *Income Sources of Malnourished People in Rural Areas: Microlevel Information and Policy Implications*. Working Paper on Commercialization of Agriculture and Nutrition 5, eds. Joachim von Braun and Rajul Pandya-Lorch. Washington, DC: International Food Policy Research Institute, 1991.

Kim, Seung-Kyung. *Class Struggle or Family Struggle? The Lives of Women Factory Workers in South Korea*. Cambridge: Cambridge University Press, 1997.

Knight, Alan S. "Mexican Peonage: What Was It? And Why Was It?" *Journal of Latin American Studies* 18, no. 1 (1986): 41–74.

Korovkin, Tanya. "Cut-Flower Exports, Female Labor, and Community Participation in Highland Ecuador." *Latin American Perspectives* 30, no. 4 (2003): 18–42.

Lama, Abraham. *Domestic Abuse Still Rampant Despite New Laws*. Interpress Third World News Agency. Article 109933, World History Archives, Hartford Web Publishing, 2000. Available at: <www.hartford-hwp.com/archives/40/172.html>. Accessed Nov 2, 2003.

Leacock, Eleanor B., and Helen I. Safa, eds. *Women's Work: Development and the Division of Labor by Gender*. New York: Bergin & Garvey, 1986.

Leal Buitrago, Francisco. *El Oficio de la Guerra: La Seguridad Nacional en Colombia*. Bogotá: IEPRI, TM Editores, 1994.

Lee, Ching Kwan. *Gender and the South China Miracle: Two Worlds of Factory Women*. Berkeley: University of California Press, 1998.

Lim, Linda. "Women's Work in Export Factories: The Politics of a Cause." In *Persistent Inequalities*, ed. Irene Tinker, 101–19. New York: Oxford University Press, 1990.

Llorente, María Victoria, and Malcolm D. Deas. *Reconocer la Guerra para Construir la Paz*. Bogotá: Cerec, Ediciones Uniandes, Grupo Editorial Norma, 1999.

Lockhart, James. "Encomienda and Hacienda: The Evolution of the Great Estate in the Spanish Indies." *Hispanic American Historical Review* 49, no. 3 (1969): 411–29.

Louie, Miriam Ching Yoon. *Sweatshop Warriors: Immigrant Women Workers Take On the Global Factory*. Cambridge: South End Press, 2001.

Lundberg, Shelly, and Robert A. Pollack. "Separate Spheres Bargaining and the Marriage Market." *Journal of Political Economy* 101, no. 6 (1993): 988–1,010.

MacLeod, Murdo J. "Historia Socio-Económica de la América Central Española." Translated by Irene Piedra Santa. *Mesoamérica (USA)* 5, no. 7 (1984): 185–87.

Maharaj, Niala, and Gaston Dorren. *The Game of the Rose: The Third World in the Global Flower Trade*. Amsterdam: International Books, 1995.

Manser, Marilyn E., and Murray Brown. "Marriage and Household Decision-Making: A Bargaining Analysis." *International Economic Review* 21, no. 1 (1980): 31–44.

Martínez Alier, Juan. *Haciendas, Plantations, and Collective Farms: Agrarian Class Societies, Cuba and Peru*. London: F. Cass, 1977.

———. *Los Huaccilleros del Peru*. Paris: Ruedo Iberico, 1973.

Mascia-Lees, Frances E., and Nancy Johnson Black. *Gender and Anthropology*. Prospect Heights, IL: Waveland Press, 2000.

Massey, Douglas S. "Economic Development and International Migration in Comparative Perspective." *Population and Development Review* 14, no. 3 (1988): 383–413.

McCann, Carole R., and Seung-Kyung Kim. *Feminist Theory Reader: Local and Global Perspectives*. New York: Routledge, 2003.

McElroy, Marjorie B., and Mary Jean Horney. "Nash-Bargained Household Decisions: Towards a Generalization of the Theory of Demand." *International Economic Review* 22, no. 2 (1981): 333–49.

Medrano, Diana. "Desarrollo y Explotación de la Mujer: Efectos de la Proletarización Femenina en la Agroindustria de las Flores en la Sabana de Bogotá." In *La Realidad Colombiana: Debate Sobre la Mujer en América Latina y el Caribe*, ed. Magdalena León, 43–55. Bogotá: ACEP, 1982.

———. *Efectos del Proceso de Cambio sobre la Condición de la Mujer Rural: El Caso de las Obreras Floristas de la Agroindustria Exportadora de Flores de la Sabana de Bogotá*. Bogotá: Organizacion Internacional del Trabajo, 1981.

Medrano, Diana, and Rodrigo Villar. *Problemas de Salud y Trabajo en los Cultivos de Flores de la Sabana de Bogotá: La Visión de las Mujeres Trabajadoras en Torno a su Situación*. Bogotá: Universidad de los Andes, 1983.

Meier, Verena. "Cut-Flower Production in Colombia—A Major Development Success Story for Women?" *Environment and Planning* A 31, no. 2 (1999): 273–89.

Mena, Norma. *Impacto de la Floricultura en los Campesinos de Cayambe*. Quito: Instituto de Ecología y Desarrollo de las Comunidades Andinas, 1999.

Méndez, José A. "The Development of the Colombian Cut Flower Industry: A Textbook Example of How a Market Economy Works." In *Antidumping: How It Works and Who Gets Hurt*, ed. J. Michael Finger and Nellie T. Artis, 103–20. Ann Arbor: University of Michigan Press, 1993.

———. *The Development of the Colombian Cut-Flower Industry*. Trade Policy Working Paper 660. Washington, DC: World Bank, Country Economics Department, 1991.

Mies, Maria. *Patriarchy and Accumulation on a World Scale*. London: Zed Books, 1986.

———. *The Lace Makers of Narsapur: Indian Housewives Produce for the World Market*. London: Zed Press, 1982.

Milgram, B. Lynne. "Operationalizing Microfinance: Women and Craftwork in Ifugao, Upland Philippines." *Human Organization* 60, no. 3 (2001): 212–24.

Mills, Mary Beth. "Gender and Inequality in the Global Labor Force." *Annual Review of Anthropology* 32, no. 1 (2003): 41–62.

———. *Thai Women in the Global Labor Force: Consuming Desires, Contested Selves*. Piscataway, NJ: Rutgers University Press, 1999.

Mitter, Swasti. *Common Fate, Common Bond: Women in the Global Economy*. London: Pluto, 1986.

Mörner, Magnus. "The Rural Economy and Society of Colonial Spanish South America." In *Cambridge History of Latin America, vol. 2*, ed. Leslie Bethell, 189–217. Cambridge: Cambridge University Press, 1984.

———. "The Spanish American Hacienda: A Survey of Recent Research and Debate." *Hispanic American Historical Review* 53, no. 2 (1973): 186–216.

Moser, Caroline, and Cathy McIlwaine. *Urban Poor Perceptions of Violence and Exclusion in Colombia*. Washington, DC: World Bank, 2000.

Nash, June, and María Patricia Fernández-Kelly. *Women, Men and the International Division of Labor*. Albany: State University of New York Press, 1983.

Netting, Robert McC. "Smallholders, Householders, Freeholders: Why the Family Farm Works Well Worldwide." In *The Household Economy: Reconsidering the Domestic Mode of Production*, ed. Richard Wilk, 221–44. Boulder, CO: Westview Press, 1989.

Newman, Constance. "Gender, Time Use, and Change: The Impact of the Cut Flower Industry in Ecuador." *The World Bank Economic Review* 16, no. 3 (2002): 375–96.

Newman, Constance, Pilar Larreamendy, and Ana Maria Maldonado. *Mujeres y Floricultura: Cambios y Consequencias en el Hogar*. Quito: Ediciones Abya-Yala.

Oman, Charles P., and Ganeshan Wignaraja. *The Postwar Evolution of Development Thinking*. New York: St. Martin's Press, 1991.

Ong, Aiwa. *Spirits of Resistance and Capitalist Discipline: Factory Women in Malaysia*. Albany: State University of New York, 1987.

Palacios, Marco. *De Populistas, Mandarines y Violencias: Luchas por el Poder*. Bogotá: Editorial Planeta Colombiana, Temas de Hoy, 2001.

———. *Entre la Legitimidad y la Violencia: Colombia 1875–1994*. Colombia: Grupo Editorial Norma, 1995.

Panopoulou, Panagiota. *Health Insurance and the Use of Health Care Services: The Case of Colombia after the Reform of 1993*. Ph.D. diss, University of Sussex, 2002.

Parreñas, Rhacel Salazar. *Servants of Globalization: Women, Migration and Domestic Work*. Stanford, CA: Stanford University, 2001.

Peña, Devon G. *The Terror of the Machine: Technology, Work, Gender and Ecology on the U.S.-Mexico Border*. Austin: University of Texas, Center for Mexican American Studies, 1997.

Peña, P. "Home Based Workers in the Garment Industry of Mérida, Yucatán, Mexico." *Latinamericanist* 25, no. 2 (1989): 1–5.

Pfeiffer, James. "Cash Income, Intrahousehold Cooperative Conflict, and Child Health in Central Mozambique." *Medical Anthropology* 22, no. 2 (2003): 87–130.

Phillips, Lynne, ed. *Dissecting Globalization: Women's Space-Time in the Other America*. Westport: Bergin & Garvey, 1998.

Pollak, Robert A. "A Transaction Cost Approach to Families and Households." *Journal of Economic Literature* 23 (1985): 581–608.

Polo y La Borda, Jorge. "Pachachaca, una Hacienda Feudal: Autoabastecimiento y Comercialización." In *Hacienda, Comercio, Fiscalidad y Luchas Sociales (Peru*

Colonial), ed. Javier Tord and Carlos Lazo, 9–84. Peru: Biblioteca Peruana de Historia, Economia y Sociedad, 1981.

Prebisch, Raúl. *Raul Prebisch and Development Strategy*. New Delhi: Research and Information System for the Non-Aligned and Other Developing Countries, 1987.

Price, John. "Regional Trends. 'Leaving on a Jet Plane': Migration in Modern Latin America." *Tendencias, InfoAmericas Latin American Market Report* (2001): 1–4. Available at: <www.tendencias.infoamericas.com/article_archive/2001/0601/0601_regional_trends.htm>. Accessed September 27, 2004.

Proyect, Louis. "Too Many Colombians or Too Many Flowers?" *The Baltimore Sun*, 1999. Available at <www.csf.colorado.edu/mail/ppn/99/msg00056.html>. Accessed: January 7, 2002.

Quisumbing, Agnes R. "Intergenerational Transfers in Philippine Rice Villages: Gender Differences in Traditional Inheritance Customs." *Journal of Development Economics* 43, no. 2 (1994): 167–95.

Quisumbing, Agnes R., and Bénédicte de la Brière. *Women's Assets and Intrahousehold Allocation in Rural Bangladesh: Testing Measures of Bargaining Power*. Food Consumption and Nutrition Division Discussion Paper 86. Washington, DC: International Food Policy Research Institute, 2000.

Quisumbing, Agnes R., and John A. Maluccio. *Intrahousehold Allocation and Gender Relations: New Empirical Evidence from Four Developing Countries*. Food Consumption and Nutrition Division Discussion Paper 84. Washington, DC: International Food Policy Research Institute, 2000.

Radcliffe, S. A. "Latina Labour: Restructuring of Work and Renegotiations of Gender Relations in Contemporary Latin America." *Environment and Planning* A 31, no. 2 (1999): 196–208.

Rahman, Rushidan I. *Impact of Grameen Bank on the Situation of Poor Rural Women*. Working Paper 1. Dhaka: Bangladesh Institute of Development Studies, Agriculture and Rural Development Division, 1986.

Raynolds, Laura T. "Wages for Wives: Renegotiating Gender and Production Relations in Contract Farming in the Dominican Republic." *World Development* 30, no. 5 (2002): 783–98.

———. "Harnessng Women's Work: Restructuring Agricultural and Industrial Labor Forces in the Dominican Republic. *Economic Geography* 74, no. 2 (1998): 149–69.

Reis, Bettina, Patricia Sierra, and Cruz Emilia Rangel. *Aspectos Relacionados con las Formas de Contratación en el Sector de la Floricultura: El Auge de las Empresas de Servicios Temporales*. Technical Report 6. Bogotá: Universidad Nacional de Colombia, Centro de Estudios Sociales, 1995.

Reyes, Alejandro. "Compra de Tierras por Narcotraficantes." In *Drogas Ilicitas en Colombia: Su Impacto Económico, Político y Social*, ed. Francisco E. Thoumi. Bogotá: Editorial Ariel, 1997.

Roberts, Glenda Susan. *Staying on the Line: Blue-Collar Women in Contemporary Japan*. Honolulu: University of Hawaii Press, 1994.

Roldán, Marta. "Renegotiating the Marital Contract: Intrahousehold Patterns of Money Allocation and Women's Subordination among Domestic Outworkers in Mexico City." In *A Home Divided: Women and Income in the Third World*, ed. Daisy Dwyer and Judith Bruce, 229–62. Stanford, CA: Stanford University Press, 1988.

Romero, Mary. *Maid in the U.S.A.* New York: Routledge, 1992.

Rozario, S. "Development and Rural Women in South Asia: The Limits of Empowerment and Conscientization." *Bulletin of Concerned Asian Scholars* 29 (1997): 45–53.

Safa, Helen. "Free Markets and the Marriage Market: Structural Adjustment, Gender Relations, and Working Conditions among Dominican Women Workers." *Environment and Planning* A 31, no. 2 (1999): 291–304.

———. *The Myth of the Male Breadwinner: Women and Industrialization in the Caribbean*. Boulder, CO: Westview Press, 1995a.

———. "Economic Restructuring and Gender Subordination." *Latin American Perspectives* 22, no. 2 (1995b): 32–50.

———. "Women and Industrialization in the Caribbean." In *Women, Employment and the Family in the International Division of Labour*, ed. Sharon Stichter and Jane L. Parpart. Philadelphia: Temple University Press, 1990.

———. "Runaway Shops and Female Employment: The Search for Cheap Labor." *Women's Work*, ed. Eleanor Leacock and Helen I. Safa, 58–71. New York: Bergin & Garvey, 1986.

———. "Las Maquiladoras y el Empleo Femenino: La Busqueda de Trabajo Barato." In *Sociedad, Subordinacion y Feminismo*, ed. Magdalena Leon, 107–19. Bogotá: ACEP, 1982.

Safford, Frank, and Marco Palacios. *Colombia: Fragmented Land, Divided Society*. New York: Oxford University Press, 2002.

Salazar, María Cristina. "Informe, Evaluación, y Algunos Resultados del Proyecto." In *La Floricultura en la Sabana de Bogotá. Proyecto Piloto en el Municipio de Madrid, Cundinamarca*. Introduction. Bogotá: Universidad Nacional de Colombia, Centro de Estudios Sociales (CES), 1995.

Sarmiento Gómez, Alfredo, Lucía Mina Rosero, Carlos Alonso Malaver, and Sandra Álvarez Toro. *Colombia: Human Development Progress towards the Millenium Development Goals*. Background papers report for HDR 2003. New York: United Nations Development Programme, Human Development Office, 2003.

Schwede, Laurel, and Hanna Papanek. "Women Are Good with Money: Earning and Managing in an Indonesian City." In *A Home Divided: Women and Income in the Third World*, ed. Daisy Dwyer and Judith Bruce. Stanford, CA: Stanford University Press, 1988.

Scott, James C. *Domination and the Arts of Resistance*. New Haven, CT: Yale University Press, 1990.

Seligman, L. J., ed. *Women Traders in Cross-Cultural Perspective: Mediating Identities, Marketing Wares*. Stanford, CA: Stanford University Press, 2001.

Sen, Amartya. "Gender and Cooperative Conflicts." In *Persistent Inequalities*, ed. Irene Tinker, 123–49. New York: Oxford University Press, 1990.

Shanin, Teodor. "Introduction." In *Peasants and Peasant Societies*, ed. Teodor Shanin. London: Penguin, 1971.

Silva, Alicia Eugenia. "De Mujer Campesina a Obrera Florista." In *La Realidad Colombiana: Debate Sobre la Mujer en América Latina y el Caribe*, ed. Magdalena León, 28–42. Bogotá: ACEP, 1982.

Silva, Marta, director. *Mujeres y Flores*. Bogotá: Documentary Video Studio, 1985.

Sklair, Leslie. *Assembling for Development: The Maquila Industry in Mexico and the United States*. Boston: Unwin Hyman, 1989.

South, Robert. "Transnational 'Maquiladora' Location." *Annals of the Association of American Geographers* 80, no. 4 (1990): 549–70.

Standing, Guy. "Global Feminization through Flexible Labor." *World Development* 17, no. 7 (1989): 1,077–95.

Stichter, Sharon, and Jane L. Parpart. *Women, Employment, and the Family in the International Division of Labour*. Philadelphia: Temple University Press, 1990.

Stoddard, Ellwyn R. *Maquila: Assembly Plants in Northern Mexico*. El Paso: University of Texas, 1987.

Suescún-Monroy, Armando. *La Economía Chibcha*. Bogotá: Ediciones Trecer Mundo, 1987.

Tiano, Susan. "From Victims to Agents: A New Generation of Literature on Women in Latin America." *Latin American Research Review* 36, no. 3 (2001): 183–203.

———. *Patriarchy on the Line: Labor, Gender and Ideology in the Mexican Maquila Industry*. Philadelphia: Temple University Press, 1994.

———. "Maquiladora Women: A New Category of Workers?" In *Women Workers and Global Restructuring*, ed. Kathryn Ward, 193–220. Ithaca, NY: ILR Press, 1990.

Tinker, Irene, ed. *Persistent Inequalities*. New York: Oxford University Press, 1990.

———. "The Adverse Impact of Development on Women." In *Women and World Development*, ed. Irene Tinker and Michèle Bo Bramsen, 22–34. Washington, DC: Overseas Development Council, 1976.

Tirado Mejía, Álvaro, dir. *Historia Política desde 1986: Vol. 7, Nueva Historia de Colombia*. Bogotá: Planeta Colombiana Editorial, 1998 [1989].

Todaro, Michael. *Economic Development in the Third World: An Introduction to Problems and Policies in a Global Perspective*. New York: Longman, 1977.

Tord, Javier, and Carlos Lazo. *Hacienda Colonial y Formación Social*. Barcelona: Sendai Ediciones, 1988.

———. *Hacienda, Comercio, Fiscalidad y Luchas Sociales (Peru Colonial)*. Lima: Biblioteca Peruana de Historia, Economía y Sociedad, 1981.

Truelove, Cynthia. "Disguised Industrial Proletarians in Rural Latin America: Women's Informal Sector Factory Work and the Social Reproduction of Coffee Farm Labor in Colombia." In *Women Workers and Global Restructuring*, ed. Katherine Ward, 48–63. Ithaca, NY: ILR Press, 1990.

Umaña, Laura. *Análisis de la Dinámica de Cambio de la Vereda de Canelón, Cajicá*. Tesis de Licienciatura, Universidad de los Andes, Bogotá, 1981.

United States Census Bureau. *International Data Base*. Available at: <www.census.gov/ipc/www/idbsum.html>. Accessed September 13, 2004.

United States Central Intelligence Agency (CIA). *The World Factbook 1996: Colombia*. Available at: <www.umsl.edu/services/govdocs/wofact96/64.htm>. Accessed September 27, 2004.

United States Department of Agriculture Economic Research Service (USDA ERS). *2004 Excel Spreadsheet format files*. Washington, D.C.: Government Publication Office, 2004. Available at: <usda.mannlib.cornell.edu/data-sets/specialty/FLO/2004/>. Accessed September 30, 2004.

———. *Floriculture and Nursery Crops Yearbook 2003*. Washington, DC: Government Publication Office, 2003. Available at: <usda.mannlib.cornell.edu/data-sets/specialty/FLO/2003/>. Accessed September 9, 2004.

Uribe, Martha Lucía. "Mujeres y Violencia." *Las Mujeres en la Historia de Colombia. Tomo I: Mujeres, Hsitoria y Política*. Bogotá: Grupo Editorial Norma, 1995.

Velez, Ligia Teresa. "El Impacto de la Entrada al Mercado Laboral en las Dinámicas del Rol Femenino en el Municipio de Suesca." Tesis de Licenciatura, Universidad de los Andes, Bogotá, 1995.

Vélez R., Humberto. *Pastrana, la Ciudad y la Guerra: Hacía un Balance de la Política Gubernamental de Paz*. Cali: Ecopaz, 2000.

Villamarín, Juan. "Haciendas en la Sabana de Bogotá, Colombia en la Época Colonial: 1539–1810." In *Haciendas, Latifundios y Plantaciones en América Latina*, ed. Enrique Florescano, 327–45. Mexico City: Siglo Veintiuno Editores, 1975.

Villar, Rodrigo. *El Proceso de Proletarización de las Obreras Floristas en la Región de Chía, Tabio y Cajicá*. Bogotá: Universidad de los Andes, 1982.

Ward, Kathryn, and Jean L. Pyle. "Gender, Industrialization, Transnational Corporations, and Development: An Overview of Trends." In *Women in the Latin American Development Process*, ed. Christine Bose and Edna Acosta-Belen, 37–64. Philadelphia: Temple University Press, 1995.

Ward, Kathryn. *Women Workers and Global Restructuring*. Ithaca, NY: ILR Press, Cornell University, 1990.

Wartenberg, Lucy. "Entre el Maltrato y el Repudio: Dilema de las Mujeres del Altiplano Cundiboyacense de Colombia." In *Mujeres de los Andes: Condiciones de Vida y Salud*, ed. Anne-Claire Defossez, Didier Fassin, Mara Viveros, 399–420. Bogotá: Universidad Externado de Colombia, 1992.

Watts, Michael J. "Life under Contract: Contract Farming, Agrarian Restructuring, and Flexible Accumulation." In *Living under Contract: Contract Farming and Agrarian Transformation in Sub-Saharan Africa*, ed. Peter D. Little and Michael Watts. Madison: University of Wisconsin Press, 1994.

Weil, Jim. "Introduction to 'Multiple Livelihoods' in Contemporary Societies: Ethnographic Sketches of Individuals, Households, and Communities." *Anthropology of Work Review* 16 (1995): 1–5.

Whitehead, Ann. "'I'm Hungry, Mum': the Politics of Domestic Budgeting." In *Of Marriage and the Market: Women's Subordination in International Perspective*, ed. Kate

Young, Carol Wolkowitz, and Roslyn McCullagh, 88–111. London: CSE Books, 1981.

Wilk, Richard. "Decision Making and Resource Flows Within the Household: Beyond the Black Box." In *Households: Comparative and Historical Studies of the Domestic Group*, ed. Robert Netting, Richard Wilk, and Erik Arnould, 55–72. Berkeley: University of California Press, 1984.

Wilkinson-Weber, Clare M. *Embroidering Lives: Women's Work and Skill in the Lucknow Embroidery Industry*. Albany: State University of New York Press, 1999.

Wolf, Diane Lauren. *Factory Daughters: Gender, Household Dynamics, and Rural Industrialization in Java*. Berkeley: University of California Press, 1992.

Wolf, Eric, and Sidney Mintz. "Haciendas y Plantaciones en Mesoamérica y las Antillas." In *Haciendas, Latifundios y Plantaciones en América Latina*, ed. Enrique Florescano, 493–531. Mexico City: Siglo Veintiuno Editores, 1957a.

———. "Haciendas and Plantations in Middle America and the Antilles." *Social and Economic Studies* 6 (1957b): 380–412.

Woog, Mario. *El Programa Mexicano de Maquiladoras*. Guadalajara: Instituto de Estudios Sociales, Universidad de Guadalajara, 1980.

Wooley, Frances. "A Noncooperative Model of Family Decision Making." TIDI Working Paper 125. London: London School of Economics, 1988.

Wright, M. W. "Desire and the Prosthetics of Supervision: A Case of Maquiladora Flexibility." *Cultural Anthropology* 16, no. 3 (2001): 354–73.

Yelvington, Kevin. *Producing Power: Ethnicity, Gender and Class in a Caribbean Workplace*. Philadelphia: Temple University Press, 1995.

Ziegler, Catherine. "Favored Flowers: Culture and Markets in a Global Commodity Chain." Ph.D. diss., New School University, 2003.

Index

Index note: page references in *italics* indicate a photograph or table on the designated page.

About the Author

Colombian economic and medical anthropologist **Greta Friedemann-Sánchez** has conducted research in Colombia and the United States. Using gender as the focal point of her research, she has studied processes of modernization among Andean peasants in Colombia and agro-industrial rural people near Bogotá. Currently she is a core investigator at the Center for Chronic Disease Outcomes Research (CCDOR) at the VA Medical Center in Minneapolis. At the CCDOR she conducts research on the social determinants of the production, receipt, and delivery of healthcare services.